# The

# PROSELYTIZER

## The Diaries of
## Panos T. Zachariou
### Pioneer Minister of the
### Gospel in Greece

by

Philemon Zachariou

*ACW Press*
5501 N. 7th Ave. #502
Phoenix, AZ 85013

Old Testament Scripture quotations are from the *Holy Bible*, New International Version, copyright © 1973, 1978, 1984 by International Bible Society. Used by permission of Zondervan Publishing House. All rights reserved.
New Testament quotations are the author's translation from the Greek text.

Publisher's Cataloging-in-Publication
*(Provided by Quality Books, Inc.)*

Zachariou, Panos T.
    The proselytizer : the diaries of Panos T. Zachariou, pioneer minister of the Gospel in Greece/ [translated, edited and compiled] by Philemon Zachariou. — 1st ed.
    p. cm.
    ISBN: 1-89-252505-4

    1. Zachariou, Panos T.--Diaries. 2. Missionaries--Greece--Diaries. 3. Missionaries--Greece--Biography. I. Zachariou, Philemon. II. Title

BV2967.Z33A3 1999        266/.009495/092
                      QBI98-990019

Printed in the United States of America

To obtain more copies please contact:
Phil Zachariou
P.O. Box 278583
Sacramento, CA 95827-8583
E-mail: pzachariou@aol.com

See the order form in the back of this book.

Dedicated to my Beloved Mother
and my Five Brothers

*In memory of my father*
*And in honor of*
*Those servants*
*Whose story*
*Unlike his*
*Will never be written*
*And name may be forgotten*
*But whose faithful service*
*Will in measureless ways*
*Continue to impact*
*Eternal souls*

# Contents

# FOREWORD

GREECE, through various periods of its history, has been a land of contradictions. It has been called the birthplace of democracy, but many times it has done poorly in handling democracy. One of those times enfolded the life, sufferings, and persecutions of Panos Zachariou; but like the Apostle Paul, Panos stood by his convictions and remained true to his Lord and his calling.

At times his "zeal ate him up," putting him in trouble repeatedly with governmental and church authorities with charges of proselytism. Nonetheless, what follows is a marvelous testimony of God's grace to a hungry and searching heart; the story of one man's intense struggle to not only find and know God in a personal way, but to get past the barriers of family members who vehemently opposed his interest in the Evangelical faith and the Pentecostal experience. His determination and persistence were rewarded, and he died with the greatest respect of his entire family and a circle of friends that reached from Chania, Crete, across Greece and to America.

I will always remember the day Panos' son Demetrios (Jimmy) and I visited the wall where Panos' father (Jimmy's grandfather) was executed by German soldiers during the occupation of Crete. We talked of the fact that his grandfather had found Jesus Christ as his personal Savior just days prior to his execution. As we talked in hushed tones that quiet afternoon, we dug fragments of still-embedded bullets from the stone wall.

I did not have the privilege of knowing Panos Zachariou, but I do know and love his dear wife and his sons. They are living testimonies to the faith of a man of God. It has been a privilege of mine also to minister many times on the island of Crete where Panos Zachariou gave so much of himself in pioneering in the full gospel ministry. His godly influence remains there.

It has been my pleasure to know the Zachariou family for over twenty-five years, and to have known of Panos Zachariou long before Phil set out to translate his father's diaries and compile this remarkable book.

As you read this exciting story of the inspiring life of a good and godly man, your life will be blessed and enriched. It begins with the exodus of the Zachariou family from Asia Minor to Greece and finishes with the exodus of Panos Zachariou from this life to his eternal reward. May God bless his memory and his dear family.

— Everett Stenhouse
Former Assistant General Superintendent
of the Assemblies of God and missionary to Greece

I became acquainted with the Zachariou family upon arrival in Sacramento, California, in May of 1978. I immediately fell in love with them and sensed the uniqueness of their family history. To now have it recorded in this book is priceless to the Church of Jesus Christ. Our Lord's apostles stretch through the centuries. Here is the record of another of that long list. With men like Panos T. Zachariou, no longer is it necessary to say, "To the unknown God." Sacrifice and determination have been exemplified through the life of this servant, ingredients that continue through the lives of his family members and the many he touched.

— Glen D. Cole
Superintendent
Assemblies of God
Northen California and Nevada District

# INTRODUCTION

WHEN my father went to be with the Lord at age fifty, I was twelve—too young to know him well. I remember him mainly as a busy preacher full of energy and joy and as a praying man. Though these indelible memories of him still permeate my life, they fit only in a small section of this book.

The countless conversations I have had with my mother, my five brothers, relatives, and others who knew my father all helped in putting various parts of this book together. What actually made this book possible, however, is an anthology of my father's personal diaries and memoirs, sermons, prayer requests, poetry, correspondence and newspaper clippings which I have had in my possession for over twenty years. Ever since his early twenties, my father wrote regularly about his experiences in Asia Minor and in Greece. He wrote at home, at work, in prison, even on his deathbed.

Examining these records over the years, I was often amazed by the nature of the turns my father's life took, whether he lived as a worldly person, a growing Christian, or a pioneer minister. The cause behind those turns pervades the story of his life, a life that helped set the course of events in the development of today's Christian work in Greece. I have long anticipated seeing these valuable records come to life in the form of this book, as a spiritual legacy not only to posterity but also to every reader who will be uplifted by it.

*The Proselytizer* is neither a paean to a man nor a record of his successful deeds; it is rather a life story that deals with the age-old questions that arise when your life turns meaningless: Who am I? What is my life worth? Who made this world? What lies in the beyond? If God exists, does He care for me?

Panos T. Zachariou, despondent and disillusioned with life, was dealing with these questions on the island of Crete at age thirty-one as he was about to throw himself into "the jaws of death." Just then, and under seemingly bizarre circumstances, he discovered "the forbidden book"—the Bible—a discovery that seemed to spell out the answers to many of his questions. Thus began the saga of a man whose quest for the truth would lead him to become a pioneer minister of the gospel in Greece; a man who, through business failures, poverty, times of war, persecution by Orthodox Church leaders collaborating with the local authorities and the media, and imprisonments under the pretext of proselytizing people to his "heresy" with gifts and money, learned unconditional obedience to God's will for his life.

*The Proselytizer* embodies the faith, service and sacrifice as well of many men and women in all parts of the world, servants whose stories will never be told. These are the unknown Pauls, Peters, Ruths and Elijahs of today, who need encouragement as they face social prejudices and opposition from family members, government, and religious authorities. In their zeal to serve God they may suffer privation, hardships, abuse, torture, imprisonment, even death by execution. In this light, my father's story is a call to intercessory prayer on behalf of today's unknown servants of God.

The book is in three parts. Part I shows Panos as a worldly young man who discovers the Bible and becomes a Christian. Part II describes the circumstances that allow him to grow spiritually in preparation for the relentless persecution he is to face, which is detailed in Part III. While portions of this book are literal translations from his daily journals, some names of individuals and places have been changed or omitted as a measure of precaution.

— Phil Zachariou

# HISTORICAL BACKGROUND

THE Ottoman Empire, weakened by her involvement in the Balkan wars of 1912-13, could not effectively control her European territories. The Greeks, Serbians, Rumanians, and Bulgarians used this situation as an opportunity to drive the Turks from their soil.

An unprecedented phenomenon in world history then began to develop between Greece and Turkey. In the beginning of 1914, the Greek premier suggested that it was possible for Greece and Turkey to engage in an exchange of the Greek Orthodox people in Asia Minor (Turkey) for the Moslem Turks in Greece. Such an exchange, it was decided, would be based on religion and would be compulsory.

The exchange did not, however, succeed. The Greek and Armenian minorities which remained within the Ottoman Empire faced the wrath and frustration of the demoralized Turks, who instead began persecuting, expelling, and slaughtering them. Thousands sought refuge in Greece—statistics indicate that an estimated 775,000 Greeks left Asia Minor between 1914 and 1918. It was at this time that the Zachariou family fled from Asia Minor to Greece.

Already by the end of World War I, rumors of war between Greece and Turkey had begun to spread. The spirit that had sparked the Greek War of Independence in 1821 and put an end to the 400-year Turkish rule in Greece (1453-1821) had been rekindled. Turkey, "the sick man of Europe," especially torn by its involvement in World War I, had again weakened. The Greek nation, on its way to recuperation from the Balkan wars and increasing in resources and stability, saw Turkey's weakness as a long-awaited opportunity. May 15, 1919 was a unique moment in the history of Greece. Authorized by the Allies (United States, Great Britain, France, and Italy), 20,000 Greek troops landed at Smyrna and raised their banners of invasion and conquest in Asia Minor, reclaiming the soil that had been theirs.

The signing a year later of the Treaty of Sèvres (1920) by the Sultan's government was an apparent victory for the Greek forces: Greece was given nearly all her European Turkey and some islands in the Aegean Sea, and the city of Smyrna was put under Greek administration. When these tidings reached the refugees in Greece, many of them returned to Asia Minor, including the Zachariou family.

With the treaty of Sèvres the Turkish nation was about to be virtually dissolved—permanently dismembered and divided among the Allies and Greece. However, a provisional government was formed in Ankara at this time, headed by the able Turkish officer Mustafa Kemal. Bottled up in the center of Anatolia,* the Turkish nationalists were determined to resist the Allies and prevent the dismemberment of Turkey. The Kemalist Turks refused to give in and recognize the treaty, so the Allies left the Greeks and the Turks to sort out their own differences.

The tides of events thus shifted. Without the support of the Allies, the Greeks became vulnerable and the Turks a more formidable foe. The Turkish nationalists were victorious. By late August of 1922 the Greek first line of defense crumbled and began to withdraw. The 1919 invasion at Smyrna was coming to a lamentable end. Sweeping westward, the Turkish nationalist armies, aided by chette bands, routed the Greek army and forced it to retreat to the seacoast. The Turks followed them, slaughtering families, looting, and pillaging as they went. The panicked inhabitants of Asia Minor watched the main Greek columns, their only protection against the Turks, bypass their homes and trudge toward the sea and the mainland of Greece.

This story begins with the second expatriation of the Zachariou family from Asia Minor in 1922 along with glimpses of the first expatriation in 1914.

---

* An ancient name for Asia Minor, including Asian Turkey.

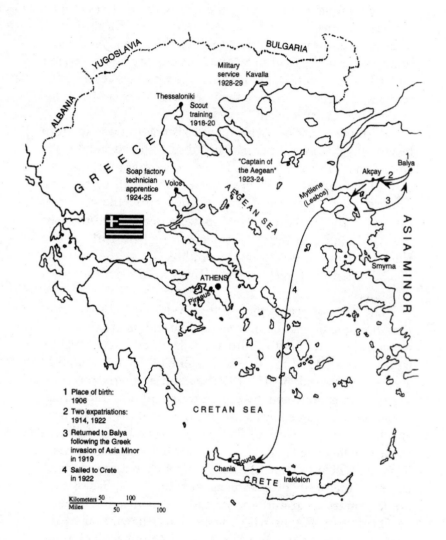

YUGOSLAVIA

BULGARIA

ALBANIA

Military
service
1928-29

Kavalla

Thessaloniki

Scout
training
1918-20

G R E E C E

Soap factory
technician
apprentice
1924-25

Volos

"Captain of
the Aegean"
1923-24

A E G E A N   S E A

Mytilene
(Lesbos)

Akçay

1
Balya

2

3

A S I A   M I N O R

Smyrna

ATHENS

Piraeus

4

CRETAN SEA

1  Place of birth:
   1906
2  Two expatriations:
   1914, 1922
3  Returned to Balya
   following the Greek
   invasion of Asia Minor
   in 1919
4  Sailed to Crete
   in 1922

Souda

Chania

C R E T E

Irakleion

Kilometers 50      100
Miles           50       100

# PART ONE

# 1

# Refugee Years

IT WAS ASIA MINOR in late August, 1922. The moonlit night was bleak and piercing, and the muddy road to the distant coast was already crowded with refugees.

Only hours earlier a communiqué had reached our village:

ABANDON THE PEOPLE — SAVE THE ARMY

I had just turned sixteen, and all that mattered to me now was how we could reach the seacoast and escape death.

We moved as fast as our legs could take us, but after a few kilometers my knees buckled, and I collapsed. A burning fever and a splitting headache had drained me. I felt hands picking me up and wiping the cold mud off my face, then I was laid on my back. Moments later I snapped out of my lethargy as I was heaved up from where I lay, then dropped heavily. Jolted joints protesting, head swimming in pain, I found myself staring at half a dozen converging spokes just centimeters from my face.

The oxcart wheel started to turn slowly. My father and my younger brother, Yorgos (George), plodded speechlessly alongside the overloaded oxcart as Mr. Silvas, the kindly neighbor who had come to my rescue, looked back to see how I was doing. Wrapped in heavy blankets, I huddled stiffly against the tailboard beside my mourning mother, whose strong loving arms cradled my newborn baby sister, Evangelia. I was sweating and shivering from my fever. Worse yet, I feared that Turkish soldiers might now be combing our village, Balya, seeking to capture genç çocuk (young lad)—a name the Turks had branded me with ever since I organized the Balya Scouts Corps in 1920.

And capture me they would. Only recently some fist-clenching neighboring Turks had vowed to "flay çocuk alive." Just before we learned that the first Greek line of defense was about to crumble, two dozen scouts, aged twelve to twenty-four, had proudly marched behind me down the main street of Balya and through its narrow alleys, carrying Greek flags and banners, shouting slogans, and singing patriotic songs. Windows were flung open, blue-and-white flags were unfurled, and a good number of young and old joined our march. Our excitement carried us past the limits of our neighborhood and well into the predominantly Turkish sector of the district. Surely those irate Turks would now go an extra kilometer—just for me.

It was now Friday, August 25, just before dawn. The few kilometers we had covered were no distance at all for the horse-riding Turks, who could charge suddenly out of the dark, spreading death. Like thousands of others, we were trying to reach the coastal town of Akçay and sail to Mytilene (Lesbos), a Greek island off the Turkish seacoast, which was my father's native land. Days and nights of fear awaited us in the more than 80 kilometers (50 miles) that lay ahead; and even if we did reach the shore, the Turks might be there, waiting.

Panos as a scout in 1922
at age 16

FLEEING to the seacoast was more than a dreadful dream, more than a haunting fear; it was the resurrection of the terror and horror of yesterday. The paradox of each present moment passed with nightmarish slowness, for we had already experienced once before the agony of running away from the Turks.

That was in 1914, at the onslaught of a draconian expatriation of hundreds of thousands of Greeks who had been forced to abandon their hearths in Asia

Minor and had sought refuge in Greece. Then, too, we had to flee to the seacoast—fortunately on a train from the French mining company in Balikesir (Palaiokastro) where my father had been working as a bookkeeper. But the expatriation, meant to be an exchange of the Greek Orthodox people in Asia Minor for the Moslem Turks in Greece, was seized by the Turks as an opportunity to persecute and slaughter the Greeks and the Armenians. Their Mehmet soldiers systematically massacred the old men, women and children, and captured all males between ages sixteen and fifty and drove them en masse to labor camps or executed them. Such must have been the fate of many friends and loved ones left behind, for we never heard from them again.

Ours seemed a better lot, for we had made it to the island in one piece—my father, Terpandros, and my mother, Terpsihori; my five-year-old brother, Yorgos; and my three-year-old sister, Elli. There on the island we found refuge among my uncles and aunts, who provided shelter and shared their meager bread with us.

But in our survival, irony set her impartial eyes coldly upon us. After we had bartered our last pieces of clothing, furniture and jewelry for anything we could put into our stomachs, our blue-eyed, dark-haired Elli, already a victim of an epidemic of influenza, complained of "funny noises" in her tummy—hunger pangs familiar to us all. A high fever, exacerbated by lack of medication and nourishment, dealt a fatal blow to our Elli. Our little angel breathed her last that cold night as she lay in my mother's arms.

That same night I realized that our greatest enemy was not the Turks. From them we had escaped. I understood then that life offers no guarantees—just itself. That which I had considered our most precious possession—our life—was not altogether in our control. The cold mystery of death awaited, ever patient, ever vigilant.

BUT more fearful than death now were the merciless Turks. At the first light of day, loud cries and awful screams reached my ears. I managed to raise my eyes over the tailboard to see. The biting cold cut into my face, sending a shiver throughout

my body. Fronted on the surrounding foothills I saw the sil-
houette of an endless column of people, young and old, some
riding on mud-splattering cattle, others trudging along with
heavy loads on their backs. The cries were coming from cold,
hungry babies, and the anguish-filled screams were from ago-
nized mothers whose children had fallen off animal-drawn carts
in the dark and been trampled to death. Every painful scream
was the scream of my mother; every desperate call the call of
my father and my brother; every helpless cry the cry of our
baby. I had to help.

As I attempted to get up, my mother, bereaved by the recent loss of her brother who was killed in action, stretched her
arm toward me and placed her hand heavily on my shoulder,
tears streaming from her eyes. She pleaded with me to remember that only hours earlier I had done all I could to save our
village, even at the risk of my own life when, still bed-ridden
with a high fever, I ran from house to house to make sure every
neighbor had heeded the warning. Her voice filled with pain,
she told me to pray to Saint George to become my patron saint,
then begged me again to stay. When she let go of my shoulder
and leaned over the baby, I could see her hand going up and
down making the sign of the cross, the bun on the back of her
neck moving with every sob. I loved her so much.

My eyes opened again at noon when the oxcart rolled to a
halt near a well. We needed w        nd so did the hundreds of
people and animals surrounding the well.

I felt uneasy. We were losing time.

After what seemed like an eternity, my father, walking tall
and poised as usual, returned carrying a bucket of water. He
raised the bucket over the side of the oxcart and held it to my
mother's lips, his pensive eyes fixed on hers.

"I've just been informed that Dukas, with your sister and
their daughter, are a bit ahead of us," he said tersely, his fingers
stroking his thick black mustache.

"Thank you, my Virgin Mary!" my mother said and burst
into tears, her hand making the sign of the cross.

Finally the rusty oxcart wheels resumed their monotonous
squeak, a welcome sign that at last we were moving again.

We had barely covered 20 kilometers altogether, just a quarter of the way. I figured it would probably be Sunday afternoon before we could reach Akçay.

Ominous clouds hung low over our heads by late afternoon. I looked at our baby and remembered how desperately my mother's tireless arms had held little Elli on the cold night she died. Suddenly I was filled with a sense of desolation and pessimism. "She's just another Elli," I muttered. "It's a vicious circle, only this time the Turks will mercilessly slaughter my parents and the baby, and they'll make Yorgos kill the Greeks and the giaours." *

All of a sudden the stream of people began to move faster, and in an instant there was an outbreak of confusion and hysteria, panicky women and children screaming and running like mad and families being scattered. That dreadful moment had apparently come.

"Run! Run, my son—run!" my distraught mother screamed. "They'll spare us—you run!"

I sprang to my feet and jumped down. My father—I had never seen him cry like that before—hurriedly took off his heavy black coat and flung it over my shoulders.

"I'll find you later, okay?" I said, and took to the nearby foothills along with hundreds of panicked men, women and children.

Not sure whether I was being followed by friends or chased by foes, I headed for the distant hills. As far as my breath could take me, I ran, hiding behind trees and ducking under bushes to avoid being spotted by Turkish farmers and shepherds who would shoot at anything that moved.

Clouds covered the sky, and the night fell hard, bringing blustering winds and ear-shattering thunder and lightning. Cold and frightened, I crouched beneath a sheltering rock.

Overwhelmed by the awesome powers that rent the heavens at such blinding speeds, I wondered if I dared ask for the intervention of a higher power. "God," I whispered, "if You do exist, spare me and my family. Spare all my scouts and my friends

* Turkish *giaour*, an infidel, especially a Christian.

and all the boys and girls of our village. . . ." I marveled then that my lips had uttered such words so earnestly, so spontaneously. But I wondered whether I should have prayed to Saint George instead.

At the first light of dawn, I set out to search for my family. After climbing rocky hills and fording the cold waters of a river, I suddenly found myself staring at three young Turks just meters away. Two of them were sitting on a boulder, one with a musket between his knees, barrel against his shoulder; the youngest one was standing nearby, holding a shepherd's staff and sporting a fez.

A chette band! I thought with alarm. Trying not to look afraid, I managed a silly smile. My appearance seemed to amuse them—feet covered with mud, pajamas rolled high, coat over the shoulder, boots dangling around my neck—or they might have shot me on the spot. Then the oldest one, perched atop the boulder, stood up, and hefting his long gun, challenged me to identify myself in Turkish.

Quickly I dashed for the river, my head down. I heard a shot as I tripped and went tumbling down the rocky bank, wondering if I had been hit. I got up and jumped into the cold water, hoping to reach the rocks near the other side before they could shoot again.

Knee-deep in the cold water, I hid behind a boulder. The trio started throwing rocks and challenging me to come out. Better frozen than shot, I figured, so I clung onto the boulder for dear life, hoping the three would not brave the freezing water and would finally give up. What an hour of icy waiting did not accomplish, however, a sudden thunderstorm finally did. That chapter of my ordeal thus ended as suddenly as it had begun.

My limbs were numb and slow to obey as I pulled myself up among the shrubs and trees. Barefoot, I climbed sharp ledges and cut through thorny bushes. By late afternoon I reached an open area from which I could see the stream of refugees moving westward. I climbed down the last slope and got back on the road, but not before devouring some watermelons and figs to stave off my hunger.

THERE was nothing moving on wheels anymore. The Greek army had destroyed every bridge. Treasures went up in smoke as refugees desperately dumped their wagons and carts by the rivers, setting dowries and valuables on fire and leaving "nothing for the Turks to defile."

I figured that if my family was still alive, they would probably be about 15 kilometers ahead. I plowed through the crowds, but soon another cold, murky night set in; so I went on plodding blindly along with the streams of people and hoping that morning would come soon.

THE exciting sight of the ocean the next day gave hope to my spirit and wings to my battered feet. I had run through the crowds since daybreak, looking at every woman holding a baby, every man wearing a black suit, every young boy. And as my ribs heaved and my legs protested, I spotted a lean silver-haired man taking laborious steps.

"Mr. Silvas!" I called.

The old man stopped. "By George! It's you, m' boy!"

"What happened, Mr. Silvas?"

"Over there, m' boy," he said in his trembling voice, pointing toward the sea. "Maybe a couple of kilometers."

My heart pounded with excitement. "But what happened, Mr. Silvas? Did the Turks—?"

"False alarm, you know. That's how we got separated...in the confusion. But you go on, m' boy. Your folks...they need you very bad—"

"But. . . Mr. Silvas—"

"You go on, m' boy," he insisted. "Your poor mom...she's got to see your face, you know. She thinks you're gone!"

IT WAS the most unforgettable moment of my life when I sighted my family that Sunday afternoon. To prevent shocking my mother, I stood back a short distance and whistled in a familiar manner. Immediately they stopped and looked back.

"Panos?" my father called out.

"It's Panoooos!" my brother shouted and ran to meet me. I hugged and kissed my brother and my father and we hopped around together for a while, tears streaming down our faces. My mother meanwhile went into an uncontrollable spell of sobbing, unable to speak. She looked haggard and spent, and so did my father, who now took the baby from her arms. Then I held my mother close and kissed her face again and again.

"Take a look at my new shoes, Mom," I said, by way of distracting her. That seemed to break the spell. She looked down at my encrusted feet and saw what I was referring to.

"My son. . . my boy!" she was finally able to cry out, and she threw her arms around my neck. And so she took comfort from me, until my nearness calmed her enough to convince her that I was still alive.

THE quay side of Akçay was another rendezvous with fear and agony, for a stampede of refugees surged around the scores of rowboats, hoping to reach the ships waiting offshore; but the men in charge had orders to rescue first the army, then the civilians. A soldier—it turned out to be one of the many women disguised in military uniform—helped my mother with the baby, and the rest of us jostled and pushed forward until somehow we managed to get into the same rowboat.

Once again we found ourselves aboard a rescue ship and amid thousands of other refugees, only this time we were as atrociously desperate and destitute as they. We had nothing in our possession other than the shredded, filthy rags that clung to our freezing bodies. Even so, we were grateful, for we were together again—and alive. And together, we had the will to live.

But the physical exhaustion, agony, and cold, sleepless nights we suffered were no match for the shuddering atrocities being experienced at Smyrna. The predominantly Greek city, with its 43,000 Greek homes, 1,000 Greek shops, 117 Greek schools, and many Greek Orthodox churches, was completely destroyed. The Greek and Armenian quarters had been turned into a huge ball of fire; only the Jewish and Turkish quarters remained. Hundreds of thousands of Greeks, young and old, including mothers holding their babies in their arms, were being beaten and driven with clubs and knives like animals toward the sea.

And there, crowded along the coast beyond its capacity, those desperate, unfortunate souls flung themselves into the sea....

THE sun was about to set. I looked at the golden shores that had been the settlements of the Aeolian and Ionian Greeks of antiquity, my aching heart telling me I was never to see my homeland again. The civilization that had culminated among the Athenians—the kinsmen of the Ionians—was born there. It was part of the conquests of Alexander the Great and the land of the Byzantine Empire that had existed for eleven centuries before it succumbed under the yataghan of the Ottoman Turk. And now Hellenic Smyrna was dead. Greek Orthodox Smyrna, too, was dead. That part of Greece where Hellenism had thrived for over thirty centuries was to be no more, its noble accomplishments and contributions alive only as history. Asia Minor had been lost to the Turks. I had to accept the bitter reality.

For a homeland and a home, I now had to look across the sea.

# 2

# Racing Anew

O UR HEARTS WERE THRILLED the next day, tears of relief mingling with tears of pain, when we met Uncle Dukas at a mosque crowded with refugees. Together, under the auspices of the Red Cross, we found temporary quarters there for a month.

Then we heard about free housing and pieces of property being offered to refugees in various parts of Greece due to a new government-sanctioned exchange of the Moslems in Greece for the Greek Orthodox people in Asia Minor, so we sailed south to the island of Crete where some of our relatives had already settled. There the government allotted us a two-story house and three parcels of land near the river-drained slopes of Perivolia, a village four kilometers from Chania, the island's capital. In 1923, however, malaria broke out in Perivolia, so we moved in with some other relatives in the refugee-filled district of Splantzia in Chania.

The capital, located on the northwest coast of this historic island, stirred a familiar vein of sentiment. It evoked within me feelings rooted in my experiences in Akçay, the coastal town which twice marked the beginning of our freedom; and in Thessaloniki, the coastal city where I was trained as a scout following our first expatriation, the seaport where my friends and I used to spend endless hours fishing and frolicking on shores washed by the Aegean Sea.

Chania was the city boxed within a moat and a wall that was built in A.D. 1252 by the Venetians, after Crete came under their control as part of the Frankish Empire. The small Venetian harbor of Chania enclosed all the northern part of the city. To form the harbor, a long wall (the chord) was stretched over a succession of rocks, built at the end of which was a minaret-like beacon. Two-thirds of the population of the old city were previously Turks, the majority of which had lived in Splantzia, a district whose narrow passes and cobblestone alleys were the vestiges of the 400-year Turkish occupation of Greece.

I loved the old city by the sea. Hard-working fishermen, fishing gear in their hands from sunrise to sunset, looked daily to its sunbathed shores for livelihood. Determined caiques (light sailing vessels) and flotillas dared the waves of the open sea before sundown, dragging freshly mended fishing nets across the golden Gulf of Chania, their shimmering lights studding the horizon by night.

I was seventeen. Disease-stricken Perivolia promised me no future except that of a petty farmer. I aspired to go to high school in Chania, but my family was poor and needed my help. So I set my sights on the sea, which seemed to promise me new horizons and new hopes.

Before leaving home to go to sea, I went to the church of St. Nikolaos in our neighborhood and lit a candle to Saint George for good luck. Perhaps some day I would be able to sail to America and claim the inheritance from the gold mines that my two Italian great-uncles had reportedly left before they died in their early thirties. And so I became a ship boy.

TRAVELING at sea from seaport to seaport on a cargo ship meant hard work, my diligence at which earned me the captain's favor. In less than two months I was given a chance at the helm under the watchful eye of the tall, imposing captain.

But aboard the ship were robust, sunbaked seamen who had long vied for the opportunity to become Captain Mitsos' right-hand man. Now they suddenly found themselves staring nonplused at a jovial, skinny teenager conversing on the bridge for hours on end with their stern captain. Soon I became a subject of resentment, a situation which, coupled with several offensive advances by homosexuals on board, made me want to quit and return home.

My heart, however, held fast to the captain's promise of some day making me "Captain of the Aegean." And so for five more months I experienced the thrill of seeing our seaworthy 800-ton cargo vessel Troas obey my commands by day and by night—in still blue waters, on the rough seas, and even in the critical moments of entering and leaving congested harbors.

By the end of my seventh month at sea, however, the repeated attempts of two homosexuals to molest me, once even at knife point, were more than I could bear.

"Did they harm you in any way?" Captain Mitsos asked, his narrowed brown eyes gleaming above his bearded face.

"No, Captain, they never did—"

"You said they wielded knives?"

"Yes, sir. This last time, they—"

"Tell me about it."

"Well, Captain, as I tried to wrest the knife from one of them, the other put his knife to my back. I...I guess it was more like revenge out of jealousy than molestation they were after."

"Go on."

"Well, I gave them my word that if they'd let me go, I...I'd never give away their names—"

"You wouldn't?"

"That's a promise I made, Captain—"

His eyes met mine for five long seconds. Then suddenly, we had a good laugh.

"Well, Panos," said Captain Mitsos, grabbing me by the shoulders, "that's what I like about you—your straightforwardness."

But in my heart I had already decided to put an end to my challenging, though in some ways unpleasant, life at sea. Besides, Captain Mitsos was aware that my parents had written me not a few letters begging me to come home. When one day he showed me a letter he himself had received from my mother, he apologized for having encouraged me to visit the red-light districts. I told him that I had decided I should leave from the sea for now and go see my family back home.

FOR the following two years I worked at the local soap factories of Ioannides-Preve and Antoniades in Chania.

Panos in Chania, Crete, at age 18

On my way home one evening I met Athena, a slender, green-eyed brunette from Asia Minor of about seventeen who lived in our neighborhood with her foster father. Once she and I established that we were cousins of some sort, she took the liberty of visiting our home often. I found her uninhibited manner appealing and her habitual giggling and spontaneous outbursts of laughter refreshing. And she was stunningly attractive.

Not many days went by before I made the heart-breaking discovery that this playful, vivacious girl was being exploited by her foster father. Crushed, I begged Athena to stop meeting with other men, promising her I would do my best to help make ends meet.

A month went by, but there was no change in Athena's lifestyle. I could not figure out why she continued to behave the same toward me as always, which made me feel pretty foolish. When I told her I was going to talk to her foster father and convince him that I loved her, she simply laughed. Utterly bewildered, I began to associate her lively spirit and enticing smiles with her foster father's evil schemes, seeing in her a helpless victim whose behavior reflected a perverted man's diabolical intents and purposes.

Downcast and dejected, one night I returned home to find my father waiting at the door, speechless, and my frightened mother in bed crying. Athena's foster father had come to my parents earlier that day and told them he feared I was going to murder him. Overcome with anxiety and fear, my mother became grievously ill for days. Her prolonged and unusual silence frightened me, and I realized that my affair with Athena was on a disastrous course. So I decided to leave Chania and head for Volos, a coastal city about 470 kilometers away.

IN order to reach Volos, I looked up Captain Mitsos. He was pleased to see me again, though this time I met him as a traveler seeking free passage rather than employment as a ship boy. And free the passage was, but only after I was charged with the helm. That was even better than I had hoped for, because I loved to helm.

"Where to, Panos?" asked Captain Mitsos.

"To the unknown, Captain!"

"We don't make stops at the gold mines of California, you know," he said jokingly.

"Just heading for that soap factory up north, I guess, Captain. You do remember the factory owner in Volos you introduced me to a while back, don't you?"

Captain Mitsos nodded. "Well, my good friend," he said, "at least I'll know where to find you."

TIME in Volos brought healing to my battered heart. It also afforded me the opportunity to learn to cut soap, a technique practiced in Chania by only a handful of specialists. After a year, it was nearly time for me to join the army, so I decided to return home to spend some time with my family.

I RETURNED home just in time for the 1927 carnival. A number of costume-flaunting friends and I entered a house where earlier in the day I had left my mandolin. Seated on the windowsill and strumming my mandolin was a girl of about seventeen, whose thick black wavy hair richly caressed her striking face. She was not dressed in holiday style, and judging by the unalarmed expression in her brown eyes, I was certain that she must have thought I was a flamboyant, garrulous woman with extravagant taste in clothes who particularly delighted in fluttering about in the company of many men. Apparently my affected voice and extremely feminine gestures concealed my identity as a male.

"I see you play the mandolin?" was my introductory remark.

"Oh, not really—" she replied in a clear, pleasant voice, as she admired the magnificent plumage atop my huge red hat.

"May I?" I asked, my hands extended.

"Certainly," she said, as she placed the mandolin onto the black leather gloves that concealed my hairy arms and hands.

My performance impressed her. "You play very well!" she exclaimed.

"Won't you join us tonight?" I inquired, taking great care to maintain my affected mannerisms.

Turning slowly sideways and looking out the window she said, "My mother won't let me go out with anyone at night."

Her modest and unpretentious character particularly appealed to me, especially as it was accompanied by a mellow voice that rang with loyalty and trustworthiness—most desirable traits to me, now. Her subdued manner of talk and resigned expression seemed void of any trace of struggle. She seemed patient and calm, looked plain and neat—and appeared to be attractively lonely.

I feared that my evident attraction to the girl and the interest I was taking in her might possibly cause my disguise to slip, but I found it fascinating to be able to meet such a fine lady from the vantage point of a "woman" and at the same time through the eyes of a man. As I was debating whether or not to reveal my identity, my friends came and grabbed me away from her. "Come on, Panos," they shouted. "Let's beat it!"

Well, no use pretending any more. "Good night. . . miss!" I called loudly in my normal voice, as loose limbs and mandolin flew in the air over the heads of those carrying me away like Helen of Troy. I saw the girl place her hands over her cheeks in utter surprise. Never mind, I thought to myself. Better if she met me in my Sunday best....

That night I learned that the girl's name was Chrysa and that she was a dressmaker from Smyrna. An only daughter, she lived in our neighborhood with her widowed mother and her grandmother. Her ailing father had been taken captive by the Turks in his home before her five-year-old eyes. That was the last time she saw him.

A SUCCESSION of unusual happenings developed during the ensuing two weeks. My mother and Chrysa's mother, Mrs. Theodora, became well acquainted through numerous visits they exchanged. Since I was not allowed to meet Chrysa on my own, without Mrs. Theodora's permission and strictly under her supervision—a rule I felt would be impossible to follow—I requested that both Chrysa and I be included in one of those visits.

My request was granted, so one night Chrysa and her mother, as well as her grandmother, aunt, and a number of other relatives, arrived at our home, along with all my aunts and uncles and every member of the grapevine. In a room filled beyond capacity, all the men managed to gather around me on one side of the room, all the women around Chrysa on the other. Soon I became aware of the meaning behind this un-precedented social phenomenon. Realizing that exchanging a word with Chrysa in private was a complete impossibility, not only on account of her mother's watchful eye but also the many other scrutinizing eyes fixed on me and Chrysa at all times—a situation that must have caused her a great deal of discomfi-ture—I heroically came to Chrysa's rescue. After preparing all ears and eyes for a proclamation, I stood up to speak.

"Mrs. Theodora," I said, "in the presence of all our honor-able guests, I have something important to say to you tonight." Dead silence prevailed, all eyes on my smiling face. "I would like to request your consent to my becoming engaged to your daughter Chrysa."

Mouths dropped, eyes opened wide. Everyone in the room looked astounded except one person—Chrysa's mother.

"We all know that you are a good young man, Panos," she said unhesitatingly. "It's all right with me if it's all right with your good parents."

"But, my son. . . soon you'll be joining the army!" my con-cerned mother responded.

"That's exactly the reason." I said. "This way, while I'm gone, I won't look for another Chrysa," I went on, my wittiness losing out to the gravity of the moment. Chrysa was fidgeting with a lace handkerchief as our eyes met momentarily. A faint blush crept into her cheeks. "There simply isn't another Chrysa," I added, causing heads to nod and triggering a crying spell among the women.

TWO months after Chrysa and I became engaged, I joined the army. I was first sent to the island of Mytilene (Lesbos) and later to the town of Kavalla in northern Greece.

Eighteen long months later, I finally returned home. Before Chrysa and I could get married, I had to find work that would support not only the two of us, but her mother and her grandmother as well. Because work at the soap factories was extremely slow, I tried many odd jobs, the most profitable of which turned out to be the auctioning of real estate property formerly in Turkish hands. Though the auctions at first were held only once a week, profits were high. Chrysa and I decided to get married and settle in Splantzia. Our wedding date: December 7, 1930.

PROFITS continued to climb, but I wondered how much longer the auctioning of properties would last. There had to be a time, I reasoned, perhaps in the not too distant future, when there would be no more properties to auction, which would mean the end of my real estate career. So I deemed it wise to invest in some kind of profitable business. Since I was known to many as an honest, hard-working salesman, building up my clientele would be simple, I figured.

Despite repeated warnings from family and friends, I entered into a partnership with Tony Zacharakis, a distant cousin of mine, the son of a wealthy businessman in Athens. We each invested 9,000 drachmas and started a private mail service business, handling the shipment of commodities for merchants, dealers, and private parties. This type of business required extensive traveling, voluminous bookkeeping, frequent personal contacts with satisfied customers, and excellent credit.

BUSINESS went well for the first eight months, but the beginning of 1932 brought a sudden and calamitous end to my dreams and hopes. The effects of the Great Depression in the

United States had already spread throughout Europe and reached Greece. By then the Greek nation itself was well into a state of economic depression that had started in 1929. By the end of 1931 the Greek drachma, which depended on the American dollar, had lost seventy-five percent of its 1928 value. Consequently travel, the lifeblood of our mail business, decreased to a record low, immediately affecting ninety-five percent of our business activity. In addition, early in 1932—much sooner even than I had feared—the auctioning of properties came to a complete halt.

The situation became hopeless: business ground to a halt, and our debtors vanished. In vain I covered countless kilometers on foot in the sweltering heat trying to collect from them. And if I happened to catch one, he would either beg me to wait a little longer and make all kinds of promises, or simply turn his pockets inside out and start talking about his starving children, tears running down his face. Then at the end of the day, irked and worn out, I would return home only to find insolent creditors at the door pestering my pregnant wife, demanding cash and threatening us with lawsuits.

And where was Tony? He, too, had vanished. He would take off for Athens without notice, leaving me to do all the footwork, the chasing, the begging. Then suddenly he would reappear, just to ask me if I had collected anything and pressure me to take matters to litigation. I threatened to break up our partnership, but Tony knew I could not afford to. Our partnership was my only hope for survival.

By the middle of 1933, lawsuits were pending against our partnership. Lack of travel had more than crippled our business. Our liabilities far exceeded our assets, and we were unable to liquidate. Having reached a state of insolvency, our partnership came to a speedy end as we went bankrupt.

My savings had been depleted; my business was lost. I was destitute.

THE rising of the sun now signaled my daily exodus. All waking hours were spent seeking work. I had to feed my one-year-old boy, Terpandros, my patient wife, her mother, and her grandmother. And myself.

Imagination had to stretch beyond its boundaries—anything to get a worthless drachma, a piece of bread. Gardening? Yes, gardening—go to it. There's a vacant lot behind the bank. It's full of junk. Clean it up and plant a garden. The bank president liked me as a bank clerk and an auctioneer; he'll like me as a gardener. Experience in gardening? As much as I had in auctioning when I first started—nil. Come on, Mr. President, don't pay me until you see a little paradise—then make me an offer. Deal? Deal! Imagination tells me I could grow vegetables. . . oh, yes! . . . and flowers, and plants, and seeds for sale!

But a junkyard doesn't turn into a paradise overnight; nor in the meantime does promised money buy bread. So dig all day, burn in the searing sun, then drag your aching feet from door to door to see if anyone wants to get rid of an old chair, a flower pot, a pair of old shoes, clothes—anything. Sell it for him, keep part of the cash. Try to catch an elusive debtor. Then lie in bed at night wishing the sun would never rise....

Sunrise! The rat race begins. Oh, God, do you care?

ᴿᴱᵁ ᴿᴱᵁ ᴿᴱᵁ ᴿᴱᵁ

# 3

# Food for Life

WANDERING EMPTY-HANDED in the valley of poverty, without the fighting sword of work in my hands to stave off the beast of indebtedness, I found myself defenseless in my fight for survival.

By Christmas of 1934 I found myself thoroughly snared in the claws of that formidable beast, a debtor to all—the landlord, the grocer, the baker, the doctor, relatives, friends. My once hopeful spirit was now weak, for all my optimistic forecasts had turned into fables, my promises into lies. Months behind with my rent, I feared I would face eviction before I could make another full payment during the cold winter months ahead. My credibility with the grocer and the baker was sagging under the weighty sums I owed them. My word of honor, which once symbolized the reliance and trust inherent in all my financial dealings, now evoked only pity. A rare opportunity to cut soap at the factory would afterward send me running to my creditors and lenders to appease them for a day or two with niggardly portions of a day's wages; but the beast of indebtedness was insatiable.

Hunger was written in the beast's mouth. I feared my family would starve. But more appalling than losing my battle for survival was the terror of its imminent outcome—my becoming a beggar. Begging for help. Begging for pity. What dreadful thoughts! I'd rather starve—I could never beg. Or would I beg, for the sake of my loved ones?

On New Year's Eve Chrysa told me that there was no food in the house. I looked at her and felt a great guilt. Stark misery was in her eyes; and she had become very thin. I responded with a nod and turned around to leave as if I were going to do something about it, but I was just trying to hide my tears. There was nothing I could do to earn a single drachma that evening anyway.

As I was leaving, she told me that our little boy Terpandros was ill and that we should take him to the doctor. I reached into my pockets. Two drachmas. The doctor's bill was going to be at least fifty! Would someone see my pitiful estate and offer me a handout so I would not have to make a humiliating plea? Would I find crumbs under anyone's table before I have to shamefully beg? "God, help me!" I murmured.

As I stepped into the alley I saw my mother, my brother, and some friends coming to our house for a visit. I wished then that I had left a moment earlier. There was nothing in the house to offer them for a treat, and I could not bear the embarrassment of not having something to offer. Then I realized they were all carrying pots and pans—they had brought dinner! I tried to welcome them with a cordial smile and laughter as usual, but I found it difficult to pretend. I was no longer the Charlie *∗ of the company; my humor and laughter had turned into tears.

That evening my mother and my brother gave me one hundred fifty drachmas. I went into the other room and fought some stinging tears. Deep inside I knew that my misery was hiding behind a veil of pride: it was not just help I was seeking to find, but rather a way to avoid begging for help. That made me feel guilty; but worse yet was the haunting fear that I might soon have to openly beg for help, the thought of which made me cringe and wallow in self-pity.

HAVE a bite today, starve tomorrow—the routine of misery. There were too many mouths to feed, though I would have fed them my very soul.

Chrysa would do some sewing, but that would barely put a bite on the plates. Poverty had of necessity taught many a home the skills of a tailor. "Come spring, there's going to be work for

---

∗ Panos was nicknamed Charlie after Charles Chaplin, a famous comedian. See photo, p. 112.

all of us," my mother-in-law and her mother would say to give me courage. Bottled up inside the house, these staunch women kept gazing resolutely at the gray sky, looking for the sunshine that would guide their footsteps to the distant hills where they might dig out greens and herbs for dinner. But they knew as well as I that, in the meantime, there would be many a cold, hungry night devoid of hope.

Many families shared the same plight, and scores of desperate people committed suicide. That scared me. It seems that everyone else in my position would have long ended his life, I thought to myself. Why not I? What stops me from doing it? Hope for a better future? My innocent boy? My pregnant wife? They'd be hurting less crying over my dead body than going on in life like this. . . .

I checked the newspapers. Special columns listed all suicides and the manner in which they were committed. Some men threw themselves down from high cliffs or buildings. Others drowned at sea or hanged themselves. Many used a gun.

The idea of suicide had been foreign to me, but as it began to pervade my mind through the news, I became fearful of it. I feared that the tendency to commit suicide was an uncontrollable obsession born within the mind as suddenly and unexpectedly as a massive heart attack. Rather than be caught by surprise, I thought that I would challenge suicide and deal with it once and for all. So I wrote a note—a suicide note. Knowing that I did not have a gun in my possession and that I could not afford one, I wrote how I would do it—with a gun.

Having established that, I was able to toy with the idea of suicide daily, though at the end of the day I would always find some excuse why I hadn't committed the act yet. All I need is a gun, I would think to myself. Maybe I can use Tony's gun. Yeah, he's got one. But no, that might incriminate him. They might accuse him of murder, or of forcing me to write my suicide note at gunpoint. That's the kind of heart I have—I care to harm no one. . . .

Soon I began to think more in terms of taking my life than sustaining it. A bullet in the head is better than a bullet in the heart, I reasoned. My heart hasn't been infected yet—I want to keep it clean. It's my head that has brought about my calamity. Why didn't I heed the repeated warnings of those who'd known Tony's character for years? Why did I turn a deaf ear to my wife, who insisted that I base my partnership on a true friend's tried integrity rather than on a distant cousin's untouchable riches? And why was I too proud to admit my growing fears of him even from the very start of our partnership? It's my head that has dug my grave. Yes, it's my head that deserves a bullet in it. . . .

But then it occurred to me that perhaps the act of suicide was not at all a thing that took its victim by surprise. Rather it was the end result of careful planning and contemplation—already my daily preoccupation.

I became filled with uncertainty and fear. I dreaded the thought that I might have already gone past the stage of simply toying with the idea of suicide and fallen victim to the norm followed by those who would inescapably commit the act. I feared that I had already reached the point of no return in a downhill path to my eventual demise.

Daily reminders now roused my fears. Whenever I saw a policeman or a soldier, I would think of a gun. But it was not only guns—if I saw the open sea, I would think of drowning; a tall building would put me in mind of jumping from its top floor. Worst of all, one day I would be talking with a friend, and a couple of days later I would be looking for his name on the suicide lists.

My mind had ballooned with the agonies of uncertainty, fear, despair and self-pity—a sure prescription for suicide. I dreaded my own thoughts. They haunted me constantly and had become my worst enemy. They were telling me that I had reached the nadir of my sanity and that I should hurry up and take my life before I turned insane. Yes, maybe that's the reason why I should do it, I thought. What a horrible thing to become insane, locked up in an asylum! I'd rather die. On the other hand, if I went insane I'd be able to commit suicide without any further ado; or could it be that I wouldn't even have the mind to think of a way to do it?

Disgusted with all the morbid, frightful thoughts I was having, thoughts that seemed to feed on themselves, I asked myself if there was indeed a reason for living. Unable to come up with an answer, I felt I needed some kind of rationale, a fabrication of some sort, for not having taken my life yet. So I managed to wheedle from my own conscience an excuse. A man who has cultivated within himself a sense of self-preservation, I began to reason, does not allow his mind to be filled with the degrading, dehumanizing thought of suicide. Then why am I waiting? Am I a coward? No. So what is it? Hope? Hope for what? I no longer have goals in this life, the life of the absurd and nonsensical, for one's goals reflect his personal values. And what personal values have I? None, except—except my pride!

My pride! Is that it? Oh, yes. My lousy pride. The pride that would prevent me from begging for help while my family starved; the kind of pride that eventually kills the conscience. So that's what stops me from finishing it all. Pride is the motive behind my survival. That's how base my sense of self-preservation is. Yet that's what prods me to hold on until, perhaps some day, I can brag about having made it on my own strength. . . .

AT LAST, in the middle of 1935, a few signs of an upward climb in business and travel gave floundering, desperate survivors like me hope for some respite.

One morning, on my way to look for work for the nth time, I was accosted by a wealthy middle-aged businessman, the owner of a private mail service firm that had survived the choking grip of the sinking economy. Mr. Mihelakis, short and slightly overweight—about my size when times were good—was a man whose fine features and thin gray hair spoke of refinement.

"Good morning, Mr. Zachariou," said Mr. Mihelakis, doffing his hat.

"Good morning, Mr. Mihelakis," I said.

"How's the hard-working man?" he said as he walked toward me, his right hand extended.

"As fine as the green plant he'll be selling you this afternoon, Mr. Mihelakis," I replied with a smile.

"Looking for a job?" he asked, his head raised so his impersonal dark eyes looked at mine right above the lower edge of his small round glasses.

"Name a job I haven't looked for and I'll name a job that doesn't exist, sir."

"Come by my office later this afternoon. I've got a job lined up for you," he said curtly.

"Yes, sir!" I said excitedly, stretching out both hands for another handshake. "I'll be there—and with that green plant, too!"

On my way home I stopped discreetly at the church of St. Nikolaos and lit a candle out of gratitude. I had on occasion in the past lit a candle to Saint George and asked for the priest's benediction, especially when I was about to cross the Cretan Sea in bad weather, but I had kept that a secret. Now I was particularly careful not to divulge this secret to anyone, for fear I might be regarded as one who, due to psycho-economic pressures, had turned religious.

That afternoon I headed for Mr. Mihelakis' office, wondering what I should expect. The possibility of a partnership seems far-fetched, I thought to myself. He knows I went bankrupt and that I have no money. Besides, he has three partners working for him—Angelos, his self-made accountant and bookkeeper; Nick, the collector and salesman; and Manolis, the shipping-receiving clerk and salesman. But I'm sure he's got a job for me—he wouldn't have talked to me about a job unless he'd meant it. I've always known Mr. Mihelakis to be an honorable man, a man who does not waste words. He might ask me to do a little bit of everything—collecting, delivering, selling. Perhaps he'll have me do some traveling and promoting, too. He'd be better off, though, giving me the freedom to use my own imagination. Well, in the beginning it won't matter to me what I do—I'll do anything. I just need a job. Mr. Mihelakis knows I can perform, and he knows my integrity. Well, everyone in this kind of business cheats some—at least there are opportunities for it. But it's the kind of cheating you do or don't do that tells you what kind of a man you are. He knows I would never cheat to harm anyone.

But it is possible Mr. Mihelakis might consider holding me hostage, so to speak? Now that businesses are improving—at least that's what everybody thinks—he might worry that I'll start my own business and take some of the most desirable clients off his list again. But he knows better. First, it takes a great deal of capital to get started in this kind of business, as well as considerable credibility, which I have lost. Most bankers won't even greet me, let alone loan me money. In any case, whatever he asks me to do, I'll do it. I'll do whatever it takes to make him want to keep me!

MR. MIHELAKIS gave me a warm welcome. Angelos, his tall, self-made accountant, leering and with a permanent smirk on his face, was the only partner present. Strangely, Mr. Mihelakis suddenly began a series of personal questions.

"How much do you owe your grocer?" he asked casually, while offering me a cigarette.

"About 950 drachmas," I said.

He signaled Angelos, who was sitting at the desk in front of an old typewriter, to jot down the figure.

"How about the baker?" Mr. Mihelakis went on.

"720 drachmas," I said.

"Rent?"

"Four months behind."

He waited.

"Twelve hundred drachmas," I said.

"Any loans?"

"Yes. About 2,000 drachmas."

"Do you owe anyone else?"

"Yes. The doctor—240."

"That's all?"

"That's all, sir," I said.

He looked at Angelos.

"It's under six thousand," reported the accountant.

"Make it six," said Mr. Mihelakis.

I began to think fast. It sounds like a loan, all right, just as I had suspected. He probably wants to be sure he's tied me down with his own rope so I'll work for him for a good long time. But I shouldn't be suspicious of this man—by this he's actually saying to me that he relies on my aggressiveness and ability to generate business for his firm. I won't let him down. After all, he's not only giving me a loan that would help me restore some of my credibility; he's going to hire me as well. I should be grateful to this man.

"Sign here," Mr. Mihelakis said, gently placing the ink bottle and pen closer to me and handing me the paper his accountant had typed on the company's old typewriter. It was a personal loan contract in the amount of 6,000 drachmas. The interest? Two hundred percent! I stood dumbfounded.

"But—Mr. Mihelakis, how am I expected to—?"

"First—" he said quickly, his eyes batting rapidly, "—first of all, you're going to be working with us. On commission, just like a partner," he said, and signaled his accountant to place the money on the desk. "Second, you don't have to start making payments until December, four months from now."

Angelos placed the money on the desk. It was all in big notes.

"At two hundred percent?" I said incredulously.

"Well, let's say that's your share of investment as a partner?" Mr. Mihelakis said through slanted eyes, his thin eyebrows raised high.

I fixed a bold stare on those dark, impenetrable eyes. I respected this man. He had helped me in the past, and now he was once again offering me help. I had no desire whatsoever to let a momentary expression of impertinence mar our relationship, but I did want him to understand how I felt about his offer. I felt like saying to him, "You very well know, Mr. Mihelakis, that there's no money on your side of the scale that could outweigh the value of my services. Yet you dare call me a partner so casually, so loosely. And not even on a contractual basis. So I'm asking you to be absolutely frank with me. . . ."

"All right, Mr. Mihelakis," I finally said. "What collateral are you asking for?"

He looked at me in surprise. "Collateral?"

"Your integrity, of course, Mr. Zachariou—" suddenly came from the leering accountant. "Your name, Mr. Zachariou, is well known among salesmen."

"That is so," concurred Mr. Mihelakis with portentous gravity.

The two men remained motionless as I re-examined the contract. The 6,000-drachma figure lying challengingly at the heart of the document took my mind a few months back, at which time my debts amounted to an even higher figure; but still today I was deep in the clutches of the deadly beast of indebtedness. By unsheathing the sword suddenly thrown into my hand, I could make a lunge straight into its heart!

My hand reached for the pen and resolutely drew it out of the ink bottle, then directed its tip toward the huge figure.

I signed.

"Five drachmas for that gorgeous plant?" said Mr. Mihelakis with a limp smile.

"It's a deal, sir. And you've got the gardener to care for it!" I said.

Six thousand drachmas—and a job! I marveled in disbelief as I left the office, my feet excitedly determined to bring good news to a dozen different creditors and lenders, starting with the landlord.

FOR the first time in months there was a respectable meal on our dinner table, one which included meat. Gratitude was silently painted on the faces of my loved ones as we all situated ourselves around the table to eat. The scene caused reluctant tears to surface in my eyes, so I looked for some diversion. I watched Chrysa, now large with our second child, feed Terpandros with great satisfaction. That didn't help the tears. Fortunately, at that moment my mother-in-law and her mother revived an unresolved problem from the past, creating the diversion I sought. Unlike their nearly-forgotten introductory dinner topic of how the meal was prepared and seasoned, they began to argue about who could have a first chance at our most worn-out household item—the broom.

The taste of our delectable meal still on my palate, I took a walk in the fresh ocean breeze and sought to relieve my mind. That's where the truth lies, I thought to myself. Where it's chewed and churned by rich and poor alike—in the mouth. All the toil, all the agony, all the strife, are really just to conquer the span between bread and bite. Nothing matters more than that which sustains life—food.

Food! The foundation island of the lofty pedestals that display the trophies of man's mind. Let this foundation of the philosopher, the theologian or the philanthropist be shaken. Let him and his loved ones be swallowed up by merciless hunger. And when his lofty pursuits have avalanched to the lowest ground, take all hope away. Then let the sea billows wash over his island's shores and carry him into the deep dark sea. Whence will his salvation come—from his ideals? His beliefs? His values? To brave life's ocean and dare its dark waves just to reach an island—a lonely rock—will be his goal. And if, half-dead, he finds himself on the shore before the tides of fortune shift, he will again seek to reach higher, more secure ground. And upon that island's plateaus and terraces he will again erect lofty pedestals to the highest accomplishments of his mind. . . .

Such thoughts occupying my mind, that night on our veranda I eased back my chair and gratefully gulped the fresh ocean breeze, while my eyes wandered to the clear, starry sky. Who made all this? I wondered. And how does all this vastness of grandeur and majesty relate to my meager existence?

Vivid images from every chapter of my life suddenly flashed before my eyes. I reminisced about Panos the scout leader and refugee, the captain, the soldier, the father and businessman, the survivor. My life—an endless strife—was all replayed in an instant. How short life really is! How ephemeral! So what is its purpose? How does the swift passing of my days relate to the meaning of my existence? To be born, to live, to die—is this the sum total of the meaning of life? And is winning my bread with sweat and agony my goal? Is there a goal beyond the winning of bread? An ultimate goal? A destiny? Could it be that, at the end of its flow, life enters into an ocean of continued existence? How can I know?

From the depths of my inmost conscience there springs a desire to know. But to have the answers may not be my lot— my lot may be to just live on, experiencing the visible, the tangible, the sensational, the real, until I die. And then, who knows? Perhaps in that ocean sublime beyond the realm of the mun-

dane, beyond the stars, lie all the answers. Meanwhile, my desire to know will exist as a feeble candle flame—weak, but burning, nevertheless—until death's cold breath reduces it to a smoldering wick. And if, perchance, amid the toil for survival this
starving flame is fed again by a rare moment of elevated thought,
rekindled, as now, by a conducive setting and allaying circumstances, then my yearning to know will burst anew into a colossal fire, its blazing tongues dispelling the darkness so as to take
me, alas, but to infinite nothingness until, consumed by its own
intensity, the fire is again reduced to a flickering flame.

I have no lofty pedestals to build, no trophies to display.
Only questions—questions reaching into infinity, seeking to
unlock the enigma of life.

Perhaps there are no answers to be had—only insatiable
questions. There may be no known purpose in living this life,
nor a destiny beyond the soil I tread and the inexplicable burning desire to know.

But such matters are for the cultivated in mind—the philosopher, the clergyman, the erudite, the learned. Why didn't I
concern myself with such matters while contemplating suicide?
Vain is my search for a meaning in life. It is void of virtue,
empty, meaningless. For it stems from my need for an emotional outpouring; a need to induce mental cleansing; a cathar-
sis of conscience that will free me from the oppression of guilt
and shame.

Even so, I cannot free myself from these thoughts. They
are a part of me, for I am what I experience and feel. My conscience is my memory. And that's just all that life may be.

# 4

# From Death's Claws

SAILING ACROSS THE ROUGH waters of the Cretan Sea from the port of Souda to Piraeus and back was a welcome routine. I was responsible for the loading, shipment, and delivery of goods. Since all transactions were conducted on a cash basis, upon my return I would count the collected cash on Angelos' desk per customer invoice, read and sign the handwritten documents Angelos had prepared, and receive my commission. Angelos kept his records, and I kept mine.

Port of Souda, Crete. Panos was familiar with all major seaports in Greece.

Mr. Mihelakis would often leave for his Athens office and return after several days. But once he was confident that business was running pretty smoothly, he began to leave for longer periods of time.

By October of 1935, Angelos was going the extra mile to ensure the best of business relationships with me. In contrast to the leering smirk on his face, upon my return from each business trip he would invariably extend his hand in friendship and give me a heartfelt welcome. He would order me coffee, offer me a cigarette, update me on all political issues and local news, and share my great excitement about my newborn son Demetrios. Greatly obliged, I of course let no opportunity slip by to return such favors.

Angelos' congeniality and obliging spirit seemed to know no limits. One day he even suggested that I have my father come and use a cozy corner of office space for the conduct of his clerical business, in exchange for errands he might be asked to run or chores to do—including killing mice. Indeed, his good will transcended my culture. The best way I knew of to repay his kindness was through an overt expression of loyalty to our friendship. Consequently, as business grew and the workload increased, making the paperwork voluminous, I figured I could save Angelos and me time by counting the cash with him and then simply signing all documents.

MEANWHILE, business boomed and profits soared. And though it meant hard work and sleepless nights away from home, I looked for opportunities to handle extra shipments, but not via our firm. Handsome pecuniary gains made the extra work worthwhile, and by January of 1937, in just one year, I had paid back nearly one-third of my loan. Were it not for my fear that Mr. Mihelakis might suspect my business exploits and surmise that I would soon become financially independent and go into business for myself, I would have already paid back more than half the loan. In any case, since the business I had generated for him in barely one year had added considerably to his wealth, a contented Mr. Mihelakis was not about to risk creating any ripples in his smoothly-run business by asking me too many questions.

Nor did he seem overly concerned about the way things were now run at his office in Chania. He would leave for Athens and not return until time to collect his money and, unlike in the past, take only a superficial look at the books. I began to fret about his new, predictable mode of operation. It left an overconfident Angelos solely in charge of all cash revenues, as well as all books and records. That made me feel very uncomfortable. On a number of occasions I came close to asking Mr. Mihelakis to let me audit the company books and check them against mine, particularly after I began to notice that Angelos had become noticeably jittery during the counting of collected cash. But I feared that this request might turn out to be a case of unfounded suspicion and mistrust, and thus cost me a relationship—and my job.

One day my taciturn father, the company's willing lackey, who on occasion would happen to be nearby to observe routine cash transactions across Angelos' desk, gave me some advice. "It's not good salesmanship to not examine what you're signing," he said. Knowing my father to be a man of no shallow character and of a keen mind, I readily concurred with his reminder, which again stirred my suspicions of Angelos.

The following day, bent over the desk ready to sign a stack of hand-written documents as usual, I alluded to the fact that we had had some pretty big figures to deal with recently, at which point I paused as if to examine a document. Suddenly I raised my eyes and, not to my surprise, faced a startled Angelos leaning over the desk, his bulging brown eyes gazing fixedly at mine. He was breathing hard and looked alarmed.

"Hey, partner—" he said, "—don't you trust a friend?"

"You've been kind of nervous lately, Angelos," I said. "Something wrong?"

"Hand that back to me!" he shouted, as he unsuccessfully tried to grab the paper from my hands.

"Just as I thought," I said, and placed the pen back in the ink bottle.

Dumbfounded, Angelos watched me put the paper in my pocket, plus a few more. His face was taut, the corners of his smirk drawn down. I looked at the freshly counted cash lying on the desk, let my eyes fly pityingly to his face, then turned around and walked away.

A short distance down the road I stopped to examine the paper Angelos had tried to grab from me. Everything seemed correct—until I read the bottom two lines:

| | |
|---|---|
| Amount per customer invoice | 166 dr. |
| Amount to be submitted | 166 dr. |

I couldn't believe my eyes! I checked one more paper. The same! I checked a couple more. Correct—no amount to be submitted. "The crafty devil!" I growled. The same figure appeared twice, but the second line read, "Amount to be submitted" rather than "Amount submitted." Had I attempted to examine one of the other two papers first, he wouldn't have batted an eye. He knew which one was dynamite!

I was outraged. I didn't know what was keeping me from going right back and tearing him apart. But I was also angry with myself for allowing him room to cheat. In the end I decided I had better let Mr. Mihelakis himself deal with his "angel."

On my next business trip two days later I looked for Mr. Mihelakis in his Athens office, but learned he had already left for Chania. That gives Angelos at least forty-eight hours to "explain" things to the boss, I thought to myself. Angelos isn't stupid—he wouldn't have gone on cheating and embezzling company funds at my expense without having weighed in his mind all possible risks. Now he'll go to step two of his scheme— probably updating the boss on my "new debt" to the company. But I doubt Mr. Mihelakis will buy Angelos' story. He knows my integrity. But then, who knows? It's really my word against his. These two men have done business together for many years and have gained each other's confidence. Mr. Mihelakis might very well swallow Angelos' story, since that could also explain to him how I was able to pay back nearly half the loan in a little over a year.

Dark thoughts assailed me as I leaned heavily over the side railing of the ship on my way back to Crete. As I looked into the awful blackness of the vast waters below my feet, I felt a wave of despondency sweeping over me. Shame and guilt engulfed me as the thought of suicide once more came to mind. Once again, it's my head that has brought about another predicament, I kept thinking. I am to blame. If I had acted like a true salesman, I wouldn't have enabled Angelos to cheat. He was lured by my own stupidity. My dereliction is the real crime. I am to blame. I am guilty. . . .

A COLD welcome awaited me at the office the following night. I found Mr. Mihelakis bent over the company books. He got up from his chair slowly, his eyes averted, eyelids batting rapidly, hands in his pockets. I stretched out my hand for a handshake, and he refused it. He turned the other way as if I weren't there. He took a few slow, short steps until he reached the back wall of the office, then stopped. He lit a cigarette.

Never in my whole life had I felt more embarrassed in the presence of a man I respected. I was anxious to have him hear my story.

"I looked for you in Athens, Mr. Mihelakis. I—I guess I missed you by a few hours."

He turned around slowly, hands clasped behind, cigarette in his mouth, his eyes riveted on blank space.

Breath caught in my lungs, I waited. If he had anything to say, I thought, he would get straight to the point.

A cloud of smoke veiled his face. "Angelos and I cleared the records yesterday," he finally said. He sounded preoccupied and irritable. Then, glaring at me, he added, "We have a deficit of twenty thousand drachmas!"

"Twen—uh—twenty thou—! Mr. Mihelakis—it can't be!"

He walked to the desk, picked up a piece of paper and handed it to me. It read:

| | |
|---|---|
| Loan balance plus interest | 10,040 dr. |
| Terpandros' rental fees | 2,060 dr. |
| Collections to be submitted | 7,890 dr. |
| Total | 19,990 dr. |

Rage consumed me. The scheming, untrustworthy charlatan! I thought. That's how much he embezzled. Ten thousand!

Surely he'd like to have me now accuse him of fraud, so he could sue me for slander. A hellish trap for me—built by that devil to protect himself!

I reached inside my pocket and produced the handwritten documents, proof in black and white that Angelos was the culprit. I handed one to the boss.

He took a quick look at it, folded it in two and flung it on the desk as if he'd seen it before.

My eyes widened, my mouth dropped. "But, Mr. Mihelakis, I—I don't get it!"

He shrugged his shoulders and took a few short steps away from me.

"For one thing, Mr. Mihelakis, neither you nor Angelos ever mentioned a rental fee for my father's corner," I continued, my voiced raised.

He nodded, but his apparent nonchalance perplexed me the more.

"Well, then?" I demanded.

I had always spoken to this man with great respect. Even now I didn't want to show him any signs of disrespect. But I was getting desperate—I needed some response, some explanation.

He moved pensively toward the door behind me, his lips pressed tightly together, his eyes batting rapidly. His troubled mind was seeking a solution. At least he knows I'm clean, I thought to myself. Good to know that this man, who has helped me so much, still trusts me. But he must think I let him down by not acting like a true salesman. The very thought kills me. Whatever the problem, I caused it. How dare I now show signs of impatience with him? I should rather stand by him and help him solve this problem—my problem!

He finished his cigarette and threw the stub out in the street. "I've arranged for you to get a 20,000-drachma personal loan tomorrow," he said suddenly as he turned around and headed toward the wall again.

"A twenty-thousand-drachma personal loan?" I exclaimed in disbelief.

I looked at the man. Either he cannot pin Angelos down or he is in collusion with him, or both, I thought. Is it possible that he means to destroy me after all? I know Angelos could hang me by my own signature. But is Mr. Mihelakis thinking the same?

He lit another cigarette. He seemed to be holding something back from me.

"Mr. Mihelakis," I said, "am I being charged with the amounts Angelos reported?"

His back turned to me, head nearly touching the wall, he stood motionless. He seemed to have come to a dead end.

"Mr. Mihelakis—"

Absolute silence.

"Mr. Mihelakis!"

"See you tomorrow, Panos!" he rasped.

"Tomorrow? There may not be another tomorrow—" I grumbled as I turned around and left.

WHEN I returned home that afternoon I found Chrysa in tears. She told me that Yorgos' brother-in-law had just passed away. I told her I needed to go for a walk.

"But dinner's going to get cold," she said, her tearful eyes looking apprehensively into mine.

I didn't know where I was headed or what I was going to do.

After a while, I found myself at a small cafe bar overlooking Faliro Beach. I drank one glass of wine, then had a second. I felt extremely depressed. "I hate myself," I muttered. "I hate myself for the hell I got myself into. . . ."

I thought of Angelos, and a flurry of anger engulfed me. "I'm so angry at him," I growled. "He rejected the best I had to offer him—my friendship. He stabbed me in the back. The same with Tony; and now Mr. Mihelakis. They all betrayed me!"

I downed a third glass of wine. I gave him too much rope, I kept thinking. The rope of my pride. Pride! What prevented me from putting an end to my life, has now become my undoing.

I drank one more glass, then gulped a fifth and stood up to walk. I did not feel dizzy. I asked for another glass—I wanted to get drunk. I wanted to drown my pain and escape the haunting fear of hopelessness. (Four glasses usually made me lean against the wall, five would lay me flat out on the floor.) When I had downed my sixth, I paid a dumbfounded bartender and walked out.

I went and sat on a large, smooth rock near the claw-like tip of a steep cliff that overlooked the jagged rocks and fierce waves of the sea below. A monument of death, that rock had seen the last breath of many desperate souls who had gone one short step beyond its cold, rounded hump. Seated on the hump, I waited for the wine to take effect so I could jump to my death. But I was not getting dizzy.

I half-arose from the rock, leaned over the edge of the cliff, and looked down into the abyss below my feet. "One step," I muttered. "No guns, no ropes. Just one damned step!"

My life balanced on the very edge, I waited.

Death snarled below my feet, spewing froth, baring his teeth. Like the vicious jaws of a raging beast, the jagged rocks below awaited their feast—vanishing, then resurfacing with every crashing wave, gushing through the foam, promising me death.

Death had one sure thing to offer: the end of bitter tears and haunting fears. No more guilt or shame, no more mortal pain.

For one last time I raised my eyes, as if to give life one last chance to challenge death's promises before I cast the decisive vote.

Just then my eyes saw a glimpse of the sun as it was setting beyond the peninsula, its enormous fiery disc spreading a veil of an iridescent rose's petal-pink that spanned the earth's dome. And when the last reflection of the sky's glorious crown had danced atop a thousand ruffles in the gulf, I found myself standing in awe before the breath-taking splendor and majesty of the heavens. There was a perfectly harmonious blending of bright and soft nuances of exquisite pink and blue and turquoise hues that brushed a gentle stretch of clouds, the glorious masterpiece of no earthly artist!

A desire swept over me to reach into the celestial heights of that matchless beauty and catch a fleeting hold of its purity and peace, and for a moment let my heart become its dwelling place.

A new realization then dawned in me that what I was seeking was a way to get rid not of my life itself, but of its filth. My head and eyes raised high, I began to shake like a leaf, and wished my tears could purge my soul.

"God!" I cried out, "do You exist? And do You care for a wretched, hopeless mortal like me?"

Looking once more down below, I saw the epitome of my hopelessness and guilt. A mortifying fear overtook me. What if there is an afterlife? I thought. What if all this majesty and grandeur bespeak the purity and majesty in the beyond? Then I am certainly doomed, for I am unclean.

As if prompted by a volition other than my own, my footsteps slowly led me away from the cliff's edge, my heart being driven by a compelling desire to preserve my life and a consciousness that someone was watching over me. Filled with awe and wonder, I tremblingly whispered, "God, You do exist? And You do care?"

A short distance down the road, I looked back, and a shuddering chill swept down my spine. The cliff's edge pointed down like the sharp tip of a sickle, as if death's claw were still threatening to harpoon my soul. "Never again!" I cried out aloud, as I lifted my eyes above and tears cascaded down my face. "Never again will I allow my mind to think of suicide. I will not kill myself. And I shall make amends for my wretched life!"

Still astounded by what I had experienced, I headed home, thinking of my wife and my two sons. I missed them terribly. Chrysa, I thought to myself, she's the one I can trust. How selfish have I been, how blind!

AS I reached my home that evening, I heard loud cries coming from inside. Women were wailing and moaning, and I surmised it was because of the recent death of Yorgos' brother-in-law. As I entered, I saw the shocked faces of a dozen relatives surrounding my wife. Then Chrysa, eyes wide and countenance filled with fear, looked at me and screamed as if she had seen a ghost.

"It's him! It's Panos!" they all shouted.

Wiping her eyes, Chrysa dashed forward and threw her arms around my neck. "Thank God you're alive! You're back!" she cried out, and collapsed in my arms.

A piece of paper fell from her hands. My brother picked it up and handed it to me.

"Oh, my God!" I wailed. It was the old suicide note I had written two years earlier and which I had placed between the pages of my diaries. Chrysa, seeing earlier that day that I was feeling unusually low, had taken my diaries out of the drawer, and the old note had fallen out from my diary pages. It had not been dated.

When everyone had regained composure, I apologized to Chrysa—for the first time ever!—and assured everyone that I had already dealt with the ignominious idea of suicide once and for all. I revealed nothing, however, about my experience by the cliff. Tears began to flow afresh.

"My son," my mother said, tears streaming down from her eyes, "I've prayed to God for you. We all know what you've gone through. We know of your disappointments in life. You have tried everything. Why not try this, too?" Having said that, she placed a book in my hands. "Go on," she said. "Take it. It will bring you protection."

I looked at the book. Engraved on the front of its leather cover, right above a large cross, was its title:

## THE HOLY WRIT

"It's a Bible!" I said in astonishment. I didn't know what to make of my mother's uncanny gesture. Why, of all things, has she chosen to give me a Bible? I wondered. The book of the priests! Does she know of my secret visits to St. Nikolaos? Had she wanted me to become a priest? It wouldn't be a bad idea for someone whose life is clean. Priests and monks seek to attain spiritual perfection early in life. But that's a state I could not hope to attain at the age of thirty-one.

Suddenly it occurred to me—I shuddered at the thought— that my mother had brought the holy book in order to place it on my casket.

THAT night, weak and spent, head throbbing, eyes swollen, I sank heavily into my bed. As I lay there, my mind kept turning back to my brush with death, my stomach now lurching at the thought. I could not believe that earlier in the day I had left home with no intention to commit suicide, yet had come closer to taking my life than ever before. Had a miracle from God stopped me from jumping to my death? I wondered. What else could have prevented six glasses of wine from taking effect?

I thought of the longing I had experienced by the cliff to rid myself of all my life's filth, and how it had rekindled the faded desire within me to find hope for tomorrow and a reason for my existence. Had God as a result heard me and intervened? For my sake? Why?

As I turned over in my bed, I looked at the flickering flame of the kerosene lamp as it was teased by the cool ocean breeze. The Bible was on my pillow, where I had laid it for good luck. Its engraved cross appeared very deep and wide. My eyelids were heavy, and my body lay inert as my fingers crawled toward the leather-bound holy book and laid its front cover open. Summoning my last ounce of energy, I raised my head over the first page of the Bible and read its first lines.

Suddenly my whole being froze. My life became trapped in my lungs, and I lay still as death. Then a charge of energy streaked up my spine, releasing my breath and conquering my inertia. I marveled as I heard my lips tremblingly speak the words that had held me spellbound for such a long moment:

"In the beginning God created the heavens and the earth."

The words seemed to be the embodiment of all the power and majesty of the dazzling beauty my eyes had beheld only hours earlier, the purity and peace of which I had so undeservedly wished to make mine.

Fingers clamped on the Bible, I went on to read that God had created everything on the earth, and also man; and that He had created everything on the earth for man.

This timely discovery overwhelmed me, filling me with curiosity, hope, and awe. It seemed to impart to me a sense of self-worth and belonging in this world, for I lived in a place made by God.

Shaking from excitement, I did not realize how engrossed I was until Chrysa walked in. She knew I had never held a Bible in my hands before, but she knew as well that my eyes spoke of an unusual experience.

THOSE circles around my eyes the next morning had been caused by an extraordinary dissipation: I had stayed up most of the night reading, of all things, the Bible! If what the Bible says about God and His creation is true, I reasoned on my way to work, then it may also say something about the very purpose of life on earth and perhaps even a life in the hereafter. But wouldn't the priests know about those things? And wouldn't they have told everyone? No one ever talks about God and religion, though. I wonder why. . . .

# 5

# The Deliverer

I FOUND MR. MIHELAKIS GOING over his books, and to my surprise, his greeting and welcome were as hearty as ever. After offering me a cigarette, he talked about the 20,000-drachma loan rather casually, only this time he gave me a different story. It was going to be not a personal loan, but a special trust-secured loan, and Angelos and I would be the signatories. He explained that earlier that morning Angelos had gone to the bank to sign, and that all that was needed now was my signature.

He then drew my attention to a document on top of the desk. As I picked it up, I noticed a grin spreading across his face. It was a neatly typed promissory note stating that Angelos was to provide the necessary company funds, with which I would be making the loan payments directly to the bank, Mr. Mihelakis being the sole guarantor of the loan. The note was already dated and carefully signed by Mr. Mihelakis.

"In effect, Mr. Mihelakis," I remarked, "Angelos' responsibility and mine with regard to this loan is primarily ethical; yours, financial. Is this the way you see it?"

He nodded. "You might say that."

Then he advised me that I should have Angelos sign the promissory note as soon as possible and that I should thereafter keep and safeguard it at all times.

The promissory note sounded safe. I could not imagine, however, that Mr. Mihelakis would let the 10,000 drachmas that crafty swindler had embezzled go forgotten or unaccounted for. Something had to be in his mind that this promissory note did not reveal.

I folded the note, put it in my pocket, and took a moment to mull things over.

"Well?" said a fidgety Mr. Mihelakis. "Aren't you going to the bank?"

Our eyes met. I always thought I could get more emotion from a wall than from this man's eyes.

"Mr. Mihelakis," I said, "since you are the sole guarantor of the entire loan, mightn't I oblige you to become a cosignatory as well?"

"Oh, certainly. Let's go!" he replied unhesitatingly, which puzzled me all the more. He got up from his chair, and together we headed for the bank.

"Well, sir," I said to a preoccupied and silent Mr. Mihelakis on our way, "I'm making another loan payment today. I thought I'd let you know."

"Oh, yes—that loan. Well, I'll tell you what. I've thought of a way to make it much easier on you, Panos," he said in an unusually friendly manner. "Why don't you just stop by my house later this afternoon, but after Angelos has signed the promissory note, and let's talk about that loan over a drink. Be sure, though—" he stopped a moment to offer me a cigarette, his lowered voice giving the matter added gravity, "—be sure Angelos doesn't know about it. In fact, no one should know about it. It's strictly a deal between you and me," he said, his eyes warily scanning the area to be sure no one had heard him.

His change of plans, shift in mood, secretiveness, unusual invitation, and the note itself—it all stirred my suspicions. Our clandestine rendezvous was bound to be revealing.

After the loan was gotten as agreed, I returned to the office. So that Angelos would not be alarmed, I greeted him with a smile. Seated behind the desk, arms folded, he nodded warily. I produced the promissory note and placed it on the desk. Angelos bent slowly forward, arms still folded, and examined it.

"Oh, man—forget it!" he said in disdain, and eased himself back in his chair. "He can sign anything he wants. It's enough I signed that damned loan this morning."

"Very well, then—" I said as I grabbed the promissory note and headed for the door, "—you tell him that!"

IT WAS Thursday, February 4, 1937. I was skeptical about my secret meeting with Mr. Mihelakis at his home that afternoon. As I was about to knock, his wife quickly opened the door and asked me hurriedly in. Standing behind her and smoking a cigarette was Mr. Mihelakis. I felt uneasy.

"He refused to sign," I said, and showed him the promissory note.

"The devil!" growled Mr. Mihelakis. "Leave it over there," he said nervously, pointing to a table. "I'll catch him later myself."

He walked to another room, at the end of which was a low, narrow door. He opened the door and turned a switch on, then beckoned me to follow as he proceeded down a wooden staircase.

From the top of the staircase I could see a half-empty wastebasket near the bottom step. Going down a dozen steps, I found myself in a dank, practically empty basement. A light hung low from the middle of the ceiling, right above a small table and a chair. On the table there was a pen and a bottle of ink.

Suddenly the door slammed behind me. I stood nervously by the wastebasket, wondering if Mrs. Mihelakis had locked the door from the outside.

Mr. Mihelakis stood by the table. Cigarette between his lips, he reached inside his jacket. A gun! I thought. No—papers. Perhaps the original loan contract? Maybe he wants to change the interest rate on my loan. But that would require Angelos' signature. So why should he be so secretive about it? Something stinks about this whole thing.

He placed two pieces of paper on the table side by side, pulled the chair out and sat down, then bent over the papers and started to examine them.

I was breathing heavily. To hide my nervousness, I took out a cigarette—my last one—and tossed the empty pack into the wastebasket. The sound broke the silence, and Mr. Mihelakis turned toward me. He could see I was searching my pockets for a match, but he continued to look at me.

The dim light seemed to enlarge his round glasses, giving his face a ghastly appearance. "Why did you do that to me,

Panos?" he suddenly said in a low, colorless voice. "Didn't you feel sorry for my children?"

Unsure what he was alluding to, I stood still and waited to hear the rest.

Dead silence ensued. I wondered whether he was intimating that I had been in collusion with Angelos. No, he was probably referring to my naiveness in my financial transactions with Angelos, I figured.

"Mr. Mihelakis," I finally said, "give me a chance to explain—"

He stood up and walked away from the table, then turned to face me from the far end of the room. He pointed to the chair and told me to sit.

Slowly, I headed for the table. I felt as though I were playing a role in a motion picture about victimization by gangsters—only this was too real. I knew he wasn't going to change his mind about anything—whatever he was determined to do, he would get on with it. Something was telling me, however, that it wasn't going to be anything nice. And it didn't look as though we were going to talk about my loan "over a drink," either.

Arms folded, eyes obscured, the ghost-like figure watched me as I took the chair. If I could only be certain that he means to harm me, I thought, now would be the time to grab him. But what if I was wrong?

I sat on the chair and bent over the papers. In front of me was a note in his own handwriting, and next to it a blank sheet of paper. As I picked up the note, he told me I was to copy everything onto the blank sheet, word for word.

I started to read. The cigarette fell from my mouth. "My God!" I breathed out. "Better dead!"

It was impossible to stop my hands from shaking. I pretended I was still reading, so I could think what to do. I'll ask if I can borrow his matches, I thought. Then I'll knock him down. I'm sorry to have to do this to Mr. Mihelakis, but he's practically asking me to commit suicide!

I turned toward him, only to see the barrel of a gun aimed coldly toward me! The blood rushed to my head, and a cold sweat covered my body. A rank darkness flooded my mind as I slowly turned my face the other way. He wouldn't dare harm me with that gun, I thought. But then, how do I know the degree of his dementia?

Shaking uncontrollably, I dipped the pen into the ink bottle and proceeded to copy the note:

Declaration

I, the undersigned, Panos Zachariou, do declare in knowledge of the consequences in accordance with the law, that the signature of Mr. \_\_\_ Mihelakis as our guarantor on the promissory note produced by Mr. Angelos \_\_\_ is not his authentic signature. The truth is that I myself placed Mr. Mihelakis' signature after being coerced by Mr. [Angelos] \_\_\_.

Chania, 4 February, 1937

The declarer

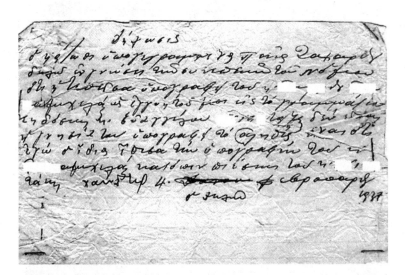

Shown here in its entirety, and torn only in half, is the original declaration note hand-written by Panos' boss, which Panos was forced to copy at gunpoint.

The machinations of the devil! No wonder that heinous promissory note was not typed on the company's typewriter, I thought. And the only fingerprints on it now are my own! All the fuss to get Angelos to sign—what a sham!

Still aiming his gun at me, he quickly placed another note and blank paper on the table and ordered me to proceed as before. I couldn't believe what was happening to me; I hoped I was having a nightmare. Head throbbing, eyes burning, I didn't even bother to read this time. I just went on copying.

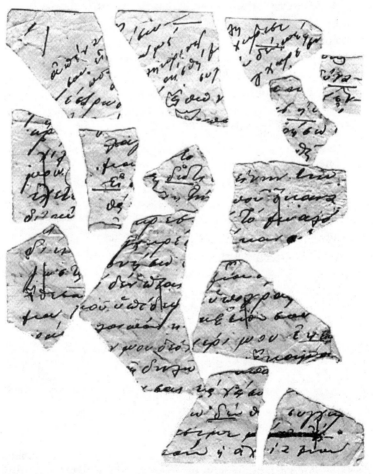

Pieces of the letter that was hand-written by Panos' boss and which Panos was forced to copy at gunpoint. (More than half of the pieces are missing.)

It was a letter, supposedly from me to him, in which I was apologizing for my deliberate intent to incriminate him for no known cause, having done so in full knowledge of the consequences punishable by law. In the letter I was asking him to forgive me, for my decision to write such a letter was the result of a deeply remorseful condition on my part, as shown by the fact that I chose to submit my forged promissory note to him in person!

Placing the pen back on the table felt like surrendering to the enemy in utter defeat. I wanted to tear those papers to pieces, but my hands would not obey.

I thought of the deadly penalty for forgery. A living death—imprisoned for life! My God!

At that moment the door opened, and someone came down the steps. I was hoping it was someone I knew, who could witness what was happening to me. It was a little old woman. I' didn't know her. He walked to her, gun in his hand, and whispered something in her ear—I couldn't make out what. He made the sign of the cross three times. Praying? I thought to myself. This maniac has just forced me to become a victim of forgery at gunpoint, and now he's praying in front of an old woman. Praying for what? Forgiveness in advance of the murder he's contemplating?

I started to pray, too. My God! Here I am, dealing with a mad man! If You are truly the one who saved me from death the other day, deliver me now from this hell, and protect me from the deadly penalty for forgery. Then I'll believe in You. I'll believe what the Bible says about You. Please, God!

I couldn't understand what the little old woman had come to do, but she left just as suddenly as she had come in.

Mr. Mihelakis then told me that we were going to have a drink. Pacing back and forth and keeping his distance from me, he told me that he couldn't trust Angelos and that he wouldn't use the promissory note or the letter unless he had to.

When he was done with his speech, he approached the table with great caution, gun aimed straight at me, and told me to lean back and not try anything bold. He picked up all the papers and walked to the wastebasket. Sorting out everything, he folded my copies and put them in his pocket, then tore the rest into pieces. He bent over the wastebasket, hesitated a moment, then picked up the empty cigarette pack I'd thrown into it. He stuffed the empty pack with the torn pieces of paper, then tossed it back into the wastebasket.

Right then his wife came downstairs, carrying two drinks. After handing him one, she slowly walked toward me and warily placed the other glass near the edge of the table, then turned around and left.

Her husband resumed his speech about this and that, but I wasn't paying much attention. I was thinking how I could grab the gun from his hand.

Suddenly he suggested a second drink and went up the stairs.

Wasting no time, I jumped to my feet and dashed to the wastebasket. I quickly picked up the stuffed cigarette pack, emptied part of its contents into my pocket, and replaced it as I had found it.

I heard him coming—there was no time for me to go back and sit down on the chair. I jumped toward the table and swung my body around to make it appear as though I had just gotten up from the chair and was slowly heading for the exit.

He came down the steps holding two drinks, one in each hand. We met at the bottom step, nose to nose. After handing me one of the drinks, which I gulped down fast, he told me I was free to go.

Less than a block down the street, I anxiously sorted through the pieces of paper I had at the risk of my life retrieved. My breath caught in my lungs, I directed my eyes skyward. "God!" I shouted at the release of my breath. "Oh, my G-o-o-o-o-d!" In my hands I had the original declaration note in its entirety, only torn in half! And I had enough pieces of the letter as well! A miracle from my God! The very thought—the thought that God should intervene on my behalf—overwhelmed me!

In the next couple of days a nervous, frustrated Mr. Mihelakis would snap his fingers at me and order me around as never before. I didn't mind making his barber appointments, buying his groceries, or running all sorts of new errands. And I didn't quite mind his demands—even in public—for bigger loan payments or longer work hours. What I did mind was that he now acted as though he had the power to control every breath I took. I couldn't trust the man at all—my picture of him had changed from that of a benevolent person to that of a dangerous criminal.

THERE was a lot of turmoil that weekend between Mr. Mihelakis and the other partners over the firing of Angelos. As the conflict mounted, Mr. Mihelakis became extremely irritable. Doubtless, I was going to be his scapegoat in the end.

The following Monday morning I questioned what he was about to have me sign and insisted that I first examine the documents. He glared at me and snarled, "Listen, you! You could very well be in prison right now, and you know it!"

"How can you be so sure?" I said provocatively.

"You want to bet?" he barked.

We exchanged a burning stare.

"If I had to choose between throwing you in jail and beating you up," I shot back, "I would gladly beat your brains out!"

"You!" he fumed vehemently, "—you will spend the rest of your miserable years in prison!"

"Brace yourself, mister, for it's not I who will wind up in prison. It's you!"

"And how might that be? Do you want to give it a try?"

"Any time, sir, any time. You show the court the copies; I show them the originals. Is it a deal?"

He gasped, his eyes ready to pop out of their sockets. "I don't believe you!" he said, his face turning pale. "You—you would have done something about it by now. Your tales don't scare me!"

"No tales, sir. Facts. Real facts. So start digging your own grave now."

Overcome by astonishment and fear, face drained of color, he continued to glare at me.

"And let me tell you one thing more, buster," I went on. "You can take your lousy business completely into your own hands and go to hell with it along with your angel. I'm through with you. I quit!"

And having said that, I walked away from the bondage of
that miserable man and his conniving consort.

As I headed home, my mind kept going back to my desperate plea and the vow I had made to God as I stared into that
gun. There was no doubt in my mind that my deliverance from
Mihelakis and my present freedom were somehow related to
my first encounter with the Bible.

囗囗囗囗囗

# 6

# The Quest

UNSHACKLED, FREE, AND THANKING GOD, I arrived home with great excitement. As I opened the door, my eyes were met by an intriguing and solemn sight. I stood still for a moment, then slowly removed my hat in reverence; for there on the dresser near my bed, like praying hands opened heavenward, lay the Bible.

Never before had I seen a Bible wide open in a home; only closed and sealed under the dust of oblivion—untouched, undisturbed, unnoticed—just as the Bible my eyes now beheld had lain hidden for years behind icons and candles. To many, simply touching the Bible would be sacrilegious; opening it, a blasphemy. It was the holy book, meant only for the priests, yet now it lay before me just as I had left it the night its first lines dazzled my eyes.

Reverently, I walked across the room and stood before the holy book. Eyes fixed on its pages, I traced the fresh imprints it had left in my heart, and I was filled with awe. I sensed a growing intuition stirring within me my questions about the existence of a spiritual reality, and the hope that that reality was rooted in the words before me which told of the God of all creation.

From that day on I read the Bible nearly every day. Starting with Genesis, I read every line, every chapter. And when I found two new partners and there was again no time to spare, I took the Bible with me to work and on my business trips.

TRAVELING by ship one day, I became so absorbed in what I was reading that only too late did I realize that I had become the cause of commotion among a number of curious travelers, who suddenly gathered around me and stared as if I had committed some crime.

"Is that the holy book in your hands?" one of them challenged.

"Why, I see you recognize it, friend," I said.

"You think you're some saint?" jeered another.

"Yeah—one without a halo!" shouted another one, as the whole bunch burst into a fit of laughter.

"Friends," I said, as I placed the Bible inside my briefcase, "you show me a better book. Then we can trade."

"You're not a priest!" blared the first one, his finger jabbed at me as the rest of the gang shouted familiar obscenities—even threats—as I walked away.

That incident was particularly discouraging, for in truth I knew of no laymen who took a personal interest in the Bible.

Another such incident took place on a bus when I was seen reading the Bible. I began to wonder then whether my own interest in the Bible was no more than a mere oddity on my part, especially since my lifestyle was certainly no match for that which rightfully belonged "in the hands of the priests alone," as some passengers on the bus had argued.

Adding to my discouragement at the same time was my inability to comprehend, let alone believe, certain things in the Bible. Why all the absurd sacrifices? Was everything in the Bible literal? Did the flood, the parting of the Red Sea, and other supernatural phenomena really happen? And where did the Bible talk about Christ, the saints, or Holy Mary?

Ironically, it was from what I heard myself say to an elusive traveler one day that I received encouragement and began to read the Bible with renewed interest. I had just sat down at the bow of the ship to read the Bible when a stranger standing behind me asked, "Do you really believe the Red Sea parted?" "Why, of course," I replied readily. "If God could—" But as I turned around to meet my unexpected questioner, my eyes barely got a glimpse of a figure hurriedly vanishing among the travelers on the main deck. That's right, I kept thinking to myself as I searched the eyes of every passenger wearing a dark suit the rest of the trip. If God could create the heavens and the earth, then certainly He could do anything the Bible says—and that includes parting the Red Sea!

I WAS intrigued by Deuteronomy 15, particularly its first two verses, which talked about creditors releasing their neighbors' debt every seven years. For a long time I wondered what those verses meant, until one day I read Job 5:19: "Six times he will rescue you from affliction; but in the seventh no evil will touch you" (NIV). This verse, along with Deuteronomy 15, was part of the same riddle, I surmised, the effects of which could benefit those who had the correct interpretation.

Suddenly I had the answer. That's it! I thought. Now I know the cause of my poverty and affliction! It occurred to me that for the past several years as a private mailman and salesman, I had lived in misery and want possibly because I had not honored my parents' advice against investing in that kind of business, especially with the wrong partner. I counted the years I had been in that business—a little over six. Another eight months or so, probably around April of 1938, I figured, and the tides of fortune would shift.

Immediately I ordered my life to go on an all-out religious alert. I got to thinking that if I became a better person before the end of the seventh year, I would find favor in God's eyes; and God, or maybe some saint, might guide me to some big money and thus rescue me from my financial affliction and martyrdom. "God will bless us," I told a stunned Chrysa that morning. "In less than one year we will prosper again."

To show God how eagerly I anticipated the day of my financial salvation, that same day I bought lottery tickets, hoping that some day soon the good tidings of a bonanza would reach my ears. That same day also, I resolved to change my life and make amends for my wretched past, so I wrote a long list of vows and resolutions I would live by, especially things I would never do again: never again cuss or swear abusing God's name, the name of Christ, Holy Mary, or the saints; never again cheat at the customs office; never again overcharge my clients; never again visit the brothels; never again get drunk; never again gamble; never again lie or stand as a false witness in the courts;

never again lose my temper and beat or bully anyone; and so forth.

Before long, however, I found myself violating my own vows and resolutions. That following Sunday afternoon, for instance, I got drunk. A born lover of fun and frolic—a trait that had always made me most desirable in the company of my buddies and peers—I was asked repeatedly to help spread smiles and laughter upon the faces of my cronies. My reluctance greatly surprised them, though I refused to reveal my reasons for fear I would be laughed at.

"It's because you went to church this morning, eh?" a friend teased.

I was baffled. I pretended I didn't hear him, but I wasn't sure whether he was bluffing or had actually seen me coming out of St. Nikolaos, where I had gone that morning for a few minutes just to see what a church liturgy was like.

"Hey, now! Charlie ain't that old yet, is he?" remarked another friend, alluding to my oft-repeated saying that religion was for the old folks and the women.

To hide my embarrassment, I sprang to my feet and shouted, "Come on, you guys, let's go!"

After walking a couple of kilometers, we ended up at a lone country tavern. At first every piquant mezes (delicacy) was washed down with a drink, but soon more drinks than tidbits were funneling down our gullets. Being more drunk than the rest, at the end of our binge I ordered the first cavalry of tipplers to mount their mules—long stocks of reeds procured from the roadside bushes—and prepare for a grand mock parade through town. Galloping and prancing, shouting and dancing, we managed to reach town, all along the way gaining other sympathetic patrons who staggered up and joined us in our revelry, clear to our neighborhood in Splantzia.

The next day I was consumed by disappointment. I can't become a religious person, I thought morosely. Religion is not for me. I am what I am, and there's no hope for change. I may for a time attain some degree of piety and godliness by reading the Bible and trying to be good; but deep inside I am full of guilt and shame. I may strive for a time to do that which is morally right, but I'll always be a victim of my own weaknesses and flaws. In the end, I'll always do that which is wrong, for I love to sin.

FOR days I felt unworthy to touch the Bible. When I finally resumed my reading, I started with the Psalms. I found them so inspiring, so enthralling, that I would at times dismount my bicycle, climb to a hilltop and, looking into the skies above, reiterate words from the Psalms: (NIV)

> Psalm 8: O LORD, our Lord, how majestic is your name in all the earth! You have set your glory above the heavens... When I consider your heavens, the work of your fingers, the moon and the stars, which you have set in place, what is man that you should be mindful of him, the son of man that you should care for him?...

Other times I would sit on a rock, let my eyes wander about the rugged terrain and mountainsides, and sing other favorite psalms:

> Psalm 42: As the deer pants for streams of water, so my soul pants for you, O God. My soul thirsts for God, for the living God...Why are you downcast, O my soul? Why so disturbed within me? Put your hope in God, for I will yet praise him, my Savior and my God.

> Psalm 104: Praise the Lord, O my soul...He waters the mountains...the earth is satisfied by the fruit of his work. He makes the grass grow for the cattle, and plants for man to cultivate—bringing forth food from the earth...How many are your works, O Lord! In wisdom you made them all; the earth is full of your creatures...These all look to you to give them their food...I will sing to the LORD all my life; I will sing praise to my God as long as I live....

And there, seated on the rock, Bible pressed against my bosom, I would yearn to slake the thirst of my soul, as tears of contentment beyond understanding filled my eyes. I wanted to know about God. I wanted to know the meaning of my temporary existence and how it related to my Creator. And I was gasping for an answer to my questions about my destiny or a life in the hereafter. Were the answers embedded in those lyrics, trapped between those lines?

IT OCCURRED to me one day that perhaps the uplifting feelings I was experiencing while meditating on the Bible bordered on the revelation of some kind of spiritual reality that might be entered into through worship in church.

In September of 1937, after much deliberation, I started going to church regularly. Whether in a city or in a remote village, I would pay homage to a saint, particularly Saint George, whom I considered my patron saint.

From the chanting of the priests I assembled a prayer, which I memorized and prayed silently each time I attended a liturgy. My prayer contained phrases and expressions repeatedly heard during liturgy, such as, "O Lord, our God. . . Glory to the Father and the Son and the Holy Spirit. . . Let us pray unto the Lord. . . Lord, have mercy on us. . . Let us confess unto the Lord. . . ." Listed at the end of my prayer were my petitions for protection, prosperity, and blessings.

Each time I tried to pray, however, I wondered whether I should pray directly to God, or to the saints, Holy Mary, or Christ. I felt awkward praying directly to God while ignoring the saints.

Soon I decided that my prayer was anything but a prayer. I knew that even the tears I sometimes shed in prayer were the result not of any profound religious experience I had undergone, but of my fear that my life would never measure up to the standards of a sincere churchgoer and that this would eventually discourage me and cause me to drift away from church.

My fears loomed large when I found myself growing tired of the lengthy liturgies. The chanting of the priests and the chanters had turned into a monotonous, repetitious chorus. On occasion there was a break in the monotony when a preacher would capture my attention, but only for a while; for no sooner would he declaim God's name than he would proclaim the church fathers, his inflated rhetoric escalating to the highest echelons of sheer oratory.

In combating my fears, it occurred to me that the pursuit of a spiritual experience in worship perhaps presupposed a systematic exercise of patience and perseverance. One ought to draw pleasure from worship rather than cope with it, I thought. In order to become a truly religious person, I will first have to learn to appreciate the chanting and the litanies, the rhetoric and the rituals. For sooner or later I may overcome the limitations of my selfish tendencies and enter into the realm of worshiping uprightly.

I envied those who could stay until the end of the liturgy, especially those who attended beginning in early morning. They were the ones, I thought, who must have conquered their impatience and discovered the true meaning of worship. So I deliberately attempted to force myself to remain in church till the end of the liturgy, contriving various methods to that end: sometimes I would try to impress a neighbor or a friend; other times I would seek a sign of approval or recognition from an observant priest. Regardless of the scheme, however, deep inside me raged an ongoing battle of impatience. Finally I decided that as long as I took communion, it was not necessary that I remain through the end of the liturgy.

Meanwhile, the pressure mounted at home and at work as it became known among relatives and friends that Charlie had turned into a regular churchgoer. Now I had to either attend all liturgies and church rituals faithfully, or risk being branded a hypocrite. And that's what I dreaded most. For while I realized that my impatience was leading to hypocrisy and hypocrisy to shame and guilt, it was nonetheless true that my involvement with church was the result of an earnest quest for a spiritual encounter in worship.

I was particularly cautious not to disappoint or provoke criticism from anyone at home, especially my mother-in-law. They all knew about my vows and that I had violated them often; but they also knew how hard I was striving to straighten up my life and better myself in any way I could, so they defended me. One day I even had to bear the embarrassment of seeing a close friend suddenly flung to the ground for having made a sarcastic remark about my religiousness—my dauntless mother-in-law had come to my defense by slapping the poor man hard enough to knock him down!

TOWARD the end of March 1938, after seven months of attending church, I found myself caught in the middle of a tug of war between my guilt and my pride. I could no longer attend church disguised behind the veil of false piety just to gain a glance of recognition or a nod of approval; nor could I bear to see my once unadulterated quest for a spiritual encounter in worship become sullied with pretense and falsehood. On the other hand, I was reluctant to suddenly quit church and become a disappointment to my family and to those who now truly admired me for my religious inclinations.

A cloud of depression followed me all day on Saturday of April 2, 1938. Irresolutely, I dragged my feet up the stairs until I reached the entrance to my study. Leaning heavily against the door, I let my eyes travel the wooden floor until they reached a little table and chair by the window. On the table lay my Bible, with a bookmark pressed between its pages. Laboriously, I staggered to the table and slumped on the chair.

After a long moment of staring half-heartedly at the Bible, I reached for my handy bookmark—a folded, worn piece of paper placed between the pages of Hosea and Joel. Skimming through a few pages, I came upon a surprisingly long succession of short books, each apparently bearing as a title the name of its Hebrew author. Along with my growing disenchantment with church, the dreadful thought then struck me that there might also be room for disenchantment with the Bible. It occurred to me that the Bible was perhaps nothing more than an anthology of Hebrew writings meant just for the Hebrews themselves. The holy book might simply be another fascinating, though inspiring, book—a history book, nevertheless. After all, wasn't the Jewish nation now extinct? "God!" I said in desperation. "I'm so confused!"

In the midst of my quandary, I became aware of my heavy dependency on the Bible. I realized that night that after weeks and months of reading the Bible, I had come to believe that the passages on God's forgiveness, such as Psalm 32:5, Isaiah 55:7, or Jeremiah 33:8, and the words of Ecclesiastes 12:7, which spoke of the destiny of man's spirit with God, were more than wishful thoughts, more than misguided hopes. Was this conviction now to vanish from my heart, like a dream never realized?

I unfolded the worn piece of paper, my eyes anxiously scanning the familiar page numbers and Scripture references I had jotted down on it over the months—mute testimony to my most intimate experiences of meditation and inspiration. An avalanche of treasured memories was then triggered in my mind. In a moment I began to see how vastly the Bible had influenced my life. It had given me a sense of self-worth and belonging in a world created by God; it had lifted my mind to higher ground where I had found refuge and respite far above the filth of the mouth and the pollution of the mind; it had brought me comfort and consolation in moments of utter despair; and it had vitalized my life and oriented my thoughts toward heaven with a sense of expectation and hope, by awakening in me the consciousness of God. There is no room for disenchantment with the Bible, I concluded. It might yet provide the answers to my questions, so I will hold it dear to my heart. It will continue to be my secret path to that which I need in order to go through this life—an inner hope. For it has taught me about God, my Creator. And in Him I have found hope.

That same night, as I turned a few more pages to determine how extensive the succession of those small books was, I found myself gazing at what seemed to be yet another extraordinary discovery about the Bible:

### THE NEW TESTAMENT OF OUR LORD
### AND SAVIOR JESUS CHRIST

"So that's where the name of Jesus Christ is—in the New Testament!" I exclaimed aloud, while wondering what "testament" actually meant. It appeared to me as though Jesus Christ had written a will, and later—before His death—had revised it. But He couldn't have written the Old Testament. Old Testament and New Testament had to be symbolical titles, I reasoned.

As I started reading the Gospel of Matthew, I marveled at the accounts of the Nativity, Jesus' temptation in the wilderness, and His miracles. But exceptionally striking to me, because of its reference not only to heaven but also to repentance in direct relation to heaven, was the proclamation made by both John the Baptist (3:2) and Jesus (4:17) alike: "Repent, for the kingdom of the heavens has come near." From this I gathered that, in order to repent and earn my forgiveness, I would have to do certain penances, perhaps in lieu of the sacrifices in the Old Testament, which I was likely to find spelled out in subsequent chapters. So I proceeded with chapter five.

At first I could not believe what I saw—never before had my eyes seen nor my ears heard such sublime words. Blessed are the downcast and discouraged, the sorrowful, the lowly, the spiritually hungry and thirsty, the merciful, the pure in heart, the peacemakers, the persecuted. They must rejoice and be glad, for their reward is in heaven (5:3-12). "God," I prayed, "could this mortal man's destiny be Your heavens? Could such promises be for an unworthy person like me? What must I do?"

Reading on, I marveled at Jesus' teachings regarding anger (5:21-26), adultery (27-30), divorce (31-32), swearing and oaths (33-37), revenge (38-42), loving enemies (43-48), almsgiving (6:1-4), hypocrisy in prayer (5-8), and a list of other points on practical living which ran the gamut from prayer and fasting to judging and being wise. The list made my own list of vows and resolutions look paltry indeed.

The night sky was giving way to dawn of the first Sunday of April. Soon church bells would ring out across town summoning worshipers to church. But I wasn't planning to go. In my heart I had already decided to stay home and find out how the words of Christ related to my own life. And I wanted to know what the Bible had to say about penances so I could think about going for a confession, according to Matthew 10:32.

I spent most of that Sunday reading the Bible and taking notes. The thought-provoking parables of Jesus and His soul-searching teachings made me pause and ponder, marvel and wonder. What manner of man was He? Was He indeed the Son of God? But who else, save God, could open blind eyes, heal the sick, raise the dead, or calm the sea? If Jesus truly was who He claimed to be, I thought to myself, all I need now is some sign that His message regarding heaven was universal and timeless and, therefore, for me.

DESPITE a busy work schedule, by Saturday of that week I finished the Gospels of Mark and Luke. I was amazed that already three accounts had been written about one and the same person, Jesus Christ; and that all three were so similar.

Excitement was particularly spelled out for me at the end of each of the three gospels, especially the Gospel of Luke, where I discovered that Jesus had aimed toward a world-wide discipleship plan involving all nations, his launching point in time and place being Jerusalem (24:47). I was quite certain now that Christ's message was for all nations and for all time; and so it had to be also for me.

That discovery made the words and life of Jesus Christ even more meaningful. As I lay in bed that Saturday night, I thought of His great teachings and intriguing parables, His unheard-of claims and supernatural miracles, His sufferings, His death, and His resurrection. All of a sudden Easter, now only two weeks away, began to have real meaning—it was not meant to mourn the death of Jesus Christ, but to celebrate His resurrection.

The words of Jesus regarding confession then came to mind from Matthew 10:32, and were reiterated in Luke 12:8. Faintly echoing in my ears as well were the words I had often heard during liturgy: "Let us confess unto the Lord!" I considered seeing a priest about making a confession before my scheduled trip to Athens early that coming week. I thought to myself, If Jesus, being so good, suffered on the cross so much, then no penance should be too great a sacrifice for me to make.

Knowing nothing about confessions, throughout the liturgy that Sunday I was preoccupied with what I was going to ask or say to the priest the very next day. Would he reprimand me for reading the Bible? Would he answer any of my questions?

What preoccupied my mind most, however, was the cost of forgiveness. So filthy was my life that I feared the priest would surely prescribe severe penalties for me. What might they be? And where were they spelled out in the Bible? On the other hand, my forgiveness would be worth many sacrifices, I thought. To make amends for my wretched life! To be free from guilt! It was going to take a true miracle of God—and a great many confessions.

EAGER to set my eyes on what had at first appeared to be another account of the life of Jesus, that Sunday I turned to the Gospel of John. I did not immediately find this gospel to be an account of the life of Jesus, however. Its beginning verses, clothed in simplicity of tone and style, had a certain profundity that escaped me. It was after pondering over the first chapter that I began to put two and two together. The Word (1:1), which became flesh (1:14), was actually Jesus Christ Himself!

Reading about Nicodemus, the Pharisee who came to Jesus by night, I thought about my impending confession. I saw myself walking to Jesus in Nicodemus' steps, posing his questions, listening through his ear, thinking his thoughts. "How is it possible for these things to happen? If entering heaven is like re-entering my mother's womb, then heaven is impossible."

And then I came upon verses 16 and 17: "God so loved the world, that he gave his only begotten Son, that everyone believing in him might not perish but have life eternal. For God did not send forth the Son into the world to judge the world, but that the world through him might be saved."

"God so loved the world!" I said, profoundly amazed at the transparent simplicity of words of such magnitude. "Might believing in Jesus be the same as being born from above?"

THE SUN rose too early that Monday of April 11, it seemed. I had stayed up longer than I had expected. Looking at my watch, I found it had stopped at two.

That afternoon I left the office and headed for St. Nikolaos, though with mixed feelings. I had just taken a fresh look at Matthew 10:32 and Luke 12:8 and realized that in my confession I was supposed to confess Christ. That left me confused—I was unsure what that meant. Too, I wondered about the role and use of penances in the light of John 3:16-17. Feeling ambivalent, I thought of putting off my confession. But I had questions, and I needed the answers. I had questions about Christ, about the saints, about confessions and penances, and there was no one to look to for direction except the priests. With Holy Week approaching, it was probably going to be many days before a priest would be available. "God," I prayed, "show me what to do!"

At that moment I happened to be passing by a watch repair shop and thought I should stop in and leave my watch for repair. As I entered, I was pleasantly surprised to see on the wall a picture frame bearing the title, "The Ten Commandments."

"I'm impressed!" I said cordially, by way of greeting Nick the watchmaker, an old acquaintance of mine.

As the white-haired watchmaker removed his eyepiece and turned around to welcome me, my eyes fell on a dusty black book lying on the shelf of his workbench.

"I didn't know you were religious, Nick!"

The watchmaker hesitated a moment. "What do you mean?"

"Well, isn't that a Bible over there?"

He looked over his shoulder. "Oh, that—sure. That's what it is—"

"You read it?"

"What if I did?"

"Nick—" I said seriously, hoping to get a straight answer from him, "—I want to know."

Nick put on his glasses, leaned over to see if the door was shut, then reached for his Bible. "Have a seat, Panos," he said as he blew the dust off the covers. "What I'm about to tell you is quite serious—and confidential." He opened his Bible and rested it on one hand, then removed his eyeglasses and looked me straight in the eye. "This is the Word of God," he said solemnly, his eyes examining mine. "It points the way to God."

I nodded with excitement.

"God so loved the world," he went on, "that he gave his only begotten Son, so that everyone believing in him might not perish but—"

"—But have life eternal!" I said in an outburst of excitement, and put out both hands for a hearty handshake. "At last!" I said, "A man who reads the Bible!"

The watchmaker's mouth fell open. "But you seem to have experienced salvation, Panos!"

"Salvation? Salvation from what?" I said with a chuckle, thinking of my endless financial afflictions, of which Nick in the past had been well aware.

"Your sins, of course."

"That I do wish."

"But you know John 3:16."

"I read it in my Bible just last night."

"*Your* Bible?"

"That's right."

"Well, how much have you read?"

"From Genesis straight through John chapter seven."

"You mean you read the whole Old Testament before you started reading the New Testament?"

"Well, you don't just pick up a book and start reading from the middle of it, do you?"

"I guess not. But—"

"But what? Was the Old Testament only for the Jews?"

"Of course not. Let me explain."

As I listened to Nick, I thought that my efforts to understand the Bible were finally beginning to come to fruition. First he explained that the Bible consisted of two parts, the Old Testament and the New Testament, and that the former comprised mainly prophecies, persons, offices, events, and rituals which foreshadowed the Messiah, or the Christ, whose person and work were revealed in the New Testament.

As he continued to talk, he perceived that I was having difficulty following him because he used certain specialized theological terms and clichés I hadn't heard before. He kindly tried to encourage me, however, by saying that if I continued to search the Scriptures, particularly the Gospel of John and the Epistle to the Ephesians, God would in due time open my spiritual eyes and reveal to me the purpose of the redemptive work of Christ Jesus, the only begotten Son of God.

The watchmaker sounded knowledgeable, profound, and eloquent. I had many questions to ask him about the person and nature of Jesus Christ; but by now I was extremely curious as to who Nick really was. Why was he so well-versed in the Scriptures? And why had he let his Bible get dusty? Why hadn't he talked to me about the Bible all these years? And why was he so evasive about the Bible at first and so secretive in discussing it with me thereafter?

"Say, Nick, what church do you go to?"

"The one right across from the courthouse, near the police headquarters," he replied easily, eyeing me amusedly. "At least, I used to."

I thought a moment. "But there is no church—oh, you mean—you're a Mason?" I exclaimed with embarrassment. (I didn't know what else to call him, though the name "Mason" was commonly used by people in Chania to refer in a derogatory sense to those who met in that building across from the court house.) "Yeah, I know where that is—"

"Have you ever been inside?"

"Nope."

"Why not?"

"Well, isn't it exclusively for the members of your sect?"

Nick did not seem offended, though it was obvious to him by now that my excitement had begun to wane.

"You've been misinformed, my friend," he said. "First, they—uh—we are not Masons, as people may call us, though I do not understand why they call us Masons nor do I know what the Masons are or believe. We are Evangelicals," he explained.

"You mean, Protestant?"

"I'm glad you know. And what's more, anyone is welcome to attend our services. They are free and open to the public."

"Well, I'll be—"

"Something is the matter?"

"I—I had no idea! Maybe that was one time I should have

ignored my mother's advice and checked things out for myself," I said. I explained then that some years back my parents and I happened to be passing by the newly-built meeting place of those referred to by that name, when I heard people singing. I told my parents to wait a moment so I could take a peek inside; but I had no sooner started up the steps leading to the main entrance of the building when my mother became hysterical, screaming and shouting that they were heretics and of the devil and that they would throw me out! When she finally calmed down, she told me that those people were Masons and that they did not believe in the saints or Holy Mary or worship icons. Then she made me swear by Saint George that I would never enter or even attempt to enter that building again.

The watchmaker was smiling, his eyes blinking rapidly.

"Is it true that you do not observe those things?" I asked.

"Observe man's traditions? Such things aren't in the Bible."

"They're not?"

"Certainly not, as you may have already found out from your reading."

I thought a moment. "Tell me what you Evangelicals believe."

"We believe and observe only what the Bible teaches."

"So you offer animal sacrifices, too, I suppose?"

Nick laughed. "I'm glad you asked that," he said. "In Matthew 5:17, Christ says that He came to fulfill the law, not to destroy it. All the Old Testament sacrifices were in anticipation of Christ's ultimate sacrifice on the cross. Read Hebrews chapters 9 and 10, and you'll understand. What's more, you'll appreciate and understand the Old Testament better if you study it in the light of its depicting the Messiah, who is the Christ of the New Testament."

I took a great interest also in what the watchmaker had to say about the format of the Evangelical services, as well as the Evangelicals' doctrine with regard to Mary, the saints, the worship of icons, baptism, communion, and a number of other things, including confessions and penances.

I left Nick's watch shop astounded—after just a couple of hours with Nick I understood more about the Bible and had more questions answered than in a year's searching on my own, I thought. And the amazing thing was that Nick had used the Bible to back up everything he said.

The timing, too, was remarkable—I had just prayed for guidance, and God led my footsteps to the right person.

And the right person Nick was. His voice filled with emotion, he told me later that God had used me that day as a reminder that he should never again let his Bible collect dust. (As I had found out by then, Nick had drifted back into the world for months, but right after our meeting that day he rededicated his life to God and started attending the Evangelical church again.)

As for my watch, I had bought it from Nick eight years earlier, and that night it had stopped for the first time. God used a seemingly insignificant thing—a stopped watch—to cause a miraculous happening.

That night I found my watch still in my fob—in my excitement, I had forgotten to leave it with Nick. But that was just as well, for there was no need to have it fixed—it was working!

# 7

# The Treasure

THE SHIP WAS WELL into its twelve-hour voyage from Crete to the port of Piraeus, the harbor of Athens. Travelers were sprawled throughout the main and upper decks, feasting merrily on their meals. There was little hope I could find any private quarters where I could settle down and read my Bible.

A thousand pardons later, having jumped over numerous legs and food, I found myself among some acquaintances who kindly invited me to eat with them. Not wanting them to know I was fasting, I told them I wasn't feeling hungry; but they insisted that I join them just for company, so I did.

All of a sudden I developed a strong appetite. Knowing that the Orthodox Church allowed only certain foods to be eaten during the days of Lent, I reached for some olives. Those who knew me to be a churchgoer perceived I was fasting and began to make sarcastic remarks about religion, while offering me all kinds of food, especially things I was not supposed to eat. The more I resisted, the more they insisted, which seemed to amuse some.

"Do you think that going to church has made you a better man?" one of them asked.

"I—"

And as I opened my mouth to speak, a man behind me suddenly forced a whole hard-boiled egg into my mouth, making me everyone's laughingstock. Humiliated, I seized the opportunity to challenge them, though not with my fists as some might have expected, but with a benign smile. That'll show them! I thought to myself with glee.

That night I asked myself whether being religious was worth the cost, and the words of Jesus came to mind: "Blessed are the persecuted for righteousness' sake." That worsened the situation, because it caused my conscience a great deal of pain—I knew I was persecuted neither for righteousness' sake nor for religion; for my benign smile had been full of vindictiveness and pride.

UPON arriving in Athens on Wednesday, April 13, 1938, I looked for some close friends who had recently moved there from Crete and who had often insisted that I visit them some day. I was looking for their house in the district of Petralona when a sign on the wall of a house met my eyes:

## PREACHING THE GOSPEL

I stood there in stunned amazement, eyes fixed on that sign. A short time later I was asking my friend Paul and his fiancée Barbara about the house down the street with the sign on it.

"God forbid!" Barbara said emphatically. "They're heretics!"

She reminded me of my mother's reaction years earlier when I had tried to go up the steps of the Evangelical church in Chania.

"Yes, they're Masons—just like those heretics in Chania," concurred Paul readily.

"You mean Evangelicals?" I said.

"They're a bunch of heretics!" Paul shouted.

At that moment Barbara's mother came out of the kitchen and redeemed the situation.

"Mr. Konstantinides—" she said with a smile, referring to the leader of the group that met in that house "—he's a very kind man. Two weeks ago he welcomed us and asked if he could be of some help."

"You've been to their meetings?" I asked her.

"—I wouldn't even consider it!" injected Paul.

"Well," I said as I got up and headed for the door, "they may have started by now."

Seeing how determined I was, Paul and Barbara followed me all the way to the meeting place, trying all the while to persuade me to stop; but when I entered, they slipped in right behind me, and the three of us found a seat by the entrance. My eyes scanned the room—it looked like a living room that had been turned into a meeting hall. Displayed on the walls were selected quotations from the Bible, rather than statues or icons. Seated in front of us was a group of twenty-four men and women facing a pulpit that was situated at the other end of the room. Behind the pulpit stood a man, who now asked the gathering to sing hymns from books. At first I thought they sounded funny because they sang uninhibitedly, like little children; but there was an air of innocence about their singing that was appealing. When Paul suggested that we leave because they were not Orthodox, I told him that I wanted to stay because regardless of what they were, they could be more sincere about God than I was.

Following the singing, the man behind the pulpit sat down and another man took his place. He, too, looked like a teacher rather than a priest or a clergyman. I reckoned he was the minister, Reverend Konstantinides—pastor they called him.

I could hardly sit still when Rev. Konstantinides opened the Bible and announced that he was going to read John 8:1-11, the passage I had just finished reading! Paul, sensing my excitement, grabbed me by the arm.

"Come on, let's go!" he whispered.

"No, I want to stay," I said.

"Come on, man! They're heretics, don't you understand?"

"I want to stay!"

Rev. Konstantinides read the passage, emphasizing the part that read, "He that is without sin among you, let him first cast a stone at her." He went on to speak forcefully on that topic. Especially driving was his point about not condemning others, but rather forgiving one another, even as God forgives us. God is always ready to accept us and forgive us, he said, regardless of who we are or how sinful we are, as in the case of the harlot whom Christ forgave. He went on to say that God's forgiveness of our sins is a free gift of His love for us through Christ, a gift that frees us from the bondage of sin which leads to eternal death, and gives us instead eternal life with Him in heaven. All we have to do, he said, is ask God for His free gift and accept it by faith.

At the end of the sermon the minister asked if anyone wanted to make an open confession—testimony they called it. A little old woman stood up and said that she had encountered all kinds of problems in life and that she had suffered much, but that all those things ceased to trouble her when she came to these meetings and learned how to find peace with God. She thanked God and sat down. Then another lady got up, and then a man, then an old woman, then again a man. I was particularly impressed by the testimony of a rich woman who said that she had experienced all the pleasures of life that money could buy, yet remained an unhappy, unfulfilled soul until she was finally led to this place, where she learned about the love of Christ and found true joy. Like all others who had stood up to speak, there was a ring of genuineness in her voice.

"Let's go, Panos. He's going to ask us to stand, too," Paul said anxiously, his strident whisper disturbing the stillness of the service.

As I looked into Paul's eyes, so negative and apprehensive, my mind became clouded with doubt. Could it be that their confessions are a kind of group therapy? Perhaps they seek to soothe their guilt-ridden consciences by comforting one another through the conviction that they have been enlightened by some divine revelation evidenced by their common interest in isolating themselves from a sinful world, while in fact they are oblivious to their being swayed by what a kind, soft-spoken man professes to believe?

Cold sweat covered my body. I detached my eyes from Paul's and again directed them toward the little gathering. As if suddenly extricated from the hold of a spell, I could hear again the words of those who continued to stand one after another, some for a second time. They spoke of God's forgiveness and of His love through Christ, the genuineness of their unpremeditated words and afterthoughts being clearly reflected on their faces. These are no actors, I thought. They are sincere people, their voice and faces void of pretense.

All but two had stood up to speak. The minister reiterated Matthew 10:32: "Everyone who confesses me before men, I will also confess before my Father who is in heaven."

I remembered then the words of the chanter at St. Nikolaos: "Let us confess unto the Lord!" So that's what it means to confess Christ—to openly tell others that you believe in Him! These are genuine people, I thought excitedly, and I wanted to tell them how much I appreciated them.

The minister noticed that my initial attempt to stand up was thwarted—Paul was holding me down by the sleeve of my jacket.

"Don't! They're not Orthodox!" Paul muttered.

"I want to!" I said, irked.

The commotion was observed by a dozen pairs of curious eyes. In a moment every head was turned our direction, and Paul was feeling like a fool.

I sprang to my feet. Paul and Barbara froze in their seats. I wasn't sure what I was going to say. There was silence.

"I have been very impressed by what I heard and observed here tonight," I said, my words reverberating in my ears as silence returned. The minister gave me a warm and encouraging smile, the gathering responding in like manner. I went on to say that I, too, had suffered and tried many things in life, until I nearly tried the worst of all things—suicide. I asked them to say a prayer for me so God would have mercy on my soul and deliver me from the whip of misery and misfortune, and then sat down.

At the end Rev. Konstantinides came down to greet us, but Paul and Barbara rushed out the door. The reverend welcomed me with a smile and a warm handshake, put his arm around my shoulder, and invited me to join him in prayer near the pulpit—the altar he called it—where others were praying.

He knelt down. I was the only one standing. Supposing he expected me to kneel beside him, I tried to bend my knees, but my kneecaps felt as if they were locked in a cast. As I tried bending them again, I glanced over my shoulder and saw Barbara holding the door and Paul waiting outside behind her. Our eyes met. Barbara began to beat her chest with one fist, with the other hand making frantic gestures bidding me to get out. "Come, brother, kneel before the Lord," came from the reverend. My knees then seemed to bend of their own volition, and I knelt on the floor right beside him. "Do you hate anyone? You must forgive, so God may forgive you also." Like dynamite, his words exploded in my ears. If these people suggest as their first step the forgiveness of enemies, they are anything but heretics, I thought to myself.

His hands on my head, Rev. Konstantinides prayed. A long list of names passed before my eyes. I forgave Tony, Angelos, Mihelakis, and all those who had wronged me. Wondering whether I had left out any names, in the end I decided I would cover everyone in one sweeping statement. "I forgive them ALL!" slipped out of my mouth, Rev. Konstantinides still praying, my head moving up and down with every word he shouted. I thought he was going to push my head all the way down to the bare floor, crushing my pride once and for all.

Following the service, Rev. Konstantinides and I sat down and talked for a good hour. He took a genuine interest in every detail of my life, and could barely hold back tears as I related to him the events that had led my footsteps to their service that night. "It is not by chance that you are here this moment, my friend Panos," he told me. "God, by His grace, has brought you here. Because you looked to Him for true meaning in life, He has guided you through such circumstances as would assure you of His love and care for you. Therefore He is now allowing His plan for your life to come into being. God has great works in store for you, as He has for every person who truly seeks Him. The Bible says, 'We are His making, structured in Christ Jesus unto good works, which God prepared beforehand so that we might walk in them' (Ephesians 2:10). God loves you enough to offer you freely an endless life with Him. So ask Him to give you that life by letting Him cleanse you from all your sins and to make you a new creation tonight. You must repent and desire to be cleansed from sin, for God is holy and hates sin."

"I hate my sins," I said. "I wish to rid myself of all my guilt."

Rev. Konstantinides then asked me to repeat after him a prayer in which I asked God to have mercy on me and save me from my sins, to lead my life the way He wanted, to protect me from evil, and to strengthen me so I would be obedient to His Word. He also encouraged me to continue to read the Bible and to consider going to the Evangelical church in Chania.

Upon returning to my friends' house, I met a disgruntled Paul at the door.

"So? Did he convert you to his heresy?" Paul said sarcastically.

"Yes. To the Bible."

"Sacrilege!"

"Is it sacrilege to know the answers to the enigma of life?"

"There's no enigma."

"You have no questions about life?"

"I am a realist."

"An agnostic at best—"

"I just have no questions."

"But you do question the existence of God."

"I said I have no questions."

You never wonder what your purpose in life is?"

"No one can be certain about this life."

"There's your enigma, then."

"Success and happiness—that's my purpose."

"I take it you are a successful and happy man?"

"I'm striving toward that end."

"There's no end to striving, only at life's end."

"The end is part of the reality of life."

"Mightn't that end be but the beginning of another reality?"

"No one can be certain."

"There's the other half of your enigma."

"I'm already getting fed up with the philosophy that preacher fed you."

"His philosophy is the Bible."

"You are a man of great reasoning powers," Paul said in exasperation. "It appalls me that in just a couple of hours you resigned your mind to the fantasies of an old heretic!"

Paul and Barbara agreed to hear the story of my life as I had just shared it with Rev. Konstantinides—from the time I drank the six glasses of wine to the present. At the end I turned my Bible to John 3:16 and asked them to read it. Barbara, her manner aloof, got up and leaned over the Bible, grinned, and quickly sat down again. Paul refused to move.

"Christ—" he said with an air of defiance, "—no one can be certain about him. He could have been a persuasive sophist, an able fakir, or a magician of some sort."

"And you call yourself a Christian?" I said.

My argument with Paul caused me to toss in bed all night. My mind was once again filled with questions and doubts. I kept thinking, Could those sincere people be innocently wrong? What if the Greek Orthodox Church is the only true religion? And how could I be sure that everything in the Bible regarding Christ is true?

Such questions and doubts continued to torment my mind on my trip back to Crete.

THE glorious sun hovered sublimely above the ship at noon the next day, shining its grace upon my misty eyes and dampened spirit. From the immense expanse of the sky's blue canopy, spread over and around us clear to the edges of the deep, I seemed to experience a visionary enchantment. I stood in awe at the prow of the ship and praised God. "In You I do believe, God," I cried out. "But Christ? Please show me what I must believe!..."

MY questions and doubts intensified my search of the Scriptures. As I took a closer look at the Gospel of John that weekend, I saw once more that no ordinary man could have spoken the words of Jesus, nor performed His works. He spoke of God and of God's supreme love, of truth and righteousness, and of eternal life. He opened eyes and raised the dead, met the poor and fed them bread, forgave sins, imparted hope—always with love, with God's love. How could Christ be a persuasive sophist or a magician? He claimed no glory for Himself, only for God.

Sunday morning I went to the Evangelical church. I tiptoed to the back and sat down. An old man sitting in front of me turned around and handed me a hymn book. The congregation, about two times the size of that in Athens, was singing to the accompaniment of an organ. The words of the hymn were inspiring: "Just as I am, without a plea, O Lamb of God, I come...." The man who led the singing sat down, and another man took his place and asked the congregation to rise for prayer. In an eloquent prayer, he mentioned different people's names and asked God to meet their needs, then prayed that God would cause the message of His servant to find room in everyone's heart. Following the prayer, a third man stepped behind the pulpit and began to preach. His sermon was about repentance. To be born from above, he pointed out, one must admit he is a sinner and desire to be cleansed of all his sins; be sincerely sorry for all those sins; repent and ask God to forgive him; and accept God's forgiveness and gift of eternal life by faith in Jesus Christ.

His words, which echoed the words of Rev. Konstantinides, fascinated me, and I was thrilled and honored to be there to hear him. One thing disturbed me, however—I knew this man. I had often done business with him. I also knew the man who had led the singing—I learned later that he had been a chanter at a Greek Orthodox church for thirty years. But neither of them had ever spoken to me about God or their services. Those "books" I kept receiving for them from Athens—they must have been Bibles!

I returned for the evening service. It was exciting to be among so many people in the city of Chania who were interested in the Bible. How I wished I had met them ten years earlier!

Following the service, Nick the watchmaker introduced me to the pastor, Rev. Karvounis.

"Mr. Zachariou, I'm pleased to see you here," the pastor said.

"I was greatly impressed by the good words I heard today, sir—" I said. The pastor nodded kindly and smiled. "—I wish I had heard such words years earlier," I added. The pastor smiled again.

"We must obey the authorities," volunteered Nick. "We're liable to be accused and jailed on grounds of proselytism."

"Proselytism? Oh, I—I think I understand, sir," I said, looking at Nick to show him that now I knew the reason he had initially been so cautious about discussing the Bible with me in his shop that past Monday. "But that's a brand new law," I felt like saying, by way of pointing out that they could have spoken to me about God in previous years, but I didn't.

The following day I went to visit Nick at his shop and found him discussing the Bible with Paidakis, an assistant minister of the Evangelical church, whom I also knew. At my request, they continued their discussion, and I listened. Before leaving, the assistant minister and Nick agreed to meet me there again the next day.

Twenty-four long hours later, I rushed to meet the two men. The assistant minister prayed that God would be in our midst and allow His Word to bring fruit, then the discussion began. Pencil in one hand, pad in the other, I jotted down every Scripture verse they mentioned.

Two blissful hours later, upon leaving the watch shop, the thought struck me that Christ went to the cross in everyone's place, including mine! I sought a place to read the Bible and pray to God to forgive my sins. Too many interruptions at the office—customers kept coming in. I went home, and there I prayed.

Thursday morning of Holy Week, Chrysa reminded me that I had promised to take communion with her in church. I told her I was going to be too busy that day and that we would do it another time. The truth was that I wanted to go to the Bible study at the Evangelical church that night.

Following a most inspiring Bible study that Thursday night, the Evangelical people made me feel very welcome. One by one, they all shook my hand and told me how glad they were that I was with them. There was no doubt in my mind that I had found the kind of people I cared to be with.

Just as assuredly, I knew that I was no longer interested in rites and rituals. But how was I going to leave the Orthodox Church and go with the Evangelicals? How prepared was I to face all the conflict and opposition at home and everywhere else? "God, show me how," I prayed.

The next day was Good Friday, and I woke up following a strange dream. I dreamed of a big, crowded ship that was permanently anchored in the middle of the harbor of Chania. None of the passengers seemed interested in getting off, except me. Leaning over the side railing of the main deck, I was relieved to sight a gangplank that led to a small rowboat meant for transporting passengers to the pier. I bounced down the gangplank, hopped into the rowboat and grabbed the oars. The plunging of the oars stirred the waters, and in an instant I found myself being tossed about by gusty winds and big waves. I thought I was going to sink and perish. Not wanting to return to the ship, I tried rowing toward the shore, but the rowboat, hopelessly tossed about and half-filled with water, would not move; it was being held back by a hook that was attached to the end of a steel cable which my eyes traced all the way up to the ship's winch. I noticed then how enormous the ship was. It was awesomely huge, and it was all black. The fierce waves, too, had now turned black.

I let go of the oars and tackled the hook, but found it impossible to lift. The steel cable was extremely taut. The hook grew bigger and heavier, looking like a beast determined to rip the rowboat apart. Meanwhile, the two oars came off their oarlocks and were swallowed by the fierce black waves. In one last agonizing effort, I again attacked the hook. Just when my muscles were about to snap and my veins ready to burst, suddenly the front of the rowboat rose high above my head. As I began sinking, my eye caught a patch of clear blue in the blackened sky. "My God! My God!" I cried out. Instantly, the hook snapped high up, swung toward the ship at a deadly speed, and slammed against its side with an earsplitting bang. The whole vessel rocked, and an opposing reaction caused my rowboat to skim atop the waves at a fantastic speed. In a heartbeat, I found myself lying safely on the shore.

I knew the significance of the dream. The huge black ship was symbolic of the Greek Orthodox Church. Anchored aimlessly in the harbor of spiritual idleness and stagnation in Chania, it was teeming with passive, spiritually ignorant passengers desperately in need of hearing the gospel. But of special impor-

tance was the dream's obvious message: in leaving the Orthodox Church, I would encounter great opposition; and in my
trials I should not rely on my own strength, but on God's miraculous intervention.

Encouraged, that day I told Chrysa that I had decided not
to attend the Orthodox churches anymore, since it would be a
mere pretense on my part.

"I'm not surprised," Chrysa said. "Do whatever you want.
Soon everyone will know where you went last night—"

"Who told you?"

"Your cousin, the French professor. He saw you coming
out of that place last night. He was here just a few minutes ago
and said he was also going to tell my mother."

I explained to Chrysa that there was nothing mystical about
those so-called Masons. They were Evangelicals—Protestants,
like those in England and America. They held Bible studies,
whereas the Orthodox priests, whom I still respected, did nothing of the sort. The reason I had sided with the Evangelicals
was that everything they believed was based on the Bible. And
in the Bible, I added, I had found the answers to the questions
I had about life. Chrysa shrugged her shoulders and said that
this new Bible-mania of mine was going to lead to nothing but
trouble.

That evening everyone in the family went to the Epitaphios
(Burial) ceremony of Christ, but I stayed home to read the Bible
and ask God for the assurance that my sins were forgiven.

Bent over the Bible, I no sooner realized that everyone had
returned from St. Nikolaos when I sensed someone approaching me from behind. All at once my mother-in-law broke into
an outburst of accusations and threats. I had betrayed my Orthodox faith and gone with the heretics; my eccentricities and
evil doings had brought nothing but poverty and misery and
now disgrace upon her and her daughter; the whole world was
at the Epitaphios, while I was home doing demonic things; and
so on. In vain did I try to persuade her that it wasn't so. She
kept cursing and damning and screaming at me.

Nerves began to gnaw at the tips of my knuckles; I was
running out of patience. Suddenly I turned and sprang to my

feet, clenched fists raised, and vehemently shouted at her to go to hell!

As soon as she left, I sat down and wept. I saw how weak I was, how vile! One moment I was reading the Bible, and the next I was telling my own mother-in-law to go to hell!

Moments later, Chrysa informed me that my mother needed me desperately. I ran to a nearby café, where I found my mother semiconscious.

"My son, I have lost you! You've gone with. . . the Masons!"

"Mother, don't listen to what others are telling you," I pleaded. "Listen to me!"

But burdened with the guilt and shame of my fury moments earlier, I found it difficult to say to my mother what I wanted to say.

As I looked around a moment, I saw the crowds of people holding candles in front of St. Nikolaos. I thought I was looking at a thousand devils mocking God!

"Mother—" I was finally able to say, "—now I know the meaning of Christ's resurrection. It's in the Bible you gave me!"

"No—no! Why? Why did I give you the holy book? All-holy Panagia—Mother of Christ—forgive me!"

"No, Mother, I'm glad you did. That's what saved my life. Now I am more fulfilled than ever before!"

But my words only seemed to add to her grief and worsen the situation.

BAD news traveled fast: Panos had betrayed his religion and turned into a Mason. Neighbors, relatives, and close friends were now quick to scoff and to sneer. Even those who would have nothing to do with religion warned me that God would punish me severely for siding with the heretics. As for my mother-in-law, she insisted that I divorce her daughter because of the disgrace and shame I had brought upon her and the family.

Easter Sunday I went to the Evangelical church again, where I was greatly moved by the simplicity in which their communion service was conducted. First, the minister reminded the congregation that communion was in remembrance of Christ's sacrifice (1 Corinthians 11:23-26). Then he instructed everyone who was to partake of the emblems to examine himself and ask God to cleanse him afresh, else he would be partaking indiscreetly and unworthily and would therefore be guilty of the body and blood of Christ (1 Corinthians 11:27-29). Though I did not take communion—it was closed communion—I prayed once more that God would cleanse me from all my sins.

Following the service, I went home and began to read the Epistle to the Ephesians. Like waves reaching the shore in rhythmical succession, verse after verse filled me with the desire to be cleansed of all impurity and sin and to allow God's love to permeate my life.

The room suddenly seemed too small to contain the heaven that was becoming mine. I looked out the window, raised my eyes skyward, and earnestly prayed to God to have mercy on me the sinner, for I hated all my sins.

I longed deeply for an open communion with heaven, for a ladder that reached from the deepest abyss of a world submerged in sin to the highest heaven of purity and love. For a long moment I remained still, tears of unutterable peace and joy mingling with a ceaseless praise that welled up within me and brimmed over my lips with gratitude: "God is my Father! God is my Father!"

I returned to the second chapter of Ephesians, teardrops falling on the pages. As I read the first half of the chapter, I became confidently aware that in His mercy and love God had seen my penitent heart and heard my earnest prayer. I knew that His gift of forgiveness was undeservedly mine; that my destiny was now in Christ and I was a new creation created in Christ Jesus. My life, in Him, had now become a treasure!

BECAUSE of a visiting Englishman, a special service was scheduled for Monday evening following Easter Sunday. The Englishman's message, though in broken Greek, took immediate root in the freshly-tilled soil of my soul. We should be living testimonies in the world for Christ's sake, he said, but that would be impossible on our own strength. We need to depend on God's strength, which comes through daily prayer and meditation on His Word. A growing personal love relationship is thus formed between us and God, which in turn generates within us the desire to please Him by reflecting Christ's character and mind through our actions, our language, and our attitude.

How could people say that the Evangelicals are heretics? I thought to myself that night. How could anyone say that they err? No, they uplift Christ, and Christ alone. I was grateful to God that He had not only forgiven my sins, but had also given me a group of believers to fellowship with and receive spiritual nourishment from. I was still unfamiliar with the sayings and terminology they used and found it difficult to communicate to them my personal experiences with the Bible, but they were still unfailingly kind and understanding, and treated me like one of their own.

Walking home after the service, I prayed that God would help me reflect Christ through my actions, my language, my attitude; and that He would help me face the situation at home in a way that would please Him.

Upon returning to my study, my mother-in-law repeated her hysterical scene. "Judas! Traitor! You betrayed Christ like Judas!" she screamed as she dashed upstairs to find me. She stopped an arm's length from my chair, still screaming and growling, her fury mounting.

I turned around. The kerosene lamp made her look like a wraith as she fell upon me. She lunged forward and punched me hard on my face.

Startled, I jumped up, my blood boiling. "God, help me!" I shouted.

She cringed and, waiting for me to slug her, remained motionless, her eyes glaring at me. I thought she'd gone into a shock. And shocked she was; for she thought I was going to knock her clear down the stairs, and instead she saw me standing there, my arms folded, simply looking at her. "Christ wouldn't have hit you back," I said calmly. "Why should I?"

Totally bewildered, she walked slowly down the stairs, saying nothing. Oh, the joy that was mine that night! God had answered my prayers once more. With His strength, I had overcome the limitations of my weakness!

I had never before experienced such joy. I tried to convey that joy to my loved ones with the new smile on my face, but they would not understand. Instead, they continued to say that I had sold Christ to the devil.

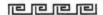

# PART
# TWO

# 8

# The Call

THREE FULL MONTHS WENT BY, months filled with
new experiences, new acquaintances, new interests, and a
new joyousness. Adding to this newness of life was the personal
attention I enjoyed getting from the Evangelicals, who commended me for my spiritual growth and my devotion to the
church.

Speaking to an admiring Evangelical friend about how God
had changed my life, I explained that in three months I had
managed to cut my smoking down from three packs a day to
only seven cigarettes a day, but that for Christ's sake I could
even kick the habit once and for all. The friend remained totally unaware of the deep conviction that fell upon me at that
moment. First, I had spoken as if it were up to me to quit the
habit—as though I could choose to do God a favor. Second, I
knew that smoking less was a poor compromise on my part.
Knowing that smoking was a sign of worldliness among the
Evangelicals, I had made sacrificial attempts to smoke less in
order to impress them, but I knew inside that I didn't want to
quit smoking—I couldn't!

That day I realized that in some of my efforts to resist temptation and improve my image as a good Christian, I had ended
up viewing certain changes in my life as personal sacrifices that
could compensate for a bit of cheating, an occasional lie, some
cussing here and there.

I fell on my knees to pray, but I couldn't—I only shed tears.
The tears caused other hidden areas of my life to surface to my
consciousness and come into focus. Beneath each tear I saw the

hard shell of an unbroken will that housed my unsubdued worldly desires, all wrapped in faulty reasoning and tenaciously lodged in the corners of my mind: cheating, pretense, lying—accomplices of greed, falsehood and pride, yet more profitable in business than honesty; bitterness, hostility, resentment—ulcerous wounds of the heart, but safeguards of my selfish intents and purposes; swearing and cussing—harmful sprays of venom, nevertheless part of a salesman's persuasive jargon; smoking—a vanishing companion, a stinking pleasure at best, but an acceptable social norm; a lustful eye—appealing snare that pampers my passions, yet not the very act itself.

I could see that Christ was not Lord of every area of my life—my commitment to Him was only partial. My love for my Creator was as wanting as my empty boastfulness, and no greater than my love for any one of my wayward pleasures; yet I expected God to watch over me and help me prosper. Conversely, I tended to view many of the changes in my life as sacrifices, even as losses. Yielding everything to God at one time was an impossible sacrifice, I figured. God could wait, I was sure.

MEANWHILE, God's conviction grew stronger in me each day. In time, I found that resisting God's conviction is plain disobedience, which leads to spiritual hardness. I also learned that obedience is more than just doing what is right; it is the joyous outcome of God's discipline learned through trying times. God saw fit, however, that in learning obedience I should first be grounded in His Word. To that end, He used a number of circumstances.

At a home gathering with the Evangelicals one evening, I decided to share how I had come to find the truth. After mentioning how God had miraculously led my steps to another group of believers in Athens, I pointed out how touched I was by those humble, sincere testimonies that night, especially by the prayer and talk I had with their pastor, Rev. Konstantinides. At the mention of that name, one of the ministers in the gathering leaned over and whispered something in another's ear. Soon the whole gathering was exchanging glances and whispering to each other.

When I inquired later about this curious happening, I was told that those people in Athens were not Evangelicals but heretics, some sort of spiritualists who erred in their interpretation of the Bible and who believed that the Holy Ghost visited them and caused them to make uncontrollable utterances which they called "tongues," and who called themselves "Pentecostals." Inquiring further whether the Pentecostals were Protestant, I was told that there were in fact many Protestant denominations in the world, most of which were in England and in America.

That night I felt discouraged. I didn't know what to think. Where could I find the true religion? Who had the real truth? Were there rungs of truth commensurate with one's degree of hunger for spiritual insight?

The following day I was accosted by a man known to be a philosopher, who had on occasion visited the Evangelical church. It was impossible for man to attain holiness, he said, since holiness is divine perfection. Man is always doomed to fail in the end. Human perfection, on the other hand, is relative; it is a matter of relative parity between one's goals and the degree of his success in achieving those goals. The greater his success, the happier he is. The resulting happiness is his gauge of his own perfection.

As if I had asked for a third opinion, two days later I was approached by a man who told me that he had attended the Evangelical services a number of times. He invited me to his home, where he spent hours pouring doctrines and ideas into my head that I had neither heard nor imagined before. Using his Bible, he turned to a number of verses he had underlined, then told me that he agreed with the Evangelicals on a number of points, but that they erred in their interpretation of the Scriptures regarding the nature and role of Jesus Christ as the Son of God and as a member of the so-called Trinity. He said that Christ was not like God, for there is only one God; that Christ was another mighty god, but of lesser power than God; and many other things. He called himself a Jehovah's Witness.

Listening to this man proved extremely damaging to me. I walked out of his place confused and afflicted with doubts. I stopped and leaned against a wall as if I had lost my bearings. Another religion? I wondered. Why? Isn't the Bible one and the same? Isn't the Bible true?

Rather than go straight home that night, I stopped by a tavern and did what I hadn't done for many months—I got drunk.

And so, back to my old life I went again—gambling, drinking, and seeking the pleasures of the world.

TWO whole months went by—two long, miserable months. I abhorred my old ways. I had been fully acquainted with the void they left, the guilt they created. Meanwhile, echoing faintly in my heart I could hear the words, "I am the way and the truth and the life" (John 14:6). The words seemed to grow louder and louder, until one day it dawned on me that my disappointment and confusion stemmed from men, not from Jesus. I got to thinking that if Jesus was the truth, I should listen to His words. But how was I to know that the Bible was truly of God, or that Jesus Christ was who He claimed to be? That I decided to find out for myself once and for all.

For many days I did virtually nothing except read the Bible. Because I lost so much weight, Chrysa and her mother became concerned enough that they called on Papasifis* to exorcise me, while my mother sent for Papaiason. I saw this as a unique opportunity to ask the priests a few questions. First I let them proceed with their ritual—reading and chanting and sprinkling me with holy water so the demons would depart from me! Then, holding my Bible, I started asking them questions.

When the priests saw that they were unable to satisfactorily answer my questions, particularly with regard to the worship of Mary, the icons, and the saints, Papasifis said, "My son, I happen to be uneducated, but I'll get you in touch with the bishop so he can direct you, because you have been deceived. Them Evangelicals accept only the Bible, you know. They reject the traditions of the Church Fathers, and so they can't fly, 'cause with one wing the dove don't fly."

---

* *Papa*- "priest" is commonly placed before a priest's first or last name.

My mother-in-law meanwhile saw how resolutely I continued to study the Bible. Joined by her mother, she once more pressed the issue of divorce. The team went as far as asking relatives, neighbors and friends to persuade Chrysa to divorce me. But I prayed that God would intervene. Despite all the negative influence from the outside, Chrysa remained patient and calm.

THIRTY-TWO days went by, most of which I spent in isolation—praying, fasting, and reading the Bible. To understand the Bible message more clearly, I filled the pages with copious notes, references, drawings and sketches. This enabled me to discover and rediscover a number of significant features about the Bible and the person of Jesus Christ.

What I first rediscovered about the Bible was its incomparable portrayal of the value of life. God created life; life is the force that emanates from Him. Throughout the Bible, the idea of life is connected with its Maker. As the Apostle Paul says, "In Him we live and move and exist" (Acts 17:28).

Furthermore, I discovered that the Bible reveals the meaning of man's life—its origin, purpose, and ultimate destiny—solely in the person of Jesus Christ, who is the focal figure of the entire Bible. It is through Christ that the Bible explains the meaning of things: spiritual principalities and powers, good and evil, nature, events, time, attitude, death, destiny, eternity. Except for Christ we would know not what life is, nor death, nor even ourselves. The reason for living would be lost in obscurity, and confusion would rule in its stead. And God would be the impersonal master of the universe.

As for the person, nature, and work of Jesus Christ, I found that He was from eternity with God the Father (John 1:1, 2; 17:5); that in form, substance, quality, and mode of being He was equal to God the Father (Philippians 2:6); and that all things were created by Him, through Him, and for Him (John 1:3, 10; 1 Corinthians 8:6; Ephesians 2:10; Colossians 1:16; Hebrews 1:2; Revelation 3:14). He is Ο ΛΟΓΟΣ (The Logos), The Word of God incarnate (John 1:1, 2, 14), the One who alone was able to explain God's mind to man (John 1:18). In His words one can see the mind of God; in His miracles the power of God; in His cross the love of God; and in His resurrection God's promise to us of eternal life.

I found the Bible to be infinitely human as well—it depicts the great drama of human life. It is the mirror of the human heart, reflecting man as he is, with all his aspirations and greatness, his afflictions and misery, his needs and wants, his weaknesses and frailty, his uncertainties and fears, his vileness and filth.

But the Bible does not stop there. It provides the answer to man's dilemma, salvation from his sinfulness. It points man to God through the only perfect Man, Jesus Christ. It shows that God, in His mercy and love for mankind, allows sinful man to be elevated from the curse of sin—Death—to holiness, in that through an active faith in the person and work of Jesus Christ, man has continuous access to God's forgiveness of his sins.

In the Bible I found a God-given word for every situation and circumstance in my life, for every crisis, for every need. In it I found words of love and wisdom, of faith, of strength, of purpose, of hope, and of eternal life. . . .

Those thirty-two days of meditation, fasting, and prayer were also days of commitment and renewal. I prayed to God for forgiveness and asked Him to give me wisdom and strength to henceforth be a Christ-like example for Christ's sake to my loved ones, to my relatives and friends, and to anyone I came in contact with. And I prayed that God would guide me and keep me from evil and use me according to His purpose the rest of my days.

IT WAS Friday night, November 18, 1938. I had just returned home from a long day's work at the soap factory and gone up to my study to pray. My number one concern was what I should do with regard to the Evangelical church. Should I join them again? I was sure the Evangelicals were people who loved God, and I missed them—I had missed their fellowship for nearly four months. But I was afraid to be disheartened again. I had just written a letter to Rev. Konstantinides about what I had read in Mark 16:17; Acts 2:4, 11; 1 Corinthians 14:2-40; and other passages, to find out why the Evangelicals did not accept speaking in tongues as a present-day experience, if it indeed were. More than ever, I now sensed the need for God's wisdom and direction.

While praying, I fell asleep and saw a dream. I dreamed that my eyes were probing the night sky while I was in some kind of distress. Suddenly a light appeared in the east. The light grew larger and brighter until its radiance permeated the far reaches of the skies, its strong rays reaching the earth. In an instant, all the sky's brightness was magnificently drawn together, then exploded into an image of a face. The image resolved into a colossal Christ, with His arms outstretched. His garment was shining brilliantly, His face shone like the sun, yet I could look at Him unafraid and undisturbed.

Then He spoke. "Only Me! Only Me!"

And with that I woke up, whispering, "Only You, Lord! Only You, Lord!"

I felt unspeakable joy and peace surrounding me. I knelt and raised my arms toward the east where the light had appeared, in my heart raising a prayer of submission and praise to the One who had spoken. For a long moment I remained on my knees, overwhelmed by the nature of the dream, consumed with its message. I understood that in times of disappointment or distress I should focus my eyes on Jesus, not on others, not even the greatest among believers, for disappointment could come from anyone; and that regardless of the situation, in looking to Jesus I would find inner strength, joy, and peace.

BEING better grounded in the Word—"loins girded with God's truth. . .feet shod with the preparedness of the Gospel of peace" (Ephesians 6:10-17)—I fully sensed God's prompting in my life to serve Him. A burning desire was born within me to obey Christ's command to reach people with His message. Unworthy of God's high calling to be His servant, I drew strength from the fact that it was God's plan and pleasure to choose men of flesh and blood to relate His message to mankind. For as Jesus prayed to the Father to keep those whom the Father had given to Him (John 17:11), so He prayed also for those who would believe in Him through their words (John 17:20). What an honor, I thought to myself, that God should choose to anoint mortal men's lips that through their spoken word others could come to believe in Him!

Awed and humbled by God's call, I was certain that the host of new trials and afflictions awaiting me in life, though of a nature and magnitude yet unknown to me, would nonetheless match the size of the room within me for the learning of patience and obedience. For I felt weak and inadequate, and of such honor undeserving.

GOD stirred my love for my Evangelical brethren, prompting me to join them again. A timely letter from Rev. Konstantinides a week later confirmed God's leading. Doctrinal differences, the reverend wrote, have always existed among believers, but God's spiritual gifts are no different today from what they were in the early stages of the Christian faith. Such differences, he said, should be no cause for neglecting the fellowship with the body of believers at the Evangelical church in obedience to God's Word, according to Romans 10:24-25.

Panos as "Charlie." An outward
reminder (insert) of Panos'
inward transformation.

# 9

# Daily Witness

A ND SO IT WAS THAT I returned to the Evangelical
church and began to openly testify of God's life-transforming love. From that point, a series of trying times, adversities
and temptations beset me, but my heart was joyous, for I knew
that God could see that I desired to lead my life in a way that
would please Him, as evidenced by the outcome of each situation. God saw fit, therefore, that through such trials I should
learn to trust Him and depend upon Him.

**A Juggling Act.** Following work at the Preve Soap Factory
one Saturday afternoon in February of 1939, I was stopped by
a policeman and a process server who issued me a warrant for
the seizure of cash. In vain did I try to convince them that I
wasn't Zacharakis, but Zachariou. More than six years earlier,
Tony Zacharakis, my former partner, had vanished from Chania,
owing over 1,000 drachmas in rental fees. In 1936, Tony's landlord had demanded the money from me in court, but the case
was found groundless. Tony's landlord had evidently not given
up; hence my present predicament.

"I'm telling you the truth, sirs. I am not Tony Zacharakis. I
am Panos Zachariou, which I suspect you do know. My accuser
is liable to be found guilty of false charges, because I never was
his tenant," I insisted, embarrassed by becoming a public spectacle.

Two fellow workers who happened by swore that they knew
me and that I was an innocent man.

"Drop it, now, Mr. Zachariou," shouted the policeman, "Did you or did you not get paid today? In the name of the law, I'm going to seize every penny on you!"

I became indignant, for I realized that my identity wasn't even an issue. I saw the specter of indigence facing me, for I had just been paid 600 drachmas—one hundred for each day of that week as a technician specialist, a rare happening. I prayed to God for help.

As I put my left hand inside my overcoat, the pair grabbed me by the arms and ordered me to remain still. They searched me for a long time, but they found only a few drachmas and my watch. I was amazed at how the situation had turned out. I looked up and offered God a silent prayer of praise.

Meanwhile, the two kept asking me whether I had gotten paid that day.

"I certainly did get paid, sirs," I would reply, my eyes raised. "You may seize only what you find on me."

And that was just what they did. Because the law did not permit the seizure of an amount less than 100 drachmas, they took only my watch.

After my two tormentors left, I spent some time looking for my money. My friends tried to help me by telling me to check maybe this pocket or that pocket. My curiosity turned first into apprehension, then exasperation.

Suddenly I glimpsed something on the inside of my left sleeve. The six one-hundred-drachma bills were wedged between the sleeves of my overcoat and my jacket!

"The nimblest of jugglers couldn't have done this," I said to my dumbfounded friends. "Only God!"

The next day I found the landlord and told him that I had no intention of bringing charges against him, but that I wanted my watch back. He informed me that the process server had it in his possession. Shaking his head, he then said, "If you were a good man, you wouldn't have changed your faith."

I looked at him with pity. The words of Titus 1:12 came to my mind: "The Cretans are always liars, evil beasts, slow bellies." "If I hadn't changed my faith," I replied, "I'd be changing yours right now!"*

* In Modern Greek, to change one's faith means to beat one up.

God saw me through once more—though I felt convicted about bullying that man.

Shortly after that incident, Mr. Preve gave me the liberty to start each day at work with a prayer in the presence of all interested workers. Usually there were a dozen, including two assertive atheists and Communists. As for my two fellow workers and eyewitnesses, they started attending the Evangelical church.

**The Stolen Pigeon.** Early on the exciting morning of March 27, 1939, God gave us our third son. We named him Thedosios (God's gift). In the midst of our celebration and thanksgiving, a man came to our neighborhood in search of his stolen pigeon. His desperate pursuit from door to door eventually led him to our garbage can, in which was revealed the fate of his fowl. Why had the evangelist, the Mason, the hypocrite, the thief, the bastard. . . stolen his pigeon? Why had the sweet-mouthed, the cheater, the pickpocket, the deceiver, the liar. . . devoured it? All the neighbors should know—because he'd changed his faith and the devil had entered his liver!

I couldn't believe my ears. Leaning over my window upstairs, I saw neighbors rushing out of their houses and my mother-in-law ready to swing a bucket over the man's head as he continued yelling and shouting all kinds of accusations and obscenities. In my anger, I was ready to shout, "Hit him over the head with it!" or, "If you're man enough, just wait till I get down there!"

In that split second, I became aware of Satan's snare. My pride trapped in my mouth, I prayed that God would help me say the right thing.

"My good man," I finally said, "what's a pigeon worth to you? Besides, hasn't it occurred to you that perhaps someone who hates me might have wanted to incriminate me by dumping those feathers into our garbage can?"

The man looked up at me, then turned around and simply walked away.

I learned that day that, in an unguarded moment, I could easily fall victim to a surprise attack by Satan; and that the defense against such an attack is the same as against any other kind—a surrendered will and the prayer of faith for God's intervention.

**Proselytizing my Wife.** Monday, May 15, 1939, I was summoned to appear in court on grounds of a new law against proselytism, 1363/38. The victim: my wife.

I had appeared in court a number of times in the past, but chiefly as a false witness or because of business-related crimes. This time I felt humbled by the awesome responsibility of making a public stand as a witness of the gospel.

According to the indictment, I had demanded that Chrysa throw away every icon and candle in the house and forced her to attend the Evangelical church. To my surprise, the accusations were traced to Chrysa's aunt, who had gone to complain to the authorities and to the bishop about me. This also explained the reason for the unwarranted search of our house by two policemen two days before the hearing.

Although Chrysa had already denied the charges during a preliminary hearing four months earlier (January 14), the examiner seemed determined to incriminate me.

"You are charged with proselytizing through unlawful means," Judge Dafermos said pointedly.

"I deny the charges, your honor. It's not true, though if such a means were effective, I would find it fitting."

"Between you and me," the examiner continued with a benign smile. "How do you view yourself, now that you have sided with the Evangelicals?"

"As an unworthy sinner saved by God's grace."

"How do you view other people?"

"According to the gospel, as ungodly, because 'He who does not abide in the teachings of Jesus has not God' " (2 John 9).

"My good man, why don't you just mind your own business, instead of this constant God, God, God!"

"That's right, your honor, His name is constantly on the lips of every believer!"

"Was it through your studies that you repented?"

"Did the thief on the cross study? He repented and believed. But I beg you, sir," I went on, "to refer to all my indictment records and confer with the judges of these courts, and you will find evidence as to what I used to be and by the grace of God who I have become."

"Certainly you have repented now, seeing that the world can no longer trust you."

"On the contrary, your honor, while I consider myself according to the gospel an undeserving sinner saved by God's grace, my peers view me as a dependable and capable man."

As the examination continued, the spectrum of accusations broadened to involve the whole Evangelical church. Many of the brethren were panic-stricken, which disturbed me. Didn't Christ say, "Blessed are those persecuted for righteousness' sake"?

Of the fourteen persons examined, only two were pronounced guilty—Nick Georgakakis (the watchmaker) and Panos Zachariou.

The date for our appeal was set in July. The district attorney sought our release without bail, but in vain. Nick and I were kept in custody.

We lost no time. Nick and I began spending practically every waking moment singing songs and sharing the message of Christ with the prisoners in the adjacent cells. Some asked for prayer. At the end of the third day, the jailers ordered us to stop talking. But that was just as well, for the next day we were released on bail, thanks to our brethren.

Two months later Nick and I were facing our prosecutors: an archimandrite (a cleric ranking below a bishop), two priests, and the two assertive atheistic Communists from my work. Prior to the trial, these two fellow workers had requested that I make no allusion to their being Communists, reminding me that it was forbidden by law to try to proselytize a Communist. They promised in turn that as friends they would not testify against me in court.

But that was just what I had planned to point out in court. I had in mind to say, "Why would it be wrong to speak to these men about God, your honor? They're not even Orthodox. They are atheists. Yes, even Communists!" But apparently God would not have me say those things in court, I thought.

During the trial the presiding judge, noticing the obvious discrepancy between the two men's deposition and their testimony in court, asked one of them whether the truth was what he was saying before the judges or the written testimony he had submitted. The man hesitated. (According to his deposition, I had suggested to him that he should pray to God, and after following my suggestion, everything went wrong in his life—he lost one of his children and his income had decreased.) The man finally admitted that he supported his written testimony, and his hesitation was at once construed by the court as further evidence of my efforts to proselytize him.

"You honor," the archimandrite stood up to say, "the Evangelicals exercise systematic propaganda, especially these two men, who fell upon my parish like wolves upon a flock!"

"You mean. . . these two?" the judge said in surprise.

"Yes, your honor. Especially Zachariou. He's capable of persuading you as well!"

"Oh?" said the presiding judge, eyeing me incredulously. "He doesn't strike me as such—"

Nick and I were led away in style—with chains around our wrists. As we left the courtroom, I saw the Orthodox zealots gleefully congratulating one another. Their hypocrisy disgusted me. It was from them I had learned to kneel during Holy Communion, though not as a professional devotee, but as one seeking to find the truth. I used to envy them, thinking that they were superior; but now I could see that their fanaticism had so blinded them that they could not even remember that a Christian should love his enemy. Raising my hands high, I said to them, "Thank you, dear ones, for allowing me, the unworthy, to be considered persecuted."

"You?" shouted the archimandrite. "You consider yourself an apostle? You—egotist!"

I remembered then the words of a man convicted of murder, to whom I had tried to speak about God while in jail two months earlier. "It's because of that pious theologian—" the convict had told me, referring to the one now calling me an egotist, "—it's because of him that I hate religion and anyone who speaks of religion!" (It was due to that particular prisoner's complaints that the jailers ordered Nick and me to silence.)

The jailers put us together in one cell and ordered us not to talk to any prisoner. Interestingly, we hadn't even heard our verdict yet!

But Nick and I found a silent way to reach the prisoners. In the corner of our cell we found two pieces of paper. On one piece we wrote the reason for our imprisonment, then cut the other into small pieces and wrote Scripture verses on them. Reaching through the bars of our cell, we passed our written messages to the prisoners in the adjacent cells, and they passed them likewise to others. Oh, the joy Nick and I shared when we heard the prisoners talk among themselves about the things they read!

Two days later our silent communications were intercepted by the warden, and I was taken before the prison director.

"Why were you brought here?" the director asked.

"So I may proselytize you, too," I replied with a smile.

"Say that again?"

I did.

Then the two of us had a good talk about the things of God. The director was quite open and receptive.

Two days later, while praying and facing the direction of the barred window high above my head, I saw the figure of a headless man from the waist up. The figure was dressed in Byzantine attire, and had his hands in chains. The chains suddenly came loose from his hands and dropped to the ground. With one hand he then picked up a quill, with the other a roll of parchment, and he began to write.

"Nick!" I said. "The Lord will deliver us!"

Nick seemed indifferent as I described my vision to him. "You know as well as I, Panos, that on Saturdays they never release any prisoners."

In less than an hour we heard our names: "Zachariou! Georgakakis! Get your clothes and get out!" Oh, what joyful sounds of freedom!

On our way out, one of the jailers leaned cautiously over and whispered in my ear, "I wasn't against you, pal."

God had once again turned adverse circumstances around. Three of the prisoners had opened their heart to the message of Christ; and the convicted murderer who had earlier expressed his disillusionment with religion, had asked us to remember him in prayer.

**An Old Debt.** The hustle and bustle of the Agora (Market) in the heart of Chania could not drown a familiar voice—unmistakably that of Mr. Mihelakis.

"So you became a godly man, eh?"

I turned around. "Mr. Mihelakis!" I said, offering a handshake.

"Time serves my memory well," my former boss said. "You owe us money!"

Thus provoked, I sensed a battle beginning inside me. I asked God to give me the right words to say.

"Why do you think I should pay you?" I said.

"That would show what kind of god you worship," he said.

Greatly vexed, I was tempted to tell him that what he hadn't been able to get by pointing his gun at me, he was now trying to get by pointing his finger at God. But I checked myself. "If God tells me to pay, I will pay," I finally said.

"Your new religious craze has blinded you, friend. You'll have no choice but pay. It's the courts that will tell you to pay, not God. They took care of Angelos, now they'll take care of you!"

I felt peaceful. I was sure this was but the onset of another trying time, and prayed that God would see me through. At dinner that evening, I recounted to my loved ones my encounter with Mihelakis, and told them that they were about to witness God's miraculous intervention once more. My mother-in-law at once pulled herself upright and exchanged a glance with Chrysa. Then she began to talk. It was a miracle, she said, that the priests hadn't been able to keep me in jail for the full two months. It was a miracle that I hadn't run out of the house to beat up the man who was accusing me of stealing his pigeon. It was a miracle that I hadn't thrown her down the stairs after she had hit me in the face....

As she continued to talk I raised silent praises to my Creator. But I knew it wasn't just those miracles that had caused my mother-in-law to mellow. She had observed the true change Christ had wrought in my wretched life, and had been especially touched by the loving and forgiving spirit I had shown toward her sister, who had instigated court action against me.

In the end, without a moment's hesitation, she proposed to sell the piece of property she owned in New Smyrna, Athens, to pay my part of the 20,000-drachma debt!

WHEN I was subpoenaed to appear in court, I learned that Mihelakis himself was not directly involved in the lawsuit. My accusers were his two partners.

The day of the trial was approaching, but the sale of the property in Athens had not been finalized. Rev. Konstantinides, who acted as our proprietor, had asked for more time. My two prosecutors suggested that I play for time by claiming to be ill on the day of the trial, so the trial could be rescheduled. Four days later—the day before the trial—they came to my home and urged me to reconsider their suggestion.

"We will testify that you were ill," they insisted. "We beg you to stay home. Just for tomorrow!"

"But, my dear friends, you don't seem to understand," I said. "I'm not the same man you used to know—not the Panos who had stood as a false witness on behalf of a child molester, then of an embezzler, then of a bribing murderer. God has transformed my life. I do not wish to lie."

At the courthouse the next day the two begged me once more. They even had their attorney try to persuade me. Seeing how adamant I remained, one of them said, "Well, then, if that's how headstrong you want to be, go eat jail for two years!"

"I'll eat whatever God provides," I said.

A short time later I found myself in the same dock as before. But I had peace. I believed God would intervene.

The presiding judge called the name of my first accuser. Silence.

He called the name of the second.

A long pause.

Tears of praise welled up in my eyes. I could see the victory of faith.

The case was dismissed!

THREE weeks later I went to see Mihelakis with the balance of the money he had loaned me four years before. All he had to do, I told him, was to produce a signed receipt that my debt to him had been paid in full, and the 3,000 drachmas I was carrying in my pocket would be his. But he refused, insisting that my debt to the company was not just 3,000 or 10,000, but 20,000 drachmas! That, I told him, God would not even allow me to imagine.

"You're forcing me to put you in jail!" he shouted.

"Don't forget who forced whom," I replied, pointing my hand at him like a pistol. "I pray that God would not have me use your own handwriting to prove that in court!"

My trial was over. God had given me the strength to be once more His faithful witness.

**Mission Unknown.** "Lord, guide my footsteps today according to Your will, and help me touch someone for You," I prayed early one spring morning in 1940 as I left home wishing to devote the day to speaking to someone about God.

"Where are you going so early?" my mother-in-law inquired.

"To Perivolia," I replied without any forethought.

When I had walked across town, I asked myself whether in fact I had any business in Perivolia, but couldn't think of any. Since I had already walked more than a kilometer, I figured I could visit my parents there, where they had resettled, and talk with my father, who time and again had rejected the message of Christ.

Upon reaching the bridge at Kastrohori, I was accosted by two policemen.

"Are you from here, sir?" asked the tall one.

"My parents live in Perivolia, but I live in Chania," I said.

"Your papers, please."

"Here you are, sirs," I said, and handed them two tracts. "As for an identification, I have nothing on me, sirs."

"Oh, it's you—" said the other, "—the one who distributes tracts. Do you have a license?"

"Is it necessary to carry a license in order to hand out Christian tracts?"

"Let's go, now," they said as they grabbed me by the arms.

"But be assured, sirs, my name is Panos Zachariou. I know better than not to tell you the truth. My parents live in Perivolia—"

At that moment a man happened by. "Pardon me, friend," I said, "do you know me?"

"No, I don't—" he said.

"I am Zachariou's son!"

"Him I know, but not you."

"Come, sir, let's go in," the tall policeman insisted. "Please know we must do our duty."

We reached a café, and I was relieved to see a man I knew. "Hey, my friend, Kosti, please tell these officers who I am."

"I know this man," my friend stated. "He's Zachariou's son."

But the policemen didn't seem to care. Proselytism! I thought. I'll be charged with proselytism again! I wonder if God has guided my footsteps here, or have I operated on my own accord?

As we continued to the police station, it occurred to me that it was perhaps the policemen I should talk to about God. That's it—the policemen!

The two officers listened as I shared with them the message of Christ. It was as though I were in the company of friends, not under arrest.

Once at the station, the tall policeman took my New Testament from my hands, checked my pockets and found more tracts, then handed everything over to the police chief, who gave me a stern look and proceeded to examine the tracts. Meanwhile, a fourth policeman came down from upstairs with a feather duster in his hand. He seemed indifferent to what was happening as he started dusting.

The police chief went upstairs, and the two policemen sat at a table to eat lunch. They invited me to join them. I told them I would if they'd let me take back my Bible and talk to them some more. They agreed.

The two policemen showed great interest as I talked to them about salvation and the forgiveness of sin. The one dusting seemed preoccupied.

"Tell me," said the tall policeman, "do we have any saints today?"

"It's God who turns people into saints, not men," I said, and turned to the opening verses of some epistles to show him that Christians are addressed as saints (Romans 1:7; 1 Corinthians 1:2; 2 Corinthians 1:1; Ephesians 1:1; Philippians 1:1).

The two finished their lunch and went upstairs. The one dusting looked at me through the corners of his eyes as if he wanted to say something. That moment the chief came downstairs.

"Please, sir, read this one here," I said, as I pointed to one of the tracts in his hands.

"Silence! I'll read everything!" he said angrily, and walked out.

The one still cleaning continued to glance at me. Is he keeping an eye on me so I won't escape? I wondered. He wiped away a tear. He must have dust in his eyes, I thought. No, he's in tears! I wonder if it's because of something he overheard.

"Yes, my good man," I said, "every Christian is also a saint. Do you desire to become a saint? Repent and ask God to cleanse your life of all your sins."

The man nodded as he wiped off more tears, saying nothing.

"If Christ was loving enough to accept the malefactor on the cross," I went on, "he certainly is loving enough to accept you and forgive you this very day."

The man nodded and wiped more tears away.

Right then the police chief and a sergeant walked in and the two other policemen came downstairs.

"Are you affiliated with the Protestants abroad?" the sergeant asked.

"We are of similar convictions, sir, though not directly linked with them."

"And what do you claim to be?"

"I am a heretic."

"And you admit it?"

"Yes, my dear sir, I even boast about it. I am a heretic according to men, but not according to the gospel."

They all stood speechless and staring at each other. Then the sergeant burst into a fit of laughter, and so did the rest of us.

The chief handed all the tracts back to me, then advised me not to go to Perivolia but straight to Chania. I shook their hands, told them I would keep them in my prayers, and left.

My mission was accomplished. God used me to reach the ears of four policemen and the heart of one.

**Filth to Faith.** While relating this incident to Nick at his shop that afternoon, a rich-looking woman came in to have some expensive jewelry repaired. When I resumed my story, Nick asked me to change the subject, because we might be accused of proselytism again.

"Pardon me, my lady, for boring you with my stories," I said.

"Blessed are those who speak the words of Christ," she said.

Nick introduced the woman to me.

"Please remember," said the lady, "that I have connections with the courts. Certainly you may be in serious trouble now."

"So much the better, my lady," I said, "for I will have a most credible witness. But since in God's eyes we are all equal, please bear with me if I address you as a close friend, not as a woman of the world."

"I cannot deny that I am a woman of the world," said the lady. "If your Lord examines my files, he will discover a person with much filth."

"The Lord knows your files. He can also burn them for good if you would ask Him."

That Sunday the woman came to our morning service. She turned out to be one of the most faithful believers.

**A Handout.** Despite the dangers involved, handing out tracts was a particularly rewarding ministry, not only because of the opportunity of exchanging a friendly greeting with a stranger, but also because of the spiritual dividends the simple gesture paid. One summer day in 1940, Nick and I visited a handful of believers in Carmelos, a community east of Chania, where Thrasivoulos, a peasant, testified that God had miraculously healed his sick body and his sick soul. From the descriptions the old man gave, I remembered stopping one day by an old shack in Carmelos to see if someone lived there. The run-down place stood like a speck against the snowy mountaintops of Lefka Ori (White Mountains). A sign on the door read, "Attention: Danger—Lodging of Tubercular." I remembered how my heart ached then. "Silver and gold have I none, but such as I have give I unto you in the name of Jesus," I remembered saying, as I placed a couple of tracts on the doorstep.

"And so," gray-haired Thrasivoulos went on, "I got to my little hut that night because the doctor had given me orders to leave the sanatorium for being a troublemaker and a hopelessly sick man."

I asked if he was the man who lived in that little house on the hill. He looked at me and said, "I suspect it was you who left those tracts by my door last year? Thank God, because God spoke to me through a tract, and He heard my prayer!"

Teary-eyed, Nick and I praised God along with the rest of the group. That day, Thrasivoulos started attending our church.

AS I looked back in the summer of 1940, I could see that by God's grace during those past two years I had become a man not only outwardly changed, but inwardly transformed. Through trying times, God had taught me to look to Him for guidance, wisdom, and strength. The joy I had found in following Jesus through trying times (James 1:2-4, 12:1 Peter 1:6-7) no longer seemed a paradox. I had learned that joy, disguised in suffering, subsists through perseverance until realized in the outcome. Obedience, patience, and a stronger faith are all part of that outcome—the substance of true joy.

I could also see the miracles God had performed in and through my life during those two years, and the many blessings He had bestowed on us. Before the end of that summer, He had brought to church my wife, my mother-in-law, her mother, my own mother, my brother and his wife, and my sister and her husband; He had healed the legs of little Demetrios from polio; He had performed other healings and wonders in my home and other places; and He had used me to reach souls with His message. And the stature of the body of believers in the city of Chania had grown in number and in spiritual blessings.

BUT there were trials of greater magnitude soon to come, trials that would involve not only me, my family, and the Christian believers in Chania, but the entire Greek nation. Already by 1938, wars and rumors of war were spreading throughout Europe. The tides of war were likely to reach our nation soon.

Suddenly on October 28, 1940, Greece was invaded by the Italians; on April 6, 1941, by the Germans. I knew that the true warfare of God's children is not against flesh and blood, but against the dominion and power of spiritual darkness in this world (Ephesians 6:12). Therefore, I knew as well that behind the specter of this imminent world-wide manslaughter was the archenemy of God and of mankind, Satan—the Master Killer who exerts his power through unregenerate and reprobate minds like those of Mussolini and Hitler.

# 10

## God's Soldier

**D**URING A GENERAL MOBILIZATION immediately following the invasion by Italian forces plunging into Greece through Albania, I was sent to Athens. I was taken ill with typhus, though, which kept me from going to the Albanian front. By the time I recovered, the last troops of our regiment had already been sent. The colonel, knowing of my experience in shipping and receiving, put me in charge of his personal supplies at his home in Patesia, Athens. This again prevented me from going to the Albanian front.

Panos during the German invasion of Crete in 1941

Mussolini's legions, which outnumbered the Greek lines of defense, soon bogged down. After their thunderous defeat in March of 1941, Germany had to go to Italy's aid, while the British sent an army to help us. Hitler's eyes were now turned on Greece.

Easter of 1941 found me in the barracks of Goudi, Athens. When I heard that the Allies were losing the war and that Greece would soon be occupied, I prayed that God would enable me to return to my loved ones in Crete. The barracks were heavily guarded, though, and no one was allowed to leave. After praying,

I picked up my bag and walked over to a lieutenant standing guard by the main gate.

"What are you up to, corporal?" the lieutenant asked.

"I request that I report for duty in my home town, sir," I said.

"Request denied," he said sardonically.

Speechless, I handed him my undershirt along with my papers.

Face filled with disgust, the lieutenant flung my lice-infested undershirt to the ground.

"I haven't taken a bath for weeks, sir!" I said.

"Then go take a bath!" he growled and hurriedly signed my papers.

THE TROOP carrier Samos sat deserted at the port of Piraeus. Hundreds of soldiers waited to board her and sail to Crete. But the only crew member on Samos, I learned, was a frustrated engineer. The rest of the crew had abandoned the ship.

Teeming with travelers going overseas and only and short distance from Samos was the passenger ship Ellas. Many had boarded Ellas hoping to avoid the Germans.

I managed to get on Samos. The engineer was relieved to see someone who had maritime experience and was willing to help. He informed me that the other crew members were afraid the ship was in no condition to sail to Crete—it had many mechanical problems, including a jammed capstan that would not release the anchor. Mainly, though, he said, the other crew members were simply fearful of an air raid by German Stukas.

After we determined the course of our voyage, I lowered the gangplank and ordered the soldiers to come on board. There were hundreds of them. It was obvious I was only a corporal, but they all obeyed my orders without question. I directed them to the belly of the vessel and ordered some armed guards to threaten to shoot at anyone trying to come out.

Within an hour Samos was filled beyond capacity—well over 1,500 men! I felt an enormous responsibility, and prayed for God's direction.

We were about to sail that afternoon when the German Stukas came. Their guns and bombs missed us, but they hit Ellas. I thought I was losing my mind! "My God, spare us!" I shouted.

Ellas was sinking. Our panicked soldiers tried to come out, but the guards kept them from making inviting targets of themselves.

The air raid was over. None of us had been hit. Fearing a second attack or wishing to aid the air raid victims, many soldiers asked to be let out—an opportunity I seized to hand out every tract I carried as the men went down the gangplank.

An hour later the soldiers began to return, and so did the captain himself, another engineer, and another crew member. The captain inquired by whose authority I had assumed control of the ship and threatened to hit me with his fists. I purposely raised my voice and said that I had hundreds of witnesses that he was a deserter, and that he had better stick to the helm all the way to Crete or he'd be arrested and court-martialed. That was enough to arouse the indignation of some brave Cretans who at once seized the captain, brought him to the helm, and kept him under close surveillance.

Because it was safer to travel by night, at daybreak the next day we stopped at the small island of Kea. When I told the soldiers to seek food and protection on the island away from the ship, they obeyed as before. I had gained their trust.

On the island I met a policeman who had moved there from Crete, and who had often accused me of proselytizing and brainwashing people with my tracts. This time, however, he not only invited me to his home for dinner, but asked me to talk to his wife and two daughters about my faith in God.

On our way back to the ship that afternoon, we saw German Stukas approaching. They dropped bombs over Samos, but our ship was not hit—the bombs seemed to follow an unpredictable path, and hit the water. When the soldiers later asked me for a religious explanation of the phenomenon, I told them that as long as we were willing to call upon God for protection, He would provide not only for our safety, but also for our stomachs. Indeed, the bombs had killed enough fish to feed an army! Freshly caught fish in their hands, the hungry soldiers swarmed around a nearby bakery, where earlier in the day they had devoured every piece of bread they could buy.

Oh, the miraculous opportunities the loving Father used to reach those hundreds of souls with His Word as we sailed on! Crammed together in the belly of the ship in absolute darkness, one after another the soldiers asked questions about the Bible, requested prayer, made promises and vows, and received the message of Christ. Never once did any soldier make any sarcastic remarks about the words that were spoken or make light of religion. Heaven rejoiced!

At daybreak we stopped at the tiny island of Andimilos, about 85 kilometers south of Kea. There we saw the smoldering wreckage of a ship which, according to some fishermen in the area, had recently been torpedoed by German submarines. As we began to evacuate we again heard the high-pitched shriek of German Stukas. Many terror-stricken soldiers jumped in the choppy waters.

The soldiers wanted an explanation again. Why hadn't the Germans dropped bombs this time? I told them that perhaps the Germans were out of bombs, but my explanations did not seem to satisfy them. "You are God's man," they said. "You should stay on the ship all the time." That was a well-deserved testing time for me, a reminder that I was an instrument of God, with a mission to direct the eyes of those men toward heaven, not to attribute God's intervention to chance.

Heavy clouds gathered over our heads by afternoon. It was windy and cold. The soldiers had returned to the ship, but our wave-lashed craft was in danger of running aground. I asked some to keep praying that God would release the anchor, while two volunteers and I lowered a boat in hopes of reaching a rock with a cable. Our intrepid efforts against the fierce waves proved fruitless, though, so we returned to the ship.

We found a fretful captain trying to release the anchor by using profanities. Then suddenly it felt as though we had been hit by a submarine, and the ship tipped on its left. We fell upon each other, and our weight caused the ship to tip even more. The prow was resting atop a reef. We had run aground.

Panic spread among us, for without an anchor we would be smashed against the rocks. "Lord," I prayed silently, "is this how far You are taking us?"

In a moment came a sudden, loud bang. The anchor had been released! "Courage, men! Courage!" I shouted. An officer of the music band praised my faith; but I, shaking my head, deplored my lack of faith. Hadn't God answered my prayer in the barracks? Had He not heard the soldiers' prayers? Had He not shown us enough signs that He would be with us all the way against all odds? Yet I had questioned Him. How could my God allow me, of so little faith, to carry out a mission this size? "Father, forgive me," I prayed. "And help me not to fail You again."

The captain asked me what ideas I had now.

"Courage," I said. "God is helping us. Let's have the men move to the other side of the ship. You get up there and move the ship back and forth with the propeller, and get us unstuck."

There was a gleam of hope in the captain's eyes. The unbelieving is comforting the despairing, I thought to myself.

The soldiers began to move to the right, and the ship suddenly tipped to the right. Pandemonium! The men thought the ship was going to capsize. Panic-stricken, they instinctively rushed to the left side, causing the ship to tip to the left, then again to the right, and so on, the degree of incline increasing with each alternate move. Finally, somehow, the ship stopped rolling and its hull floated free.

The sun went down. Our craft set sail again, in absolute darkness. Our bodies were bruised and aching, our hair stiff with salt, our eyes red from lack of sleep; but we knew we were halfway home.

Toward midnight we heard the roar of warplanes. They circled over our heads and sent us bright signals.

"The Germans!" some men shouted. "We're lost!"

I raised my eyes in prayer and stood still. I sensed no fear.

"British! They're British!" shouted the captain, who signaled back with a flashlight that we were fugitives. The planes were en route to the port of Souda in Crete. And, by God's grace, so were we.

By afternoon the next day we reached the port of Souda. The port was a minefield. Losing heart, the captain asked me if I knew the way. To comfort the man, I said that I had sailed those waters not long ago and thought I could still manage; but truly, it was I who needed God's comfort and reassurance now, for I knew nothing about those mines. I believed that God leaves nothing half-done and therefore was going to help us until the end, but still my head was telling me that we could be blown into pieces any second. My hands on the helm and my agonizing heart in my throat, I hummed songs of praise and asked God to strengthen me and my faith.

An hour later, our maritime adventure was over. Samos lay securely at anchor in our home port, and not one of us had been lost.

Now I could see how God used my experience as a ship boy for a purpose and my relationship with Him for a mission. In the midst of the hundreds of soldiers coming ashore, I unreservedly raised my hands and voice toward heaven and magnified the name of Almighty God!

LIVING daily under life-threatening conditions, I prayed for every step I took and every decision I made. Completely resigned to God's guidance and protecting hand, I learned to live each moment overshadowed not by my own fear, but by God's mercy. I saw each life-and-death situation as another trial, another testing, as well as the root of another manifestation of my growing relationship with my Master.

After a blessed reunion with my loved ones, I reported for military duty. Being among the first to report, I exercised the option to join the battalion commanded by Maj. Papadakis, a family friend. Strangely, the recruiting officer insisted that I be transferred to another unit, which disturbed me. My desire was that God would overrule that decision, but in the end I still had to concede to the recruiting officer's authority.

Due to a lack of military personnel, I was promoted to sergeant major. My area of operation was near the bridge of Alikianou, where heavy air raids were anticipated. Already by May 14, 1941 the Germans had begun a systematic bombing of ports, cities, roads, and central areas of defense on the island.

Violent bombardment of the airfield at Maleme, near Chania, began the morning of May 20. We were attacked by air on May 21, and learned that day that all of Maj. Papadakis' men had been killed, including the major himself.

After the attack, I ran to the headquarters in Chania to report the casualties. As a reward for my perilous 11-kilometer run from Alikianou, I was given a 15-hour leave, during which I managed to get my family moved to the village of Perivolia.

When I reported for duty, I was issued a written authorization to recruit men from the surrounding villages to perform noncombatant service and to supply food to the fighting units. Going through Fourne, I felt hot bullets hissing past my ears. As I ducked beneath a bridge, I thought of Psalm 91:7: "A thousand may fall at your side, ten thousand at your right hand, but it will not come near you." Realizing what was happening, I prayed that God would intervene. My hands acted as if ordered by a will other than my own, and waved a white handkerchief in the air. In moments I was surrounded by German soldiers.

THE prisoners exchanged not a word as the camion jounced its way toward the unknown. I looked at those despairing, exhausted faces and found it difficult to accept the idea that I, too, was a prisoner of war.

The camion finally stopped in a German concentration camp in Ayious Apostolous. At first I couldn't recognize the area—barbed wire and German guards were everywhere, surrounding a large number of working prisoners.

I knew very little about concentration camps, but from what I had heard I suspected that hard labor, torture, starvation, uncertainty about tomorrow, and even execution lay in store. I thought of my wife and three children, whom I had not seen for several days. "Lord," I prayed, "revive in me the flame of my conviction that You have a definite plan for me in this life. Lay Your protective hand upon all my loved ones, and also upon me."

Our first task that afternoon was to restore a huge tent that had blown down over the first-aid equipment. The captives were yelling confused instructions to each other, and after a period of frustration I yelled out, "Let just one, not everyone, give orders here!" The men froze, staring at me. The only stare that gave me a sensation of uneasiness, however, was coming from under a German colonel's hat.

Working together, we at last drove the final peg into the ground. But I had no sooner caught my breath and gazed into the twilight to see the first stars, when the German colonel and a guard came up and signaled me to follow. The colonel stopped at his headquarters and turned around, looking at me as if he meant to say something friendly. Then he pointed to his guard, who stood a couple of meters to my right and was holding a machine gun.

"You are to go with him tomorrow morning," he said firmly, in broken Greek. "I am giving you twenty-five prisoners. Your task will be to walk into every food store and every garden as far as Chania."

Vandalism! I thought. Extortion! But I had no choice.

The condition in which I found Chania the next day was beyond description. Buildings had been bombed. People were burying their dead. The city was nearly deserted—everyone who could had sought refuge in nearby villages. Those who had stayed behind now witnessed savagery at the hands of their own friends, for they were people I knew. None dared object to what was happening, though; none dared protest as he watched his food, the food his family needed, being forced away. With heavy, aching hearts, we stuffed the truck with all the edible goods we could find, until there was barely enough space for us.

As we approached Splantzia, I felt cold chills all over my body. I began to shake. "Just in time!" I whispered with trembling lips, and a prayer of gratitude to God rose within my heart for His protecting hand. Had the Lord not provided that 15-hour leave for me to move my family to Perivolia, all my loved ones would most assuredly have been killed, for an incendiary bomb had exploded inside our house!

That evening we returned from our foraging with great quantities of meat, fish, fruit, and vegetables. Shouts of joy rose from the hungry prisoners, most of whom had not eaten for days. But my own heart was breaking.

This venture gained favor for me in the eyes of the Germans, as well as the captured men. The German colonel announced that night that I was in charge of the prisoners. Immediately I divided the men into groups to facilitate the rationing of food and the organization of labor.

When the British bombed our concentration camp two nights later, the men ran to my tent and found me on my knees, praying and singing praises to God. Surprise replaced their panic, and in moments I was sharing with them God's message of salvation.

But what I had been forced into doing during that food-gathering expedition did not fit in the picture of a Christian's testimony. Knowing that I would soon be sent out again, I brought the matter before God for a solution. Of all solutions, the most satisfactory one was also the most impossible—escape. I knew this would be a matter of life and death, but there was no other way out of my predicament.

The next day I assigned another prisoner to take charge of the rations. When I explained my intentions to him and to some of the prisoners, they reacted with fear.

"But how are you going to escape, Panos? You know they'll mow you down!"

"Certainly not over the fence," I said with a smile. "God has His way."

That afternoon I looked half soldier, half civilian. Sack over my shoulder, hat on my head—a gift from a civilian who wished protection for me from the hot sun—I began to whistle "Onward Christian Soldiers," and walked toward the well-guarded gate of the concentration camp. I saluted the guard, he saluted back, and I exited. So I would not be suspected as an escapee, I purposely passed near a company of German officers standing outside the gate and engaged in conversation. After saluting them, still whistling, I continued my escape with no further complications. Like Peter walking out of prison under the noses of the guards, I walked under the noses of the German soldiers and was free.

Only when I found myself with my wife and children and the rest of the relatives in Perivolia did I realize, with incredulity, the apparent absurdity of my action. Logically speaking, it was absolutely impossible! Most assuredly, God had barred every suspicion from the minds of my captors.

My six-day ordeal in captivity was over. God was my Captain, and I was His soldier—a soldier of the Cross.

GOD used my deliverance from the Germans to draw ears and eyes to His miracle-working power. While bombs fell all around us in Perivolia and machine guns raged, the Spirit of God fell close upon me, prodding me to intercede for the souls of those I loved. In a house filled with loved ones, neighbors, and friends, I fell on my knees and asked God to have mercy on each one of us and to draw us by His Spirit, to cleanse our souls, and to protect us from harm and evil. One by one, they all fell on their knees and asked God to have mercy on them. What a moving sight it was to see those especially close and dear to me seeking God with all their hearts! The only person who refused to kneel and pray, however, was my father.

We studied the Bible and prayed every day. In less than a week virtually all the neighborhood joined us, including a policeman and once even Papayannis, the priest of Perivolia who in the past two years had persecuted me for telling the villagers that forgiveness of sins was not possible after death. But the fear of imminent death was too real now to allow room for disagreements, let alone for solving any differences. Everyone listened to God's Word, everyone prayed. And God saved souls.

Dive-bombers kept flying by at ear-breaking proximity, spreading terror. Homes nearby were blasted, and the earth heaved under our feet with every blast, making our house tremble. But for each bomb aimed at our rooftop, there were dozens of prayers lifting it away, as we continued to give ourselves to prayer.

On June 14, God performed a miracle in my father's life. As we were praying, he humbled himself before God on his knees and asked Him to forgive him of all his sins and save his soul. As tears of joy and peace coursed down his face and all of ours, we all hugged him and kissed him and praised God together. It was a miracle we all had been hoping for, and God performed it through the importunity of prayers of faith.

ON the morning of June 20, 1941, looking out of the upstairs window, my boys Terpandros and Demetrios saw German soldiers kicking doors open and forcing men out of their houses at gunpoint.

"Baba, Baba! Wake up!" they shouted as they stamped their feet on the wooden floor, shaking me out of my sleep. "The Germans are coming and they're carrying machine guns!"

God helped me sense the urgency of the moment. I grabbed my pants and shoes, dashed out of the house, and threw myself over the wall into the adjacent vineyard. I heard the Germans ordering men out of their hiding places, then a few shots. "Protect Your people, my Lord!" I prayed, realizing it wasn't hard labor they had in mind.

Two gunshots were fired near my ears, and a pair of hot bullets ripped through the grape leaves next to my hiding place. Slowly, I raised my head, and saw a German officer's eyes and pistol staring directly at me. Holding my breath, I waited. The German officer looked to his right and walked away.

Grateful to God for His miracle, I collapsed among the grapevines, fully aware that He had caused the enemy's eyes not to see me.

I was grateful to God also that my father and Uncle Dukas had gone to work in the garden early in the morning, and that my brother and cousin had already left for Chania. When I had heard the Germans kicking doors, shouting, and searching every corner, I knew they would find no men in the house, only women and children.

I remained hidden among the leaves for a long time. Meanwhile, from the window upstairs, Chrysa could see Germans rounding up the dozens of captured men and herding them away. Was I among them? She didn't know.

Later I heard men shouting helplessly in the distance—I couldn't make out what. Then the rat-a-tat-tat of gunfire, followed by dead silence—then one more shot. "God, are You allowing our people to be killed?" I said, my heart breaking.

Moments later I heard a town official assuring the residents of Perivolia that it was all over. He urged them to come out of their houses immediately so they could bury their dead within one hour, or the Germans would penalize them. Mothers, wives, and young girls rushed out of their houses, screaming and weeping and wailing hysterically, and heading for the gory scene of the execution of their own husbands, fathers, brothers, and sons.

Totally broken, I could do nothing except cringe in agony and let my bleeding heart weep and pray. God had protected me from sure death; but our village of Perivolia lay decimated.

"Pano? Pano?" I heard my wife's trembling voice calling me. "Are you there?"

She had just returned from the place of execution, and having not found me among the dead, was hoping to find me still alive.

"Over here!" I said, and came out of my hiding place.

Her face was drained of color, her lips white, her eyes filled with horror. "Hide! The Germans! All they caught, they killed!" she said, stumbling over her words. "Everyone! Sabbas—and Pispisis—and—and your father!"

I began to shake like a leaf. I felt disoriented, and didn't know which way to go. Chrysa dragged me here and there until we reached the house. I poured a bucket of cold water over my head, as if to try to wake up from a nightmare I was having. Then I wept bitterly, and talked to my heavenly Father.

I learned that the Germans had found three of their soldiers killed and buried in Perivolia by noncombatant men, presumably some villagers from Perivolia. By way of retribution, for each of their dead the Germans had to kill eleven men from Perivolia who were caught within an area they had cordoned off, one end of which happened to be our very house. My father, unaware of the danger, had left Uncle Dukas in the garden and headed home earlier than usual in order to surprise us with some fresh squash and other vegetables. That's when he fell into the hands of the Germans.

Of the men captured, those who had produced evidence of residence outside Perivolia had been released. My father, too, had been released for a while, after a German-speaking interpreter from Switzerland, wife of the assistant minister Rev. Paidakis, spoke to a German officer on my father's behalf. But after the men were lined up against the wall and counted, the German officer in charge of the firing squad discovered that he was short one man from Perivolia, so he ordered my father to stand against the wall again.

Finally my mother returned from burying my father. I held her blood-stained hands, kissed her pain-filled face, and pressed her bleeding heart close to mine. She told us that the bullet in her beloved's lower abdomen did not bring immediate death; so a coup de grace to the head did. I remembered then the single shot I had heard at the end of the execution. My mother's agony now pulsated inside the void that shot left in my heart.

Heaven now seemed closer, as God comforted and strengthened us with His Word. We all knelt to thank Him for the comforting assurance that my father had so timely become a child of His.

The monument in the village of Perivolia where Panos' father was executed by the Germans along with other innocent civilians

# 11

# Obeying the Command

FOLLOWING THE EXECUTION at Perivolia, we found temporary lodging at the home of Koronis, a hospitable friend from church. Because the factory where I worked had been destroyed, Koronis and I started a small grocery store, usually in the form of a fruit-and-vegetable stand. Because of the war, the black market was now rampant, so we had to do a great deal more bartering than selling of goods. I did all the footwork, the traveling and the bargaining, which I considered to be God's plan in that I found numerous opportunities to speak to people about Him in many parts of Crete, especially in the province of Irakleion. Such opportunities strengthened an existing nucleus of believers in the city of Irakleion, about 110 kilometers (68 miles) from Chania, and led to the eventual formation of a church there.

The desire to share Christ's message burned in my mind. And the harvest was ripe. Because of the war, battered souls needed to hear words of peace, comfort, and hope. Seeing the Bible in my hands and hearing the words I spoke, priests and churchgoers took me for a visiting Orthodox preacher. This afforded me invaluable opportunities to preach in Orthodox churches, particularly in the villages of Irakleion. I prayed that God would help me keep my identity as an Evangelical unknown, so that my ministry would not be hampered.

ON my way to preach at an Orthodox church in Irakleion one Sunday morning, the priest of the village told me that a policeman had informed him that I was an evangelist—Evangelical, he meant. "Haven't you heard?" I said to the priest as though I had received a compliment. "The Bible says that some are apostles, others are teachers, others are prophets, and others are evangelists." The priest agreed. God moved among us that day. The priest himself was moved to tears, along with every other soul in that thirsty gathering. Oh, that our war-torn nation might have ears to hear God's message, was my prayer.

AFTER preaching at another Orthodox church in Irakleion, a visiting chanter from St. Nikolaos in Chania, who fortunately did not recognize me, shared with me a complaint some church-goers had expressed.

"You know," he said, "the women here have noticed that the preacher never worships the icons."

Praying that God would prevent a scandal, I said to him, "Well, you are a chanter, right?"

The young man nodded.

"Then you must know that God says you should not worship anything in heaven, on earth, or in the water beneath the earth, right?"

The chanter nodded again.

"Well? Are we going to do the women favors, or are we going to do what God says? Just don't listen to them," I said.

The chanter agreed.

WHILE climbing up a hill in Irakleion on a Saturday afternoon, a villager asked me who I was. "A son of peace!" I said.

"Whose son?" the villager asked, wondering if I had mentioned a person in the village he didn't know. After I talked to him about God's love through Christ, he told me that he and his family had waited for years for a man like me.

Before preaching at the local church the next day, the priest offered me wine to drink. "Have one or two," the priest said. "It'll help you s-s-slur the words through the s-s-side of your mouth." To which I replied that we should not be drunk with wine, but rather filled with God's Spirit (Ephesians 5:18), but the priest was clearly ignorant of such a verse.

That day, and on several occasions thereafter, a good number of villagers there confessed Christ as their Savior.

MY ministry in Irakleion was extremely blessed. God saved souls, comforted lives, and healed the sick. One winter day, while I was in the village of Lagouta, Irakleion, a lady came running to tell me that her neighbor, Tzirakis, a retired policeman, was dying of pneumonia. The man had been told of God's love and forgiveness through Christ, and he had now requested prayer for his soul. I found him on his deathbed, surrounded by weeping relatives and friends. I asked the man if he would be willing to tell everyone in the village about God's healing power if he became well through prayer, to which he readily agreed. So we prayed.

The next morning I heard the good news. Despite the cold weather, Tzirakis had run out of his house to tell the world that Christ had healed him. I advised him to stay home because of the bad weather, but he told me he feared nothing, because God had given him eternal life. Oh, that God might have mercy on me for my small faith, I prayed. He looked good that day and continued to live in good health thereafter.

IN sharing my experiences with the Evangelical brethren by way of bringing words of encouragement and requesting prayer for people, I was careful to draw attention only to God's work and the fruits of my ministry, not to solicit undue sympathy or praise for any hardships I encountered. One cold winter day, however, Koronis, whom I considered also a spiritual partner, came to Irakleion with me to observe a typical business transaction, as well as to enjoy the fruits of my ministry there. As we were going uphill, with him next to the driver and me hugging the front fender of the truck, the overheated radiator suddenly blew up. As boiling water sprayed us and hail rained down upon our heads, poor Koronis moaned that he couldn't stand it any more. He was astonished to hear that experiences of that sort were not uncommon during my trips, and marveled that I had never complained about my hardships and privation.

For some unknown reason, as I traveled throughout Crete I used much of our nearly worthless Greek currency to purchase plant seeds, flower seeds, and grains of all sorts. Koronis often scolded me for my "seedomania," saying that I had turned our cash into a "dung heap."

By June of 1942 the black market had crippled our business. In addition, heavy restrictions on travel and communication enforced by the Germans caused our partnership to come
to an end. Koronis offered to let me keep all those sacks of
seeds in the shop, if I agreed to let him take the cash, to which
I agreed.

Since I could no longer travel to Irakleion, where I was
able to freely minister in Orthodox churches, I prayed that God
would give me opportunities to reach souls in Chania.

IN SPRING of 1942, at the suggestion of our kind pastor,
Karvounis, my household moved to the lower level of the Evangelical church. Shortly after that, God blessed us with our fourth
son, Timotheos (God-honoring).

That year I was given charge of the upkeep of the church,
and became a communion member and a member of the church
council. Because of my many questions about the Pentecostals,
as a condition to my becoming a communion member I was
asked to affirm that I did not believe the Pentecostals were
correct in their beliefs with regard to speaking in tongues. (That
made me want all the more to get in touch with Konstantinides
again—a thing, unfortunately, not possible because of the war.)

Knowing that God would have me serve Him mainly in
Chania, I risked visiting Judge Dafermos at his residence to ask
him to be lenient to us in the courts.

"Our sole purpose, sir," I said, "is to preach the message of
the Savior of mankind."

"That is why we have churches everywhere."

"Our nation remains ignorant of the message of truth."

"That is the task of the priests."

"Our priests must remain aware of the need to relate to our
people the essence of the message of Christ, through whom we
have forgiveness of sin and eternal life."

"Such things are personal convictions and should be kept
within your own circles."

Clearly, I might as well have been talking to a brick wall—
the man wasn't hearing me. I did not feel, however, that he was
totally unsympathetic toward us.

Before leaving, I reminded him that two of the men who had accused me in the past were in fact Communists, and that if we did not take the gospel to the Communists today, we would be chasing them up in the mountains trying to take their guns from them tomorrow. (How prophetic those words were! For that was exactly what happened immediately following the defeat of the Germans two years later.)

I also visited Papantonis, the priest who had so ardently persecuted me in the courts.

"The peace of God be upon you!" I said by way of greeting Papantonis, whom I found seated in his backyard under his grapevine. The priest looked alarmed for a moment. "Those who are not ashamed to be accused in our courts today for Christ's sake will not be ashamed to stand before the Judge of the world," I said.

"Oh, Mr. Zachariou!" Papantonis exclaimed, still not sure what to make of my unexpected visit. "Mr. Zachariou—uh—how many children do you have?"

"Four."

"Four?" he repeated sadly.

"Why?"

"Mr. Zachariou, there's this woman by the name of Zambio," the priest said seriously. "She says that God will give you lots of money, but will take one of your children and—she's demon-possessed, you know, and she can tell."

Amazed at the turn of our conversation, I almost told him that Satan had no business being the messenger of God's will on earth, and that as a priest he ought to make sure that he himself was not Satan's servant. Instead, I asked him to continue.

"You see, three other priests exorcised her, and now she's saying that the devil goes to the Evangelical church transformed into an old woman who sometimes goes to Karvounis' house and hides among his tomato plants and damages his house."

Curiosity gripped my mind. I wanted to see to what degree superstition saturated the minds of some of the so-called spiritual leaders of our nation—who actually were victims of spiritual ignorance and devoid of the Spirit of God.

"Say, Papantonis, would you permit me to meet you at Zambio's with a friend this afternoon?"

Papantonis agreed.

That afternoon, an Evangelical friend by the name Karakatsanis and I met Papantonis and his young deacon at Zambio's house. A tiny woman in her mid-thirties, Zambio was sitting on her bed and holding a baby.

First I asked the young deacon to go find Rev. Karvounis at his residence, then come back to tell us whether indeed the devil had caused any damage to the pastor's house. Meanwhile, we had Zambio recount her experience of exorcism to us.

"Oh, you should have been there!" Zambio said, her eyes rolling in horror. "The demon wouldn't come out! Papapetros shouted at him to come out through my mouth, but the demon wanted out through my eye. He was going to ruin my eye, so Papapetros kept reading his exorcisms, and the demon was driving me crazy. My body was shaking like this. Finally, he agreed to come out through my little finger, so the priest pierced my finger a bit until it bled, and then the devil shot out through it and I was rid of it. But he told me lots and lots about them Masons, you know. And about a Zacharias, he said that God will take his second child!"

Noticing how gullibly Papantonis swallowed all that garbage, Karakatsanis and I exchange a pitying look. Then Zambio stared straight at me and said, "Woe, my God! You don't happen to be that Zacharias, do you?"

"Keep your peace, my lady," I said calmly. "Satan's lies are useless."

At that moment the deacon showed up. "Lies—" he said, trying to catch his breath. "Mr. Karvounis welcomed me—and told me that—there's no room for—the devil in his house because—Christ dwells there!"

Karakatsanis and I had a good laugh! It was a story worth telling to show the naiveté, ignorance, and superstition of many of our priests.

LATE on the night of December 15, 1942, a policeman arrested me at my home. Incredible though it seemed, Lefteris the blacksmith, a friend of mine, had reported to the police that I had violated the law by selling him imported food without first itemizing and declaring the food stock to the police. Suspecting this to be the work of some priest, I became indignant. I felt my anger giving way to the counsel of the enemy, who whispered in my ear to simply deny the charges and go free. "No, Satan," I said, quoting Scripture from James 1:2-4. "I will honor God's righteousness. I will confess the truth."

I had obtained about five kilos of sardines from a fishing boat for 18,000 drachmas and sold them for 20,000. The courts did not consider this to be some sort of sordid profit, but a violation of inspection regulations—a technicality of the law which, because of the war, was openly disregarded. I was sentenced to two and a half months in hard labor.

Three of the jailers who knew me from the past asked me to speak to them about God, but under the circumstances— feeling distraught due to the cause of my imprisonment—I found it difficult to speak to them.

The second day, as I was about to speak to them, I was transferred to a different section of the jail. Oh, the misery that became my lot that day for having allowed my personal shame to prevent me from speaking to those jailers about God!

As I approached the prisoners in my new cell with God's message, my mind kept going back to the cause of my imprisonment. I prayed God would imbue me with boldness, and I began to speak to them.

"You sound okay, too," a prisoner shouted from the adjacent cell. "But you should have heard the guy who was here before the war. He was something else!"

Moments later, face buried in my hands, I shed bitter tears of sorrow and repentance as I asked God to have mercy on me and to rekindle the first flame of my love for Him.

During hard labor, I took special pains to ensure that my words matched my actions by not appearing slothful at any moment. While digging a ditch in Souda before Christmas, I turned around to answer a friend when the German guard suddenly hit me with a pike. My back ached all night, and I brought the matter before the Lord. Early the next morning, as we lined up to get on the camion, the guard stayed right beside me, as if looking for an excuse to repeat his uncalled-for action. I prayed earnestly that God would intervene, because I still had more than two months left. As we were about to get on the camion, two jailers came and escorted me outside, where a lady and two men were waiting to see me. To my surprise, it was Mrs. Paidakis, her husband, and a tall German officer by the name Mattis, a captain of the German army in the camp of Pedion tou Areos, the athletic stadium in the heart of Chania. The handsome captain was as well an Evangelical preacher, I was told, a thing that touched me profoundly. From that day on Captain Mattis would call on me for this or that, sometimes to decorate his Christmas tree, other times to enjoy a meal with him.

Once he even came to our house for dinner. We had a good laugh that day when I told Captain Mattis with humor that as God provided for the fowls of the air, so would He forever provide. . . seeds for us, pointing to the dozen sacks of seeds and grains stored in our house—in my mind all the while wondering about that so-called "dung heap."

ON January 25, all prisoners who had not served a sentence within the last five years were released.

"You're lucky again!" the announcing attorney said to me. "All you have to do is come up with two witnesses who will testify under oath, and out you'll go."

"I was jailed on grounds of proselytism in 1939," I said.

The attorney went out a few moments. When he returned he said, "You need not worry about that kind of offense. It doesn't count."

"But the fact remains that I was sentenced," I said.

"The court can overlook that."

"I cannot lie. Nor can I cause others to lie under oath on my behalf."

"How stupid!" the attorney shouted in front of the other prisoners.

So for one more month, God used me anew to accomplish a great work among the dozen souls who remained in jail. Three prisoners openly asked God to cleanse their lives and accepted

Christ, while the rest received the seed of the Word in their heart. At the end of my jail term, a teary-eyed prisoner said, "It must be because of us that you were jailed, Panos."

Chrysa, her mother, and my mother, who with tears two and a half months earlier had begged the arresting policeman to postpone my arrest for just a couple of hours, now stood amazed at how God had used me throughout my term in jail. Because I had offered Him in humility my will, He turned my shame into blessings.

As for the attorney, he apologized for insulting me in front of the other prisoners, though he asked whether by staying in jail I felt I had saved my reputation as an honest man. It wasn't my reputation I was concerned about, I told him, but how I could live a life pleasing to God.

Penniless and jobless, but with my faith strengthened, I knew that my heavenly Father would find a way to help me meet my responsibilities at home and provide for the needs of my loved ones, as He had provided us with shelter. I knew as well that He would sustain me spiritually by leading me to opportunities to minister to needy souls.

THE night of March 2, 1943, two days after my release, a German officer was sent to my home by Captain Mattis. Speaking flawless Greek, the officer asked if the sacks of seeds (often referred to by my former partner as "a worthless dung heap") were for sale, and if I could procure additional supplies. I pondered a moment over the fact that no one until now had been interested in buying any of those seeds from me, let alone all at once, and wondered if the offer was God's answer to my prayers to help me find ways to provide for my family. I told the German officer that those dozen sacks of seeds—sunflower, squash, mustard, sesame, and various kinds of flower and fruit seeds—represented countless kilometers of footwork in severe weather, hitching rides on buses and trucks, and spending sleepless nights away from home; and that the possibility of finding more supplies would now be extremely remote and risky due to travel restrictions. The German officer thanked me and left.

The next day brought an awesome sight. The kommandant from Kreis Kommandantur came to our house, accompanied by attachés and SS men, and handed me a signed authorization for travel privileges throughout Crete in order to procure seeds. The interpreter placed some cash on the table as the kommandant shook my hand, then they all left. At once I saw that God had used those sacks of seed to provide sustenance for my family and opportunities for ministry throughout Crete. What a miracle-working God! He who turns water into wine also turns "worthless dung heaps" into bread; and as well treads down enemy barricades and turns them into open highways for ministry and service.

And so God enabled me once again to share Christ's love from one end of Crete to the other—in villages, in cities, even in German camps. In Chania our church became packed with Germans worshiping God, Captain Mattis leading church services in sermon and in song. Oh, the bond of God's love that allows man and his "enemy" to become one!

ON SEPTEMBER 7, 1943, Karakatsanis and I were questioned by the authorities about Zambio's demons, and a trial was scheduled for November 11, 1943. The accusations were based on an eight-page letter sent to Irakleion through Mrs. Grafanakis, a believer from there, in which I described the Zambio episode. The letter had evidently fallen from Mrs. Grafanakis' apron while she was at the market, and somehow landed in the hands of the priests. I couldn't figure out what part of my letter could have been construed as libelous and censured.

The day before the trial I gave myself to fasting and prayer. As I was praying, I saw a bridge that spanned a dry river, the riverbed being a work of exquisite white masonry. Coming slowly down the riverbed was a procession which comprised the entire patriarchate—bishops, archimandrites, priests, deacons, chanters, emblem bearers and icon bearers, and the rest of its venerable retinue—all pompously clothed in sacerdotal vestments, and chanting. Suddenly a roaring stream of crystal-clear water swept the procession with torrential force, stripping all of their attire and causing them to stand shamefully in absolute nakedness. "God!" I exclaimed, as I became aware of the message of my vision. "You are exposing them?"

Outside the courthouse the next day, I met an outraged Papantonis and his young deacon. Looking me up and down imperviously and with disgust, Papantonis said, "I can tell you are an egotist by the way you're standing—just like a Pharisee!"

"You are calling Pharisee the Zachariou who can pray for you," I said. "You're lucky you're not talking to the old Zachariou right now. He wouldn't have left a single whisker on your bearded face. Can you imagine the anguish your rumors could have brought into my home if I hadn't kept secret the scores of sympathy letters I received from Kastelli and as far as Ierapetra for the loss of one of my sons? It wasn't my letter that spread those false prophecies throughout Crete, you know."

The courtroom setting was reminiscent of my 1939 trial. The same place, the same chief accusers—Papantonis and Strongylakis, the archimandrite. The two dozen priests present reminded me of my vision.

According to the indictment, in my letter I had misspelled once the word *diakaki* (little deacon) to read *dikakaki* (the extra *k* apparently giving the word a pejorative meaning); and I had called the priests "naïve."

So that's it? I thought to myself.

My defense attorney spoke, but unfortunately the accidental error in spelling was misconstrued as intentional and therefore derogatory; and the word "naïve" was given undue emphasis.

"Defendant, you may stand up," announced Judge Dafermos—the judge I had risked visiting at his residence the year before.

I stood up.

"Why do you write such things?"

As if expecting my vision's message to become fulfilled that very instant, I wondered what I should say. "Your honor," I finally said, "my accusers have spread rumors that according to a demon-possessed woman one of my four children will soon die, and that—"

"Wh—what? What? Who said such things?" said a perturbed judge, and called the archimandrite to approach the bench. "You said such things?"

The archimandrite's face fell. "Zambio—the demon-possessed—she told us these things, your honor—"
"You should be ashamed of yourself for believing such things
and disturbing the people. This is a disgrace! And you call yourself a theologian!"
"Hallelujah!" I said—nearly shouted—to praise the name
of Jesus! He had suddenly laid bare the shame of the accusers
in one sweeping stroke. And I went home free!

MEANWHILE, I became acquainted with Stavros Yannarakis,
a gentle, reputable Orthodox preacher who was greatly favored
by the bishop of Chania and who seemed to take a great interest in the doctrinal convictions of the Evangelicals. Yannarakis,
who had recently learned about my ministry among the Orthodox churches in Irakleion, informed me that he had been
assigned by the diocese of Chania to preach in the Valley of
Mesara, Irakleion, and suggested that he and I meet in Irakleion
for a joint outreach ministry there. Rather than be suspicious
of Yannarakis' motives, I accepted the opportunity as God's
direction and prayed that He would guide me and give me wisdom throughout our itinerary.

In Irakleion I introduced Yannarakis to the Evangelical
brethren as an enlightened, liberal Orthodox preacher, truly a
partaker of the gift of God's salvation through Christ, whose
two brothers-in-law, both Orthodox priests, and truly enlightened and born-again children of God, shared a favorable stance
toward the Evangelicals and their convictions. (The bishop of
Chania had in fact denounced the two priests' liberal preaching for being patterned after that of the Evangelicals, and accused me of trying to proselytize them.)

The following day Yannarakis and I stopped at a village
where we learned of the scandalous action of two itinerary
Orthodox preachers, who had recently asked for two kilos of
fruit per villager for their services. The war-oppressed villagers had no appetite for another such experience, for they were
poor, and now disenchanted. Yannarakis and I were shocked.
Immediately we went from door to door and invited the villagers to come to hear God's Word—for free! A short time later

our eyes witnessed one of the most touching sights on earth—
men, women, and children, some with tears in their eyes, flock-
ing around us like sheep to hear words of comfort and hope.
Oh, that God would satisfy the longings of their souls with His
Spirit, was our prayer.

When we finished, a woman came to offer us a basket full
of eggs. "God sent you our way to comfort us!" she said with
tears in her eyes. "These are for you. We're offering them to
you from our hearts!"

"Impossible!" I said, looking at Yannarakis. "We will not
receive any gifts!"

Despite her persistence, we did not receive the gift. That
truly impressed the villagers, some of whom ran to their houses
and returned with more gifts. We received none, however. The
villagers sent us away with expressions of gratitude and love,
and asked us to return soon.

Our next major stop was the town of Moires. There we
met some people from Chania who knew me, so Yannarakis
assured me that he would be the one to speak at the Orthodox
church. The next morning I was dismayed when I found
Yannarakis holding his stomach and writhing in pain. He was
suffering from colic. "Courage, friend," he said. "God is allowing you to speak." Indeed, my fears were of the devil, for the
Word was received, and no one questioned my identity. A trustee
brought the collection of money in a tray and handed it to me
in the presence of the priest, a policeman, and part of the congregation. I asked the trustee to name a person in the community most worthy of a gift, and he named the priest. So I handed
the tray to the priest, who received it with gratitude.

Yannarakis' condition did not improve, so I did all the
preaching. As a rule, my messages in the Orthodox churches
were on repentance and salvation through Christ, so as not to
create a scandal and be accused of any biased doctrinal views.
Priests and laymen alike received the messages with gratitude,
for they were God's words of life and hope in a devastated,
war-ravaged world.

"You know, Panos?" Yannarakis said to me after a service at
an Orthodox church one Sunday morning. "The people like

your style. It's different." Yannarakis was referring to the manner in which Evangelicals preached, usually using a semi-conservative mode of delivery focusing on repentance, salvation through Christ, and righteous living, presented matter-of-factly with illustrations and the use of Scripture verses. This was in contrast to the style of the Orthodox preachers, who typically presented performance-based speeches sprinkled with eloquent archaisms and references to church traditions, holy mysteries, and rituals.

"It's really the message that's different," I said. "As for style, you should have heard this preacher I met in Athens back in 1938. He drove every word home with authority and force. He was Pentecostal."

"I've heard of those Pentecostals—"

"They're like the Evangelicals, except they also emphasize the manifestation of the gifts of the Spirit. Just like in the days of the first Christians."

"Wouldn't that be something!" he said, his eyes glowing with wonder. "To have miracles, prophecies, tongues!"

"That would certainly have an effect on one's style, wouldn't it?" I said with a chuckle.

TOWARD the end of our 24-day itinerary, we reached the village of Haraka. Because of festivities in progress, the Orthodox church in Haraka was well attended by young and old, including an archimandrite as well as a number of Germans. While preaching, I noticed a German officer taking a pad and a pencil out of his pocket. Momentarily distracted, I prayed that God would give me wisdom and courage. After all, I had said nothing derogatory about the Germans when I pointed out that our true enemy was the enemy of our soul, not the conqueror, though God often uses the conqueror to cause sinners to turn to Him.

Following the service, we dined with the archimandrite, five priests, two monks, a dozen armed German soldiers, and the German officer who had attended the service, who now introduced himself to us ostentatiously and in fluent Greek as a philosopher. With subtle sarcasm, the Nazi philosopher alluded to my performance and delivery, then to my message.

"Hurling words among the masses with unfounded passion is an art, indeed," he said sardonically.

"'Living is the Word of God,' sir, 'and energizing and sharper than any two-edged sword' (Hebrews 4:12). As for my passion, its substance is the force with which this life-transforming sword is thrust into men's hearts."

"An undernourished mind more easily falls a victim to big fantasies when subsisting in the fear of imminent annihilation."

"The sayings of Jesus Christ are spirit and life (John 6:63), not fantasies, sir. They are the spirit of power and of love and of a sound mind, not of cowardice or fear (2 Timothy 1:7). And certainly 'undernourished' does not necessarily mean of inferior intellect—at least not among the progeny of the greatest philosophers."

The Nazi philosopher felt he was losing ground and became irritable. "You realize, of course, that I have other means of persuasion," he said, staring coldly at me.

Suddenly there was tension in the air—the German soldiers became alert. I prayed for wisdom.

"After all," he continued, "I can prove to you that the idolatry of your contemporaries is no different from the worship of the Olympian gods of antiquity. And as their contemporary intellectuals and great philosophers, one being Socrates, found the veneration of those so-called gods to be the product of childish fancies, so any wise and logical man's mind today cannot possibly tolerate a religion of dead men, stone statues, and color paintings!"

I could have easily shown him that my message and my faith had nothing to do with idolatry or man's traditions and fantasies, only with the purity of the Word of God, by revealing to him my true identity, an identity shared in Chania even by his own superiors. But then I would have had to face the priests and monks, who would immediately drag me to the courts.

"Let it not surprise you, sir," I said, "that our people have been misinformed due to a lack of enlightened teachers, first during the Venetian conquest, and then the 400-year Turkish occupation of Greece, when the country was completely passed over by the Protestant Reformation. It is difficult to detach a people just in a short time from idolatry, which you quite well characterized as a thing patterned after the practices of ancient Greece."

Taking issue with this Nazi philosopher, I learned later, was risky business. Earlier that week a villager had barely escaped being executed by him for challenging his philosophy of the superiority of the Aryan race. That "other means of persuasion" was nothing but force—among fanatic Nazi intelligentsia, a common substitute for reason. It was the hellish philosophy of a demented Führer, whose manifesto of racial superiority defied the bounds of reason and which, when challenged, uncoiled in the form of brute force.

But God protected me from that man, and He protected me from the archimandrite and the priests. Rather than accuse me for anything I had said, they in fact commended me for God-given wisdom.

God had given me words of truth, and the truth had set me free.

ꄦꄦꄦꄦ

# 12

# The Awakening

IT WAS THE MORNING OF September 3, 1944, and
Chrysa was about to give birth to our fifth child. I stepped
out of the house and headed downtown. The neighborhood
seemed unusually quiet, its stillness broken only by the crow-
ing of a rooster in the distance. An eerie coolness hovered over
the empty streets as the big town roloi (clock) in the clock tower,
just a five-minute walk from home, struck six.

Just then two German motorcycles came roaring out of the
barracks and down King Konstantine Street, between the roloi
and the fenced stadium of Pedion tou Areos. Within seconds
there followed a formidable, disquieting motorcade. By the time
I got to Agora, the city was infested with German machinery
and arms, and guards were posted at every street corner.

Two Germans ordered me to stop, and I found myself
among hundreds of bewildered men being driven en masse,
like sheep, toward the stadium. Women were wailing and faint-
ing in the streets, little children looked terrified. "God, protect
us and our families!" I kept praying.

The stadium of Pedion tou Areos had turned into a sea of
men. A mass execution? I wondered. But why?

I found some church brethren and we joined hands in prayer.
More brethren joined us. As some of us raised our hands heavenward in prayer, our circle was spotted by a German officer,
who came to talk to us. It was Captain Mattis. An instant answer to our prayers, Captain Mattis told us confidentially not
to worry, and that we would soon be free to go to our homes
because we were not Communists. Tears of relief ran down

our faces, and we praised God for protecting our lives. We felt like sheep being separated from the goats on Judgment Day.

When I returned home, God blessed us with a son. We named him Philemon.

But our tears of relief and our rejoicing were no comfort to our aching hearts that day when—ironically, just prior to the end of the German occupation of Greece—we saw truckloads of helpless men, young and old, being taken to be executed.

BY MID-November the last German soldier had left northern Greece, though a large concentration of German forces remained fortified in the province of Chania until early spring of 1945.

But while the end of World War II was at hand, our war-wracked Greek nation now faced a new threat and menace—Communism. The first menace, Italian Fascism and German Nazism, defied God's justice; the second, God Himself.

Already by December of 1944, the Communists systematically raided the police and the army in northern Greece, ransacking villages and cities, killing civilians, taking hostages, and destroying railroads and bridges as they went. Their treacherous tactics, plotted and carried out by Greek rebels under the vigilant eye of Soviet Communists, would ravage the Greek ideals of democracy and freedom the rest of the decade. By spring of 1948, the Communists' diabolical plot of wrack and ruin would culminate in their paidomazoma (child-gathering), when more than 25,000 Greek children, aged three to fourteen, would be snatched from their homes and taken to the lands behind the iron curtain.

With the Communist Rebellion looming over our hearths, a strong desire fell over me to pray that God would raise praying hands throughout Greece and around the world that would intercede for our needy people and prevent our devastated nation from falling into godless hands. (Those prayers were honored by God. Because of Great Britain's military and economic aid to Greece until April 1, 1947; then through the Truman Doctrine on May 22, 1947; and the four-year Marshall Plan on April 1, 1948, Greece was spared from Communist rule and a direct confrontation with the Soviets.)

SUCH was the backdrop of my challenge at the end of World War II, as I tried to eke out a living for my loved ones and continued to fellowship with my Evangelical brethren, whom I loved so dearly. At the same time I pleaded with my Creator to imbue me with His Spirit, so I could minister to battered souls more effectively and be better equipped to counteract my weaknesses in the face of adverse circumstances.

Shortly after the war, I rented a small room in downtown Chania, where I conducted a floral business.* The hours were long, the demand sporadic. Most people were extremely poor and considered what I had for sale a luxury they couldn't afford. To strengthen my business and to defray some of the cost, I shared the rent with Kalogerakis, a business acquaintance, who set up a glassware business next to mine and with whom I started a partnership.

Despite the endless working hours, our partnership barely survived the first year. Poverty, the black market, thefts, casualties, non-payments—it was all a daily risk. And as if I had time to spare, in the spring of 1946 I extended our partnership to include a second partner, Eleftheriou, who would help me restart a private mail business. Our new partnership bore the acronym ZEK (Zachariou, Eleftheriou, Kalogerakis).

In April of the same year, God blessed us with our sixth son. As it was customary to name the last child in a family after one of the parents, we named him Panos.

LATE in 1945, I received a magazine from New York which described the work of a Greek missionary by the name Peponis. I was moved by the testimony of this man. Formerly a commissary of ships, he had felt led to work among the Chinese in Shanghai, China. His work in Shanghai before and during the Chino-Japanese war (1937-45) was brimming with accounts of miracles among the Chinese—massive conversions to Christianity, manifestations of spiritual gifts, miraculous provisions

---

* I sold flowers, plants, seeds of all sorts, and horse manure. I would put dirt in an empty can or a ceramic pot, plant seeds in it, add manure, and water it. Days later I would have new flowers or a plant for sale. I had purposely set up my floral business right next to a ceramic sales shop.

of food and supplies, and also his own miraculous escape from death, when he was found buried in the debris of his residence after a shelling by the Japanese. His life inspired me and rejuvenated me, and I mailed him a letter at his residence in New York. His response came about the same time I received the first letter from Konstantinides since before the war. I was filled with excitement as I read the words of both men, who advised and encouraged me to seek the gifts of the Holy Spirit according to 1 Corinthians 12-14. Not wanting to create a problem among my Evangelical brethren who espoused a different view on the subject of spiritual gifts, I shared the letters with no one except Yannarakis, who time and again had expressed an interest in spiritual gifts. Yannarakis read the two letters with enthusiasm.

Thereafter I exchanged a good number of letters both with Peponis and Konstantinides. Yannarakis and I consumed those letters, and searched the Scriptures relating to spiritual gifts. The excitement we shared was intensified partly by our clandestine meetings—as an Orthodox preacher, he was cautious about being seen with me—and partly by the challenge of the mysteries we were exploring. We each felt like a boy hiding in the pantry with his hand in the cookie jar.

ONE day late in 1946, Yannarakis returned from a trip to Athens, where he had gone with his devout follower, Baletakis. He had been unable to visit Rev. Konstantinides, he said, but he had a secret to share with me.

That evening the two of us met inside my shop. I pulled the corrugated door all the way down the floor, then removed my hat. Yannarakis kept his hat on.

"The Lord has branded me with his seal," said Yannarakis, as he bent forward and looked straight into my eyes from under his hat brim. "See?"

"Where did God brand you, Stavros?" I said curiously.

"Right here—on the forehead," he said, his eyes widening, the brim of his gray hat nearly touching my nose.

An alarming sensation flitted through me. "I don't see anything," I said dryly. Has Satan played a trick on this quiet and harmless man? I wondered. "I don't understand you, Stavros. Explain yourself better. I see no marks on you."

"Here—can't you see?" he insisted. Still bent forward, he quickly removed his hat and pointed to the front of it, where the mark of a small cross was barely visible. "Right here!"

I began to shake inside, wondering if I was responsible for this innocent man's strange behavior. "But, my dear Stavros, this is done with a pencil. Who did this to you?"

"I did," he said and picked up his Bible. He turned to Ezekiel 9. When he had read a few verses, he said, "I shall come with my forces and you with yours and together we shall meet for a common cause. Then this chapter will be fulfilled!"

There was no doubt in my mind now that Satan had duped this man. "Say, Stavros, if you and I are going to work together for the cause of Christ, let's have a word of prayer right now," I said, placing my hand on his shoulder. No sooner had I opened my mouth to pray, than I heard Yannarakis making incomprehensible utterances. Immediately I stopped. My heart was trembling for my friend. I asked him if he was all right.

"You know, Panos, I wanted to tell you that I have been baptized in the Holy Spirit and speak in tongues," he said with a smile.

My eyebrows raised, I nodded. "You almost make me envy you, Stavros," I said. But in my heart I had no assurance that this was a manifestation of a gift of the Holy Spirit.

A few weeks later I was in bed with a cold when Yannarakis' follower came to visit me. Toward the end of our joyful reunion that day, he invited me to kneel for prayer. As we prayed, I heard tongues again.

"So—you, too, received the Holy Spirit?" I said to Baletakis, incredulously.

"Well, yes," he said, and promptly continued to pray loudly in tongues.

Again, I discerned no gift of the Spirit. Perhaps my heart is hard, I thought to myself.

THOSE two peculiar encounters were emotionally and spiritually taxing. I cared for those two friends, especially Yannarakis, with whom I had spent many precious moments ministering the Word and searching the Scriptures. Now it appeared as though he and his cohort had fallen victim to deception. How did this happen to them? I kept wondering. Did something bizarre take place during their two-month sojourn in Athens? If not, was it a front? But why? What's to be gained if their claim is not genuine? No, Yannarakis isn't that kind of person. He wouldn't mislead or deceive others with ill-founded zeal. Besides, such spiritual claims and expressions, even if genuine, would not hold water within Orthodox circles. They would be viewed cynically and with contempt by the priests.

But what if their experience is genuine? Then I am the loser, for it was I who first challenged Yannarakis to seek the riches of God's spiritual gifts. So then I must be envious. Am I? No, not on a conscious level; not even subconsciously. For I consider Yannarakis my brother in the Lord, and in God's family there's no room for jealousy and envy, because those are of the devil in the first place. After all, who am I to question God or offer Him advice as to whom He should or should not give His gifts? God shows no partiality to persons (Acts 10:34). He grants His gifts as He sees fit to those who seek Him, whether they be Orthodox, Evangelical, or Pentecostal. Then I should rejoice, rather, for my friends who may have received what they had sought after.

I sensed no need to gather up my courage to ask the church ministers their opinion in this particular case, for although it concerned the claims of a reputable Orthodox preacher and his religious follower, I was pretty sure that would touch off a storm of reaction. Besides, it was not the existence of spiritual gifts in our present day that I was questioning, as did the ministers and the rest of the church council; only their authenticity and genuineness.

I did not see Yannarakis again for many months. When we accidentally ran into each other in downtown Chania, he hurriedly informed me that he had a successful ministry going in a nearby village, in which miracles and manifestations of the Spirit took place—tongues, interpretations, prophecies, visions, healings—alluding to the Biblical church of Ephesus. I visited his meetings twice, but unfortunately witnessed nothing of the sort. Thereafter, I wrote Yannarakis a half-dozen letters to tell him I cared for him and his ministry, but I never got an answer.

MY business ventures, meanwhile, were in a pitiful state. As I once again worked with partners and others who were ready to devour one's soul, I pondered the hard lessons of the past, experiences that can sap the pith of the heart and leave it encrusted in layers of hate. But those painful memories did not seem to be a helpful guide for the present, for it was God's wisdom I needed to heed—wisdom which I had, alas, disregarded. "Do not be unequally yoked with unbelievers," God's wisdom had been crying out to me now for nearly two years, "for what partnership does righteousness and lawlessness share?"(2 Corinthians 6:14).

By January 1948, ZEK was dissolved (though Kalogerakis continued to rent half the room a little longer). Shipwrecks, losses, thefts, the black market, debts, and poverty, all aided by the gamut of human vice, caused the partnership to topple. Two shipwrecks resulted in losses worth hundreds of thousands of drachmas. A single theft wiped out 300 gallons of olive oil. It was I who bore the brunt of our misfortunes, with losses exceeding nine million drachmas altogether, as I had invested more capital than the combined totals of my two partners.

In the midst of my disappointments, God's soul-searching conviction flooded my mind with a crystal-clear awareness that my disobedience was cradled in my weakness and swathed in selfish reasoning. I realized that my short-lived business success had sired a desire to eradicate the haunting memories of my business failures of the past, a drive that gradually prevented me from recognizing the dire spiritual needs of those around me, as well as my own. The culprit was my greedy business pursuits, disguised under the banner of success, while I bemoaned my lack of time for family and ministry. And rather than select God-fearing men to work with, in my hasty decision to form a partnership I had ended up depending on worldly men, whose aggressiveness knew no ethical bounds. My behavior was now yielding its inevitable dividends—huge losses and, once more, two heartless men to deal with.

In my weakness, I had allowed my godless past to drag me down. But, whereas ten years earlier under similar circumstances I might have been suicidal and wallowing in self-pity, I now saw the situation not as a personal failure, but as God's merciful reminder that I was His child and that in my life and ministry I was to put Him, not earthly treasures, first.

Awakened by God's intervention in my situation, I fell on my knees and begged Him to forgive me and cleanse me. I implored God to strengthen me, and to shield me from any selfish tendencies that might otherwise cause me to fail Him again.

In the labyrinth of my economic woes, I ran a floral shop and resumed work at a restored soap factory. The days were long, the work strenuous. Somehow, however, I now had time for family, for friends, and for countless opportunities to minister and be ministered to.

Heaven was never so real, the Word never so clear. How well I now understood the words of the Apostle Paul, who said that every spiritual blessing in the heavens is ours in Christ (Ephesians 1:3), and that God's hidden plan and wisdom are realized in Christ and now revealed through His Church (Ephesians 3:9-11), which is the body of His believers. And how I desired to be even a speck in the grand unfolding of God's plan for mankind through His Church. It was the grandest privilege bestowed by God Almighty upon man—the authority to proclaim God's divine plan of salvation for mankind.

# 13

# Blessed

SPRING of 1948, I FLEW to Athens, fulfilling my ten-year-old dream to visit Konstantinides. The opportunity also seemed to be God's way of letting me join other brethren in Athens for a grand celebration of the restoration of the Jewish nation, as prophesied in Isaiah, Jeremiah, Ezekiel, Micah, and Zechariah and fulfilled on May 14, 1948—the main talk among Christians everywhere.

And so God enabled me once more to visit the church where ten years earlier my relentless pride had first been challenged to bend before God. It was there I first learned to forgive and to receive forgiveness, to pray, and to seek God's purpose in my life; and there that I first felt the bonds of Christian love surround me. Back then, God led my footsteps to that place because of my quest for the truth; now, because of my quest for greater insight.

"Have you received the infilling of the Holy Spirit?" Konstantinides whispered in my ear at a prayer meeting with other brethren that Friday. His words exploded in my mind with the same force as the words he had spoken into my ear ten years earlier: "Do you hate anyone? You must forgive, so God may forgive you also."

His voice still echoing in my ears, I thought of the challenging letters he had written me, the words in which I used to simply toss back and forth in my mind for as long as I wanted. Now his words were all too real. I looked at the man whose faith had defied the odds of sudden death from the German bullet lodged in his lung right by his heart since 1918, when he fought in the American army in France during World War I.

"No, not yet—" I said.

Konstantinides nodded. "We must seek the Holy Spirit," he said matter-of-factly. "God's gifts equip us against the enemy and empower us to serve Him more effectively."

I wasn't prepared for the challenge. For one thing, I was afraid of an experience that might cause others to question my spiritual integrity, as I had questioned that of Yannarakis and his follower. "I may not speak in tongues, brother Konstantinides," I said, "but I consider myself a Pentecostal at heart."

"Tongues are as well a manifestation of God's Spirit in a Christian's private life," Konstantinides said as he opened his Bible, "for it is also a gift for personal edification (1 Corinthians 14:2). . . . But there are other gifts we must seek as well (1 Corinthians 12:4-11). . . . So we must earnestly wait upon the Lord, who apportions His gifts according to His will" (1 Corinthians 12:11).

Meanwhile, I could hear others praying in tongues. I felt uncomfortable. Was this truly the gift? Was this what I had sought in the past few years?

What if Konstantinides or someone lays his hands on my head and I begin to sound the way they do? I kept thinking to myself. Do I want that? On the other hand, what if this is the real gift?

Perhaps there is a Pentecost different from Paul's days, a Pentecost tailored to the needs of today, I reasoned. After all, today we don't meet in catacombs nor are we in danger of being torched on a cross like the first Christians. The gift may be different today from what it once was. . . .

THE believers in Petralona loved to spend time in prayer, so we met again the next day. The sound of tongues and interpretation was commonplace by now. The words of the Apostle Paul kept coming to mind: "Therefore tongues are a sign not to the believing, but to the unbelievers, and prophecy not to the unbelievers, but to the believing" (1 Corinthians 14:22). As a believer, however, I felt nothing. Oh, I must be hard, I kept thinking to myself. Harder than doubting Thomas!

Going through downtown Athens later in the day, I reluc-
tantly got off the trolley and headed for the house of close friends
from Balya (the place of my birth), whom I had not seen for
over ten years. Since the purpose of my sojourn in Athens was
to pursue matters of spiritual edification and enrichment rather
than visit friends, the visit was going to be short, I decided—
only long enough to plant the seed of the Word in that household.

After the initial excitement of our surprise reunion, I explained that I was on a tight schedule because I needed to get
ready for church. The mother, surprised at my mention of
church—apparently a poor excuse for a worldly man wanting
to bow out of a cordial social event—said, "In that case, we
insist you stay for dinner. My husband is not here, but my two
daughters, my son, and I all love to talk about church."

Pleased by the sudden twist in conversation, I said, "Well,
then, I suggest tomorrow we all go to church, but—to an Evangelical church!"

"Agreed!" happily said the younger daughter, to my utter
surprise.

"We—we are now Evangelical, you know," the mother
added.

"Well, praise the Lord!" I exclaimed, looking heavenward.

Their mouths dropped as they heard words of praise coming from the mouth of ol' Charlie.

When they told me that they attended the church of Pastor
Mamalis, a Pentecostal minister in Athens, I asked if anyone
had received the experience of Pentecost.

"Most certainly!" the older daughter replied, the rest nodding and smiling at me.

God had led my footsteps to these family friends as an added
sign that the experience of Pentecost today was real.

Following the Sunday morning service at an Evangelical
church, I tried to prepare for the evening service at Pastor
Konstantinides' church, where I was scheduled to preach, but I
found it impossible to concentrate. My mind was preoccupied
with new questions—questions that had whirled through my
mind all during the morning service. I wonder if it should mat-

ter that the visitation of God's Spirit today is not fashioned after the day of Pentecost (Acts 2:3), I kept thinking to myself. Perhaps that shouldn't matter, though. What should matter is that today's manifestations are by the same Spirit—God's Spirit—regardless of the manner of expression. One may not see cloven tongues on people's heads today, but—but neither did Cornelius (Acts 10:45-46), nor the Ephesian believers (Acts 19:6), nor the Corinthian brethren! So it may well be that the manifestation of the Holy Spirit today is the same as in the times of Peter and Paul, except—except that sounds too good to be true.

. . . Then I shouldn't judge the manner of expression among my Pentecostal brethren. They are genuine Christians. Questioning the validity of their claims and experience would be downright blasphemous. But why am I not as fortunate as they? What prevents me from experiencing what so many common folk seem to enjoy so readily? Is it my motives? Is there a foul desire in my heart to use God's gifts to elevate myself above others? No, none of that garbage—that's only of the devil. I will serve the Almighty with whatever He apportions or does not apportion to me in my humble ministry. My sinful pride has been crushed, my empty boastfulness buried at the Cross.

. . . But what triggers the release of God's Spirit upon one's life? The degree of his spirituality? God forbid, for then we would all be anathema in God's eyes for becoming judges of God and of one another. And I would be the first one to point a finger and judge most of my Evangelical brethren for not knowing how to bend the knee, let alone talk about such spiritual matters.

. . . I certainly do not doubt today's manifestations of God's spiritual gifts. I have seen God release the power of His Spirit in and through my own life, now in the form of healing, now in the form of preaching, counseling, teaching, or some other variety of ministry, a word of wisdom or of knowledge, the discerning of spirits—all according to 1 Corinthians 12:4-11. What, then, prevents me from speaking in tongues, if indeed that's what God would have for me? I have long sought this gift—though, admittedly, on my own terms. For I have personal doubts that this particular gift would not hamper my ministry, in that it would cause an uproar among my Evangelical brethren.

. . . So that's what's preventing me from receiving God's blessings—my fears and doubts! I have been seeking God on my own terms—conditionally. I am actually telling God what He should or should not do with the ministry and life He has given me. Why? To protect myself from the fiery attacks of my Evangelical brethren? Am I then asking God to build my ministry upon my personal fears of what others might or might not do or say? It's no wonder that I always come up with this or that excuse for not receiving the baptism in the Holy Spirit, when in fact I am fearful of the consequences!

After a blissful time Tuesday night at Mamalis' church, where I preached, and a special time of prayer and sharing with a church group Wednesday night at a believer's home, I flew back to Crete. Going back to the cares and snares of my business world was like being suddenly shaken out of a beautiful dream and thrown into a dungeon. "Lord," I prayed, "help me in the midst of life's storms not to flounder and falter, but to be faithful to You as You are faithful to me."

" 'AND which father among you, if your son asks for bread, will give him a stone? Or if he asks for a fish, will you instead of a fish give him a serpent? Or if he asks for an egg, will you give him a scorpion? If you then, being evil, know how to give good gifts to your children, how much more will the heavenly Father give the Holy Spirit to those who seek Him?' " Everyone in our congregation was captivated by the words spoken by Rev. Kyriakakis, a visiting Evangelical minister from Athens, as he brought to life the passage of Luke 11:11-13 on the Sunday morning of June 6, 1948.

"A loaf of bread, a fish, an egg." These words kept ringing in my ears after the service, my heart craving for heavenly food. At the same time my mind was preoccupied with my partner. He was probably moving out of my office now, tearing down walls and taking the high metal shelves I had so laboriously obtained.

I got home and went straight into my prayer room. "Lord, have mercy on me!" I prayed. "Do not let this injustice come upon me. Do not let Kalogerakis take the shelves. And forgive me, God, for having not learned to avoid being equally yoked with unbelievers."

Then the words from the message my soul had been fed only a half-hour earlier came to my mind, and I felt convicted. It was as if I could hear someone say to me, "The words of the Spirit of God are still fresh in your ears, yet you are concerned about shelves. Doesn't the Word provide comfort for daily cares? Doesn't the Lord promise He will be with you? Time and again you brought wonderful words of comfort and strength to hundreds of people and witnessed many coming to God with tears of repentance and joy. God directed your path to places where you received spiritual nourishment and strength. And you asked God to send someone to speak to the body of believers in Chania about the Holy Spirit. Have you thanked God for it?"

Humbling myself before God, I asked for forgiveness. A longing was born in my heart to praise and thank Him. Raising my hands heavenward, I let tears flow, as my lips uttered praises to my Redeemer. Nothing else mattered now, for God's presence and peace filled the room. Overwhelmed by His holiness, I nevertheless became aware that this was a visitation of the Holy Spirit according to Acts 2:4. As I continued to worship in audible praise, I perceived that the words I was saying were words I had never spoken before, yet I was fully aware that they were the river of praises flowing from within me.

As I turned around, still praying in tongues sprinkled with Greek, I found myself being stared at by loved ones. Their faces were pressed sadly against the glass on the door, and tears streamed down their faces because of the seemingly pitiful state in which they had found me. They thought that my business failures and pressures had surely caused me to go insane.

They opened the door. "Panos?" said my sister-in-law, curiously examining my face. "You've got to stop this, or you're going to drive us all crazy!"

"It must be what he's been praying for," explained my wife, as she, too, examined my face curiously—it glowed, she explained later. "It must be the Holy Spirit he's been talking about for years!"

"Come, my dear ones," I said. "Come, kneel with me. Come and taste of the goodness of God's Spirit," and I began to hug and kiss each one of them, smiling and encouraging them to kneel for prayer.

When they realized nothing was wrong with me, they all knelt and, with tears, sought to worship God. After a blessed time of prayer together, I instructed each one of them not to spread the news about my spiritual experience.

The next day I went to a hospital to visit one of my mother-in-law's relatives, who was paralyzed on one side. I touched her as I prayed for her. The next day she walked out of the hospital, and came to my house with other relatives to ask me whether the thing that went through her body as I prayed was electricity.

The news about my spiritual encounter soon reached the church leadership. Following the morning service one Sunday, three church elders kindly advised me to beware of the snares of the enemy, for tongues were of the devil. The following day I was accosted by one of the ministers who, in a surprisingly unbecoming manner—he raised his hand and yelled at me in the middle of the street—forbade me to speak in tongues!

For a long time after that, no one from the church approached me about the subject of tongues. And God so led my steps as to assure me He was with me, guiding me in new paths of service and preparing me for the planting of spiritual seeds that would be fruitful and blessed.

# 14

# Standing Up

THE SHADE OF A FIG TREE offered some relief from the scorching sun as I stopped a moment to wipe the perspiration off my brow. The droning sound of cicadas filled the air, a lullaby for the neighborhood's midday siesta.

It was the hottest Saturday of August 1950, and I was walking uphill in Amberia, a suburb of Chania, looking for the house of a friend who had ordered a bird cage from me. I thought I was walking up the alley to the right house when I saw a woman coming to meet me, one whom I remembered seeing at the Evangelical church in the past.

"Yes, Mr. Zachariou. Welcome to our home. Please come and see my husband, who is in bed."

That's strange, I thought to myself. Was she expecting me?

I entered the house. A man was lying in bed and breathing hard, suffering from chronic respiratory complications of an undetermined nature.

With much effort, the man turned in his bed to see me.

"It's you, Antonis?" I said in surprise. A machinist near downtown Chania, Antonis had faithfully attended the Evangelical church in the past.

"I was really desperate about my husband's condition, Mr. Zachariou," said his wife, "when suddenly I heard someone calling me three times—'Thaleia, Thaleia, Thaleia!' I came out, and there you were."

"God is about to perform a miracle in this home today, for the voice you heard is a sign that God is with us," I said.

Thaleia stood in awe as she realized what had happened.

I turned to Antonis. "Do you believe God can heal you today?"

Antonis nodded. He coughed. "I—I believe," he said with effort, his eyes closing, ready for prayer.

"We are going to ask God to heal you," I said.

Antonis nodded, tears flowing down his cheeks.

I considered Antonis an enlightened man, ready to receive the Word, so I was open with him. "You know, Antonis," I said, "I must advise you that, as I pray, you might hear me say words you do not understand. That's because I wish to pray in the spirit according to 1 Corinthians 12."

Antonis sat bolt upright, his eyes wide open. "What do you mean?" he said.

I turned to 1 Corinthians 12 and asked Antonis to read.

Moments later, Antonis looked up at me in amazement, his hands pressing my New Testament against his chest. "It's been there all these years and—and I never saw it?" he said. Deep inside me, I knew that God had already started to heal this man.

After we prayed, we read the Scriptures together and talked more about the gifts of the Spirit.

As for the bird cage, upon leaving Antonis and Thaleia I delivered it to their next-door neighbor.

The next day Antonis and Thaleia were at the Evangelical church. As I had expected, Antonis was completely healed—never again did he suffer from that chronic disease. The couple could hardly wait to see me after church to urge me to visit their home the next day.

Meanwhile, they spread the news about Antonis' miraculous healing to neighbors, friends, and relatives everywhere, and when I visited their home again the following day, I found a dozen people waiting. Among them was Chrysaki, a faithful Christian woman from the Evangelical church, who testified that years earlier I had prayed with her for her sickly son to return from the Albanian front and that within a week her son was home.

Antonis and Thaleia took me aside that day to tell me that they thought the Evangelicals erred in attributing tongues to the work of Satan and saying that he twists people's tongues and causes them to fall to the ground. They said they had examined the Scriptures over the weekend and found that tongues and healings and all the gifts were listed side by side, and that they believed no one had any business today trying to take any one of the gifts out of that list, let alone attribute them to the work of Satan.

AS THE Lord added souls to our group, we started meeting regularly every two weeks at Antonis and Thaleia's home. People were hungry for the Word, and eager to learn about the love of God through Christ. Many were the miracles the Lord wrought within our nucleus as we prayed, sang spiritual songs, and shared the Word.

When I shared the news with the church council and invited them to visit our home group, I sensed a restrained reaction. One elder asked what the size of the group was, and another whether anyone in the group was a regular church member. No questions about tongues. Nor did anyone advise me at the time against holding such meetings.

Two months passed, and I became concerned about the possible ramifications of our home group meetings. Our group was growing—20, then 30, then 40. Each time we ran out of room, we sought a bigger place. Soon no place was big enough. Where do we go from here? I wondered each time.

Outsiders became suspicious of our peculiar gatherings and threatened us with sabotage, while the priests and the police made sure we knew we were under surveillance. A cat-and-mouse game thus began, and my primary concern now became how to elude the priests and the police each time, rather than how to fit more than fifty persons in one house.

As an active member of the seven-member Evangelical church council in Chania, I had personal concerns as well about our home group meetings. As more brethren from the Evangelical church joined us, I began to dread the idea that I might be accused of enticing away church members and creating factions within our church. Never once did it occur to me to start a group or a ministry in Chania separate from, independent of, or in conflict with our Evangelical church. In fact, I always encouraged our group to attend the Sunday and Thursday evening services at the Evangelical church, which actually brought about a sudden growth in church attendance for which the ministers and council members showed me great appreciation. At the same time I had no doubt that our gathering was ordained by God, and that disbanding our home group meetings would not only be a disobedience to God, but also an injustice to the participating believers and a fatal spiritual blow to other eternal souls in our hopeless and godless community.

I brought the matter before God through prayer and fasting. God impressed upon me that the group was like a lonely wild flower that sprang out in the middle of a spiritual desert from a single seed He had provided. The flower was God's—not mine—my responsibility was to plant and water it; His, its growth (1 Corinthians 3:6). Strengthened, I prayed that God would enable me by His Spirit to carry on the work with the flock He had entrusted into my care, and help me to be faithful and obedient to Him in the days ahead, regardless of the cost.

ON A cold January night in 1951, I was summoned to appear before the church council. Upon my arrival, I was met by the pastor, the officiating minister, and five laymen. After starting with prayer, the minister began to talk about the fallaciousness of tongues. Those victimized by this so-called "gift" are often an embarrassment to the gospel of Christ, he said, and he himself had heard from the very mouths of those deceived, including Pentecostal leaders in Athens such as I was acquainted with, that it was possible for one speaking in tongues to fall to the ground and go into convulsions for as long as eight hours.

I was dumbfounded. Is this what this meeting is all about? I wondered. Accusations? What had happened suddenly to this man? Where is the expression of true Christian love? Or is it now doctrinally conditional love? As he continued to talk, I prayed within me and sensed tremendous boldness in my spirit.

"Tongues are a deceitful tool of Satan," he went on to say. "The true gift of tongues was only for the first Christians, until the church was established, and those who claim to possess the gift have regrettably allowed themselves to be deceived and are themselves deceitful, and true Christians should shun them."

His words are harsh, his claims unfounded, I thought to myself as I opened my Bible and began to speak.

"Have you ever sought the Holy Spirit for the gift of tongues?" I asked bluntly.

"No!" the minister shouted. "And I never will!"

"Well, then, you will never receive it," I said.

"You're filling souls with deleterious ideas," a member interjected.

"You call the Word of God poison?" I said calmly. "Let me ask you this. Do you consider the Pentecostals to be Christians or not?" (Recently he and a couple of other members had spoken with admiration about the work of a charismatic evangelist from Puerto Rico by the name of Robert Fierro.)

There was silence.

"Well?"

"Some of them are genuine, but they err," said the assistant minister.

"Do they err when they bring souls to Christ?"

"They err in their interpretation of the Scriptures regarding tongues," said another member.

"Right," added the pastor. "You need to be able to understand the original text, but your education is limited."

"Peter was not educated, but he was enlightened by the Holy Spirit," I said. "In any case, 1 Corinthians 12 and 14 are clear enough. It's all a matter, not of education, but of believing or not believing the Scriptures."

"In other words," said the pastor, "I do not believe the Scriptures? Is that what you're saying? Let me tell you, friend, I have studied the Word for over thirty years!"

"Thirty? Then, as a minister of the Gospel, do you believe the gifts of the Holy Spirit are given to Christians in our time?" I said.

"No, I do not believe it—"

"How can you say that you have studied the Word for over thirty years, yet not believe it? Your very words declare your unbelief!"

"Well, now," challengingly cut in another member, who had been flipping the pages in his Bible and who on occasion spoke from the pulpit. "Do you speak Chinese when you speak in tongues, or just—tongue twisters?"

"I speak as the Spirit gives me utterance, according to Acts 2:4 and 1 Corinthians 12:11," I said.

"But in Acts 2:8 it says that people heard the disciples speak in those people's native language," he said.

"Well, that's not too hard for the Holy Spirit, is it?" I said.

"Absolutely not, for that's what the true gift was. No nonsense. If you claim to have that gift, then you should speak in other people's native language."

"There has been no need for that yet, for all those around me speak my native language."

"Then why do you blather and babble if nobody can comprehend you? You call that a gift of the Holy Spirit?"

At that point I welcomed the opportunity to talk about the purpose of tongues—though, alas, I sensed no room for spiritual enlightenment in their minds, only a contentious spirit. "First, tongues may be in the form of a known language, as in the case of Acts 2:4-8. Second, tongues may be in the form of unknown utterances as part of the believer's individual worship or intercessory prayer—"

"The word *unknown* is not found in the original text," quickly interjected the pastor.

"That doesn't matter, for it says 'He who speaks in an unknown tongue speaks not to men, but to God, for no one understands him, but in the spirit he speaks mysteries,' " I said.

"Where does it say that?" the former member said.

"Here," I said, holding out my Bible, my finger on 1 Corinthians 14:2. "See?" The man kept looking at the verse for a long moment. There was silence.

"But it says also that it's all a mystery," he went on, "in which case we—uh—we should leave that alone—"

"That, what?" I said.

"God's mystery!"

"No, my friend, that's in a different Bible, not mine," I said, shaking my head. "That's why you flubbed when you spoke this time."

"So you're saying that when you hear tongues you understand God's mysteries?" he said with sarcasm.

"No, but when tongues are given not in the hearer's native language, God speaks through the gift of the interpretation of tongues."

The man looked at me in unbelief. "Where do you see that?"

"Further down," I said, and once more I held out my Bible and asked him to read 1 Corinthians 14:3-5.

The man began to read. Everyone remained speechless. It was a moment of silent victory for the Truth.

When the member handed me back the Bible—everything he had read was boldly underlined—I said, "It is not right, brethren. It is not right for those responsible to God for eternal souls to strip the Word of Truth."

"Be careful what you are saying to this council," the minister warned, "for you should not be here anymore."

"I am careful about what I'm saying, and I must say also this one thing: you have stripped Christ of the power of His healing and of His miraculous manifestations, and now of His love, and have left Him shamefully naked."

The session suddenly took a different turn, as the officiating minister sought to change the subject. No allusions were made to the home group meetings I held, perhaps in the interest of time. A more pressing issue on their agenda was obviously to order me out of the church premises, where my family had gratefully found shelter for nearly ten years now. They did not have the right to evict me, I told them, for it was unchristian. Where would my family go during the severe winter months?

That night my die was cast. Having made my stand, I felt relief, for I knew God was with me. At the same time I was profoundly grieved, for I was being persecuted by my own brethren, whom I dearly loved.

The next day I didn't have the heart to break the news to my loved ones—my children looked pale; my wife had lost weight; my youngest son couldn't understand why there was no milk in the house. My oldest son wrote from Athens, where he was studying to become a radio technician, that for days he had eaten nothing but roasted chickpeas and sunflower seeds.

At the same time, I thought of the needy souls in our home group meetings. A miracle of God was needed there, too, for I felt unfit to lead them.

Back to the routine, I said to myself with humor, as I went once again into one of my frequent bouts of fasting and prayer. In my walk with God I had learned that, in the lives of those who prayerfully and patiently wait upon Him, a desperate situation signaled an opportunity for His miraculous intervention.

Under pressure from the council, I searched all over town for a two-room rental house that would provide shelter for my family of nine. The only places I could afford were like dungeons. God would not have me dump my loved ones into such rat holes—I couldn't. So I kept praying and looking.

UPON returning home one evening, I was met by an unexpected visitor, who greeted me in the name of the Lord and who introduced herself as Kyparissia Antonopoulou. Kyparissia explained that she had recently returned to her homeland for a visit after having lived most of her life in America, and that she had come to meet me at the recommendation of Peponis, the former commissary of ships and missionary to China. She had already spent a few days with close relatives near Chania, she said, but had felt unwelcome there because of her "strange" religion.

That night our simple meal of bread, oil, and green onions was enriched by our visitor's uplifting accounts of God's work among the Christian believers in America.

The following night a dozen believers joined us at our home for fellowship and prayer. Just before midnight, still on our knees praying, we felt the room shake. Thinking it was an earthquake, I got up and went to check on my two youngest boys, who were tossing in their sleep in the corner of the room. At that moment, we heard steps—the familiar sound of someone setting foot on the three portable wooden steps that led into the room through a low window. As we all turned toward the audible steps, my twelve-year-old son Theodosios, still on his knees praying, shouted, "It's Jesus! It's Jesus!" his arms reaching upward as if to touch the Master. Overwhelmed by God's presence, our spirits and voices lifted praises unto God until the wee morning hours.

The event did not go unnoticed—two days later the church council demanded that I vacate the church premises at once, because the American prophetess and I were of a different spirit. The spirit was different indeed, I told them, as evidenced by the fact that their demands were made not in the spirit of Christ's love.

Upon returning home from a day's search for a place to live, I felt compelled to share with Kyparissia the story behind my eviction. Kyparissia showed extreme interest. As I continued to talk, I noticed tears in her eyes. She began to praise and thank God that He had honored her desire to visit her homeland for a specific purpose, and went on to explain that for years God had impressed upon her to some day dedicate the house she had in Chania to God's service!

Two days later my family witnessed once more God's miraculous provision—a five-room house in the outskirts of Chania near the sea!

# PART
# THREE

# 15

# A Lighthouse

THE SECRET POLICE KNEW to no longer expect to find me walking down the same street at the same hour, mandolin in one hand, briefcase in the other. Instead, they would wait until I closed the shop and then follow me through town all the way home, even if it meant lurking outside my house for an hour or longer, waiting for me to launch out in the dark, if I did. Then, late at night, they'd find me in the middle of town heading home, and they'd wonder if I was bluffing or they had been outsmarted again.

Why did they follow me? To earmark the houses I entered? To intimidate innocent souls for opening their hearths for a time of sharing, prayer, and singing?

On one occasion the sleuths discovered our meeting place because of our singing, and they barged right in. After scanning the startled gathering, they threw a sharp stare at me and left.

The situation brought to mind the persecution a few years back of Demetrios Kastritsiotis and other brethren in the village of Vaya in east-central Greece, who were imprisoned for reasons even the attorneys could not explain. Forbidden by the police to hold meetings, four faithful men of God, each a father of four or more, endured humiliation and imprisonment in Thebes, then in Leivadia, and finally in Piraeus, where they were threatened with exile to the isle of Makronesos.

The pressure from the police fueled our fervor—we saw each meeting as a precious opportunity to worship together. We were over sixty souls meeting in small groups in staggered fashion, at times on very short notice.

THE chief of police did not hesitate to explain that it was the bishop of Chania who had my movements monitored. Asked about the unnecessary scare tactics his men used, he simply shrugged his shoulders.

I tried visiting the bishop, but he wouldn't meet with me. Meanwhile, I discovered that goading the bishop was an alliance of four priests, who wished to see me behind bars. Behind those priests was Xanthoudakis, a man who had been a chanter in an Orthodox church for thirty years before joining the Evangelical church for a time. This man had often led the Evangelical congregation in song; now he was siding with the priests in instigating action against me, accusing me to the bishop of trying to establish a heresy in Chania by proselytizing his Orthodox parishioners with American money. Their charge included the accusation that I held religious services without a license.

The platform of their operation now enjoyed legal status— the police could arrest me for giving an informant a tract or simply talking to him, or for holding meetings without a church license. Though nothing would prevent my persecutors from seeking ways to stop me, I thought that getting a license might alleviate part of the problem.

In applying for a license, I realized that I had to fit into the mold of a man-made, government-sanctioned religious taxonomy. What am I? I asked myself. Orthodox? That, I am. For an Orthodox Christian is a person who worships uprightly. Evangelical? That, I am, too. An Evangelical is a Christian who agrees with the gospel. Pentecostal? Most certainly. A Pentecostal Christian is one who has experienced and believes in the manifestation of the gifts of the Holy Spirit. I am each and all of these; but the name Christian alone suffices, for I wish to be identified only with Christ. However, no Greek would deny he is a Christian, for in his mind being Greek traditionally means being a Christian, regardless of his personal relationship with Christ. Therefore, I would want our group to be identified with the kind of Christians who adhere to the teachings of the full gospel.

MY proposal early in 1952 to the Pentecostal ministers in Athens to petition for a church license in Chania was received warmly. The first step was to have the members of our group present themselves at city hall to sign the petition, pending verification of their signatures. Pulling teeth would have been easier, for not only were they leery about openly identifying themselves with a non-Orthodox religious movement, but the person they had to face at city hall was a former police officer who was now a chanter at an Orthodox church. He was skilled at making them go back a second and a third time for no apparent reason. In most cases, I had to go find members at their homes and escort them all the way to city hall. Over thirty signatures were finally gathered—more than the required minimum, to the bishop's dismay. The petition was submitted to the Ministry of Education and Religions by a faithful Christian woman in Athens, Mary Orphan.

Immediately we chanced holding Sunday services openly at my home, the designated meeting place shown on the petition. The living room was filled beyond capacity. Neighbors and passersby crowded at the door and the window to hear the preaching and the singing. During the week we continued to meet secretly in smaller groups as usual.

AS I fasted and prayed that the license would be granted, I prayed also that God would put a burden in the heart of an experienced minister like Konstantinides to help with the tremendous opportunities among the growing flock of believers in Chania. One day Kyparissia, who had often heard me make mention of Konstantinides' name, informed me that she and Mary Orphan, as well as a number of other Pentecostal ministers and laymen I had met, were affiliated with the Assemblies of God, a large Pentecostal denomination with headquarters in Springfield, Missouri; and that Konstantinides belonged to another, though similar, Pentecostal denomination.

I stood dumbfounded. Different Pentecostal denominations? I kept wondering. How could it be? Why couldn't they be the same? But no, I thought in the end. I will not allow the enemy to fool me. However wrong, such differences existed in the early church as well. Paul advises against such claims among believers as "I am of Paul, and I of Apollos, and I of Cephas, and I of Christ" (1 Corinthians 1:12). (I came to understand later that differences between genuine Pentecostal denominations were not related to doctrine, but to minor ideas and organizational technicalities.)

As I prayed that God would send the right person, I wrote letters to churches and individuals requesting their assistance. A letter I received from Springfield advised me that there was no one they could send now, but that one of their workers, Mary Orphan, was already in Greece. Orphan and leading Pentecostal ministers such as Spyridon Diktos (Diktyopoulos) and Nikolaos Karakostanoglou were particularly supportive of our ministry, but I was thinking in terms of finding someone to help with the pastoral duties on an ongoing basis.

Prior to her return to the United States, Kyparissia showed me a photograph of some individuals in California, and pointed out a woman whose father and other relatives lived in Chania. Inquiring further, I learned that this woman, Evangelia, and her husband, Joseph De Julio, had faithfully given themselves as a team to a wonderful ministry among the Greeks in California. In my spirit I knew that I should write the De Julios immediately, which I did.

Meanwhile, rumors spread outside our circles that the American woman had left me her house and given me thousands of dollars to help me proselytize. To prevent a scandal within our group, I explained to them that they needed to know the truth in full detail, in case people pointed a finger at us. The house was not given to me, I told them, but rather I was renting it for 200 drachmas a month. I had not received any sums of money, and in fact had refused to accept monthly support offered by sympathetic brethren in America; just as I had prayerfully refused to accept support back in 1948, when a visiting minister from America proposed that I receive 600 dollars a year on account of my poverty as well as a ministry I was to spearhead in some islands of the Aegean. Then, as well as now, I dreaded the thought of mingling serving God by faith with dependence on guaranteed support. Since about the time I moved to Kyparissia's house, and despite my objections to receiving support, three individuals had faithfully sent me independently a total of twenty-five dollars a month. That was the only source of income I had during the four months the soap factory had closed in the summer of 1952, plus God's welcome provision of work as a full-time gardener at the orphanage for just those same four months!

The believers in our group knew I had no hidden riches. They were poor, too, so they understood well, for instance, why my good wife would often hide an egg or a piece of bread so she could feed it secretly to the son who needed it most.

These people trusted me. They knew that my love for them sprang out of my love for the Savior and a desire to obey His command to spread His message. They knew that we met week after week, month after month, for the purpose of ministering to one another and growing together in the knowledge of the Person of Christ and in the blessed hope of His coming. And they knew that my main interest was to see the kingdom of God on earth extended, rather than establish one of my own.

Too, like Moses, I felt inadequate, and often wished that someone would take the reins of this ministry, or for an Aaron to share the burden of the flock God had entrusted to my care.

IN AUGUST of 1952, four months after we submitted our petition for a church license, the government notified us of the need for additional and immediate verification of membership. That meant that I was to have all members of our gathering show up at city hall again, an embarrassment most members would not relish. My repeated recommendation to government officials that the police visit our church service on a Sunday morning by way of verifying membership fell on deaf ears. Sensing the urgency of the moment, I fasted and prayed. My fast ended four days later when the police agreed to come to our service and take a count.

OUR church license was granted just before the De Julios, a delightful couple in their early thirties, arrived in Crete on September 5, 1952. It was a time of rejoicing for the church, for God's providing hand was very evident as He rewarded our diligent prayers in such a timely fashion.

The De Julios, who came on their own, had already in-
curred enormous out-of-pocket expenses at customs, and staying in a hotel for any length of time would have added to their
financial burden. Renting a place also was difficult for them,
since landlords demanded six, or more, months' rent up front.
Finally, they decided to check out a housing facility that belonged to Evangelia's father. Located on the second floor of a
two-story building in the heart of Syndrivani in the port of
Chania, the facility had been vacant for two years; apparently a
sign on the wall facing Syndrivani's Eleftheriou Venizelou
Square had discouraged potential tenants from inquiring, for
they assumed the building was the headquarters of a political
party. "Remove your hat a moment," I said to Joseph, as
Evangelia's father and another relative considered letting the
couple move in. "We're going to pray that the Lord will turn
this place into a house of worship."

Joseph played his guitar and Evangelia her accordion, as
the couple ministered in sermon and in song. Souls continued
to be added to the flock of believers, and Kyparissia's house
was already too small to accommodate our numbers. Inevita-
bly, we considered moving our services to the facility occupied
by the De Julios in Syndrivani Square, to which Evangelia's
father agreed. Our petition to relocate was sent to the Ministry
of Education and Religions in Athens through a cousin of mine
who worked there. Incredibly, the permit to relocate was granted
within a week!

Shouts of joy slipped from our hearts as we once more witnessed our loving Lord's providing hand. We had already held
two services at our new location in Syndrivani, when we received a letter from my cousin in Athens saying, "Cousin, you've
got to reapply for a permit to relocate, because they've lost the
petition I hand-carried to them, and no one here knows what's
going on!"

THE presence of our beloved De Julios in the city of Chania,
particularly in this central part of town, could not go unnoticed. Our hearty singing and music echoed in the square, and
the delivery of the Word, especially through Evangelia's voice,
penetrated the surrounding shops, cafes, and taverns like the

clear sound of a church bell. Curious people rushed up the stairs to hear us. New souls, like Christos the retired policeman, confessed Christ as their Savior and were added to our flock. A number from the Evangelical church joined us as well. Attendance reached capacity proportions nearly from the start, and we had to tear down part of the middle wall of the building.

Because the De Julios carried out most of the pastoral duties, I had opportunities to travel and participate in various church synods and councils, visit other churches and invite ministers to Chania, and do outreach ministry.

IN the midst of expanding ministries and an upward climb in numbers and spiritual growth, I wondered what would happen when the tidal waves of persecution were unleashed; for I was certain that the unprecedented declaration of the Word of God in Chania was bound to challenge the city's so-called spiritual leaders. The church license shielded us from the front, so to speak, but our sides remained vulnerable to attacks, particularly now that Americans were visibly involved in the daily ministry of the church. My word of caution to the De Julios was never to give anything to anyone, not even a pencil to any of the little children.

The first waves of persecution came in January and February of 1953 in the form of libel through the Athens-based newspaper *Allage* (Change), in a series of eight articles titled "The Dreadful Spider of the Foreign Heresies." The author, Spyridon Dendrinos, aided by Nikolaos Xenos, a reporter who claimed to have had first-hand experiences with Pentecostals in Greece and in America, targeted the Pentecostals in Greece and their "heresy," and accused them of systematically ravaging the Orthodox churches and proselytizing devout Orthodox Christians by Satanic means.

According to Dendrinos, the Pentecostal "pastor" carefully takes a naive, God-fearing woman, for example, through progressive stages of brainwashing, after which a torturer, also called a pastor, subjects the victim to twenty-four hours of prayer while kneeling on a piece of wood. The victim repeats what she is told and has to resist all kinds of temptations brought before her eyes. The helpless victim is further subjected to hideous and shuddering experiences as she is forced to sit naked on a coffin and face a skull and crossbones while undergoing other indescribable experiences. The victim must endure all this pain and horror in hopes of becoming a true child of God and having the Holy Spirit descend upon her head so she can speak in a foreign and unknown language.

Vexed by these disgraceful lies, I wrote to Dendrinos and suggested that it was his duty as a reporter to present the truth only after personally visiting our Pentecostal churches and talking with our ministers. But that did not stop Mr. Dendrinos. As Diktos pointed out, editorials of this nature get their support from the forces that are behind them—in this case, the priests. Curiously, the editors in Chania now had no space in their newspapers for our articles, they said, not even for the tenets of our faith—clear evidence of an organized plot against us.

ΣΥΝΕΧΕΙΑ
ΕΚ ΤΗΣ 1ης ΣΕΛΙΔΟΣ

'Αλλὰ ἂς ἀφίσουμε τὸν κ. Ξένο νὰ μᾶς ὁμιλήση.

**ΟΜΙΛΕΙ Ο κ. ΞΕΝΟΣ**

«Τὸ δωμάτιο, ὅπου θὰ ὑποστῆς τὴ φρικτὴ δοκιμασία μᾶς λέγει ὁ κ. Ξένος, γιὰ νὰ καταστῆς ἄξιον τέκνον τοῦ Θεοῦ καὶ λάβης τὴν ἐπιφοίτησι τοῦ ἁγίου πνεύματος, εἶναι ὁλοσκό-τεινο. Καὶ τελείως γυμνό. Μόνο στὸ ἐπάνω ἀνατολικὸ μέρος, ὑπάρχει μία μεγάλη νεκροκεφαλή, καὶ χιαστὶ δύο ὀστά. Αὐτὰ θὰ τὰ δῆς ὅταν τελειώση ἡ δοκιμασία καὶ ἀνάψη ἕνα ἡμίφως. Στὸ δωμάτιο σὲ ὁδηγεῖ ὁ «καλὸς ποιμήν», ὁ ἀνελέητος δηλαδὴ δράκος. Σὲ τοποθετεῖ στὸ κέντρον. τοῦ σκο-τεινοῦ δωματίου. Τάρταρα σωστά. Δὲν βλέπεις οὔτε τὴ μύτη σου. Σὲ εἰδοποιεῖ νὰ ἀποβάλης τὰ ἐνδύματά σου. Καὶ μετά, σύξυλος, ἔτσι, ὅπως σὲ γέννησε ἡ μάνα σου, σὲ βάζουν ἐπάνω σὲ μιὰ σανιδένια κασέλλα, ποὺ μοιάζει μὲ φέρετρο. Ἡ ἀτμόσφαι-ρα εἶναι βαρειά, ἡ ἀναπνοή σου πνί-γεται κι' ἔτσι, ἐξηντλημένος, ὅπως εἶσαι ἀπὸ τὶς νηστεῖες καὶ τὶς προσευ-χές, οὐρχεται νὰ λυποθυμήσης.
— Καὶ μετὰ τί γίνεται κ. Ξένε;

(See translation on next page)

## The Dreadful Spider
### of the FOREIGN HERESIES
_____ CONTINUED
FROM THE 1st PAGE

#### MR. XENOS SPEAKS

"The room, where you will undergo the horrid trial, tells us Mr. Xenos, in order to become a worthy child of God and receive the enlightenment of the Holy Spirit, is pitch-black. And totally bare. Only on the upper place facing east there is a large skull and two crossbones. You will see these when the test is over and a dim light goes on. The "good pastor" leads you to this room, who is the merciless ogre. He places you in the center of the dark room. True hell. You don't see even your nose. He tells you to take off your clothes. And then totally bare, that is, the way your mother bore you, they put you atop a wooden trunk, which resembles a casket. The atmosphere is heavy, your breath is being choked and so, exhausted from your fasts and prayers, you are about to pass out.
— And then what happens, Mr. Xenos? ..."

[excerpt from Feb. 8, 1953]

Dendrinos and I exchanged a number of letters, through which he became well informed as to the true views and practices of the Pentecostals. He welcomed me with a warm embrace at his home in Athens one day, and we enjoyed each other's company just like old friends. But when Diktos, Karakostanoglou and I waited for Dendrinos in downtown Athens for an official interview as agreed, he simply did not show up. We were not surprised.

SHORTLY after Dendrinos' articles were released, Papagiorgis, rector of the local cathedral and a member of the four-priest alliance shadowing my moves, began to take a chair at the front of a cafe just across from the door of our church building. He would arrive prior to our Wednesday night service, then write

ΕΝΑ ΑΠΟΚΑΛΥΠΤΙΚΟΝ ΡΕΠΟΡΤΑΖ ΠΟΥ ΕΝΔΙΑΦΕΡΕΙ ΟΛΟΝ ΤΟΝ ΚΟΣΜΟΝ

# Η φοβερὴ Ἀράχνη τῶν ΞΕΝΩΝ ΑΙΡΕΣΕΩΝ

"Ενα θῦμα τῶν «πεντηκοστιανῶν» ὁμιλεῖ διὰ τὰ βασανιστή-
ρια ποὺ ὑπέστη γυμνὸς εἰς κατασκότεινα ὑπόγεια κατὰ
τὴν διαδικασίαν τοῦ προσηλυτισμοῦ.-Σφράγισμα καὶ... χάπι

## Η ΑΙΡΕΣΙΣ ΤΩΝ «ΠΕΝΤΗΚΟΣΤΙΑΝΩΝ»

ΠΕΡΙΛΗΨΙΣ ΠΡΟΗΓΟΥΜΕΝΩΝ

Τοῦ Συνεργάτου μας κ. ΣΠ. ΔΕΝΔΡΙΝΟΥ

Additional excerpts from the libelous articles by Spyridon
Dendrinos and Nikolaos Xenos which appeared in the Athens-
based newspaper *Allage* (Change) titled "The Dreadful Spider of
the Foreign Heresies"

down the names of those coming to worship. At first we figured that sooner or later he would tire of this activity and stop.

But Papagiorgis did not stop. In fact, he began to show up
before and after every single service we had, including Sunday
evenings, often carrying a stick. Eyeing every man and woman
coming in or going out, he would threaten that he would not
be willing to accommodate them if they ever needed public
assistance or the issuance or verification of certain documents.*

One of Papagiorgis' first targets was Joseph the mailman.
Joseph delivered our church mail and had frequent contacts
with the De Julios, and as a result, the De Julios led him to
Christ. Joseph looked unusually low one day, and I asked him if
there was something troubling him. Joseph explained that he
had sold his shop and spent all his money trying to save his
hemophilic daughter. After the De Julios and I laid hands on a
napkin and prayed according to Acts 19:11-12, Joseph took the
napkin home and by faith placed it on his daughter. That same
day, the girl was healed. "God used these people for a double
miracle in my life," Joseph said to Papagiorgis. "I found Christ,
and my daughter was healed! Why shouldn't I come to this
place?"

On my way to the church office one Wednesday morning,
some friends (who did not attend our church) informed me
that Papagiorgis was plotting to threaten and even harm us.
Before the service, I looked down from the church balcony and
saw a stick-toting Papagiorgis already occupying his spot. I
hurried down the stairs and approached Papagiorgis peacefully,
with a smile on my face. Surprised, Papagiorgis sat straight up
and froze in his chair.

"What are you doing there, elder?" I said in a friendly manner.

"Well—Ah'm sittin' over here tuh. . . to sanctifah mahself!"
he said with put-on humor, causing a fit of laughter among the
half-dozen men in the back of the small cafe. Were they the
bullies he had brought along to harm us? I wondered, as I looked
their way and greeted them.

---

* To obtain certain verification or identification papers, one had to be registered first with the Orthodox Church.

I leaned over Papagiorgis and whispered into his ear, "It does not become a clergyman to do what you are doing, sitting here and thinking that those who come to us are corrupted with money. Come upstairs and observe in person, rather than sit here while even your own parishioners speak shamefully of you."

"What do you care about my own? You' re proselytizing them!" he said aloud, so his bullies could hear.

I stood straight up and said, my voice raised, "If you wish to perform watchdog services on those losing their souls, follow me and I'll show you the red-light houses where marriages fall apart, the casinos where hard-earned wages are squandered, and the cabarets where our young men are getting soused right this moment!"

Papagiorgis felt disarmed as he lost his grip on the argument that proselytes from his parish lose their souls, so he skirted the issue. "Do you worship Holy Mary?"

"We worship God," I said, suspecting he wanted me to slip in front of his witnesses. So I leaned close to his ear again and whispered, "No, we don't worship her, nor do we reproach her with four-letter words."

The priest understood my conundrum, for on Greek lips the name of Holy Mary is commonly subjected to daily abuse. "It's not your fault," he rasped. "It's the fault of those who issued you the license!"

"Did you know, Papagiorgis, that I can make you stand before the judges tomorrow? Are you aware that what you are doing here is against the law and our constitutional rights?"

"So, why don't you sue me?"

"Because God's command to love one another does not allow me to," I said, and turned around to welcome those arriving for the service.

"I don't want you to love me!" Papagiorgis shouted as I went up the stairs. "I don't want you to love me!"

The Lord protected us from harm that night. And a short letter I wrote to the governor and to the district attorney the next day put an end to the elder's three-month-old practices and gimmicks.

LIKE the wave-lashed lighthouse in the port of Chania, our church continued to emit to lost souls signals of hope and peace. During the summer of 1953 the church experienced tremendous spiritual growth, as the Spirit of God brought men, women and young ones to the saving knowledge of Christ.

It was at this juncture of our ministry that our church was to stand as a wave-breaker as well. The dark waves of persecution, already visible on the horizon, developed a much greater magnitude and force, and were of a nature that would challenge the very foundation upon which our ministry stood—the Rock of Ages.

A view of the port of Chania, Crete, as seen from Syndrivani Square. The church building was within a few yards of this port.

# 16

# The Battlefront

IT WAS LIKE A SURPRISE AIR RAID! Freshly read passages from the Acts of the Apostles describing Paul's persecutions by the high priest pulsated in my mind at the shop that morning as I picked up the *Nea* (News) and read:

---

**THE PENTECOSTALS
ARE PROSELYTIZING**

CHANIA, 14 September [1953]
(By our correspondent) —Following repeated reports to the local Sacred Bishopric about acts of proselytism by the Pentecostals at the expense of credulous and naive citizens, the Very Reverend of Kydonia and Apokoronou, Agathangelos, has requested that the office of the District Attorney intervene in order to close their church, which is housed in a very central hall in Syndrivani Square, driving out at the same time all of the heresy leaders.

**ΟΙ ΠΕΝΤΗΚΟΣΤΙΑΝΟΙ
ΕΝΕΡΓΟΥΝ ΠΡΟΣΗΛΥΤΙΣΜΩΝ**

ΧΑΝΙΑ, 14 Σεπτεμβρίου (Τοῦ ἀνταποκριτοῦ μας).— Κατόπιν ἐπανειλημμένων καταγγελιῶν πρὸς τὴν ἐνταῦθα Ἱερὰν Ἐπισκοπὴν, περὶ διενεργείας προσηλυτισμοῦ ἐκ μέρους τῶν Πεντηκοστιανῶν, εἰς βάρος εὐπίστων καὶ ἀφελῶν πολιτῶν, ὁ Θεοφιλέστατος Κυδωνίας καὶ Ἀποκορώνου κ. Ἀγαθάγγελος ἐζήτησεν ἀπὸ τὴν Εἰσαγγελίαν ὅπως ἐπέμβῃ καὶ κλείσῃ τὴν ἐκκλησίαν των, τὴν στεγαζομένην εἰς κεντρικωτάτην αἴθουσαν τῆς πλατείας Συντριβανίου, διωκομένων συγχρόνως ὅλων τῶν αἱρεσιαρχῶν.

---

"Something is the matter, Mr. Zachariou?" asked George the cobbler, a disabled man who had for a year now used a corner of free space at the front of my shop. George, known to be a cynic and one who delighted in poking fun at religion, had recently begun mellowing and didn't mind my telling him that I was still praying for him.

"Well, yes, my friend," I said, and read the news to him.

Looking earnestly at me, George said, "Why, Mr. Zachariou, does God torment those who love Him?"

"George," I said. "It's called training. After God washes us thoroughly with a bath in the sin-cleansing blood of Jesus, He enlists us in His army. Then the training begins. To help us conduct ourselves as soldiers, He uses different trainers to tame and teach us. Naturally, the less trainable need to train harder. And then there are those in God's army who go for additional responsibility. That means extra training for them. In my case, not only was I one of the most untamed recruits God had to deal with, but one who now loves to serve all the way. Wouldn't it be unfair if God gave me additional responsibility without the proper training? So He has lots of trainers around me to prepare me for the battlefront. And sometimes it's at the battle-front where the real training begins. You read me?"

George kept looking at me and nodding his head for a long time as if waiting for his mind to clear. "Battlefront, eh?" he said holding an awl in his hand and making a grim gesture at his amputated leg, an unfailing reminder of his war injury. "Your battlefront is the courts; your enemies, the priests."

"There's only one enemy Christians have, and that's the enemy of God, who is also the enemy of our souls—Satan. The priests are not my enemy. The Bible says that we wrestle not against flesh and blood, like fighting the Germans or the Com-munists, but against Satan and the powers of darkness, for ours is a spiritual battle" (Ephesians 6:12).

George put his awl on a piece of leather in the middle of a portable workbench that fit over his lap. Pensively, he folded his arms and eased his lean frame against the chair. A grin crept over his gruff face as he said, "Judging them by their looks, some of them do look like the devil. You're telling me now they're not your enemy? Whose side are they on?"

"The priests' battlefront and mine should be one and the same: the enemy of darkness. Any other conflict or enmity be-tween men is rooted in man's jealousy, selfish ambitions, greed, lust, pride, hatred, etc. We can't blame anyone except ourselves for many of our problems—not God, not even the devil. Just ourselves. That's exactly what James tells us (James 1:12-15; 4:1). Anyone who purposely sides against the children of God or God's will becomes an agent of Satan."

George looked at me as if he'd been hit by lightning.

"Look here, George," I said, holding out my Bible, my finger on the passage.

"I can't—I don't read, you see. But I believe you, Mr. Zachariou," he said. "But—"

"But what?"

"Are there any God-fearing priests?"

"I'm so glad you asked, George," I said. "Yes, I do know priests who are truly children of God and who serve Him with all their heart. They may wear their clerical frocks and I my suit, but that doesn't put us in two different camps, for in God's eyes we are the same—children and servants of the Living God. On the contrary, I've known some who call themselves Pentecostals or Evangelicals and who shouldn't even call God their father!"

George nodded as he reached for his cutting knife. He seemed content.

HIS mind filled with false reports and accusations, the bishop of Chania launched a wrathful attack on us the next day through *Ethnikos Kiryx* (National Herald):

## Η ΑΙΡΕΣΙΣ ΤΩΝ ΠΕΝΤΗΚΟΣΤΙΑΝΩΝ ΚΑΙ Η ΔΡΑΣΙΣ
### ΤΩΝ ΤΡΙΩΝ ΑΡΧΗΓΩΝ ΤΗΣ ΕΙΣ ΤΗΝ ΠΕΡΙΟΧΗΝ ΤΩΝ ΧΑΝΙΩΝ
### ΜΕΤΕΒΑΛΟΝ ΕΙΣ ΕΚΚΛΗΣΙΑΝ ΜΙΑΝ ΑΠΛΗΝ ΑΙΘΟΥΣΑΝ

ΧΑΝΙΑ, 15. (Τοῦ ἀνταποκριτοῦ μας). — Ἡ ἀποκαλυφθεῖσα δρᾶσις τῶν ἀρχηγῶν τῆς αἱρέσεως τῶν πεντηκοστιανῶν, οἱ ὁποῖοι κατηγγέλθησαν ὅτι ἐνεργοῦν προσηλυτισμὸν εἰς βάρος ἀπλῶν, κρατεῖ εἰς εὔλογον συγκίνησιν τὴν κοινωνίαν τῆς πόλεώς μας. Ἡ καταγγελία ἐγένετο ὑπὸ τοῦ θεοφιλεστάτου ἐπισκόπου Κυδωνίας καὶ Ἀποκορώνου κ... Ἀγαθαγγέλου, φαίνεται δὲ ὅτι ἡ πολιτεία Ἱεράρχης κατέχει συστηματικὰ στοιχεῖα τὰ ὁποῖα θὰ γνωσθοῦν κατὰ τὴν διεξαχθησομένην προσεχῶς δίκην.

Ἡ αἵρεσις τῶν πεντηκοστιανῶν ἐμφανισθεῖσα ἀπὸ διετίας ἐνταῦθα, κατώρθωσε χάρις εἰς τὴν δραστηριότητα τῶν ἀρχηγῶν τῆς Πάνου Ζαχαρίου, Στ... Για... ὁ κη καὶ Εὐ... ου Βαλ... ἀκη, νὰ ἀποσπάσῃ σημαντικὸν ἀριθμὸν ὀπαδῶν ἀνερχομένων εἰς ἑκατὸν περίπου. Οὗτοι ἔχουν ἐνοικιάσει εἰς τὴν πλατεῖαν Σαντριβανίου μίαν αἴθουσαν τὴν ὁποίαν καὶ μετέβαλον εἰς ἐκκλησίαν.

Ἡ ἐν λόγῳ ἐκκλησία ἱδρύθη κατὰ τόπιν ἀδείας τοῦ ὑπουργείου Παιδείας διότι ἡ αἵρεσις τῶν πεντηκοστιανῶν εἶναι ἀνεγνωρισμένη.

Ἡ τελευταία ὅμως ἀποκάλυψις ὅτι ὁ ἀριθμὸς τῶν μελῶν τῆς αἱρέσεως αὐξάνεται διὰ προσηλυτισμῶς, ἐμπλέκει τοὺς ἀρχηγοὺς τῆς εἰς τὸν ποινικὸν νόμον ὁ ὁ...

ποῖος τιμωρεῖ αὐστηρότατα τοιαύτας πράξεις.

Οἱ ἀρχηγοὶ τῆς αἱρέσεως ἰσχυ- ρίζονται ὅτι γνωρίζουν τὸ θέλημα τοῦ Θεοῦ δι' ἐπικοινωνίας τοῦ Ἁγίου Πνεύματος τὸ ὁποῖον ὁμιλεῖ πρὸς αὐτοὺς εἰς διάφορα γλώσσας, ὅπως συνέβη κατὰ τὴν ἡμέραν τῆς Πεντηκοστῆς, ὁπότε τὸ πνεῦμα ἐπεφοίτησεν εἰς τοὺς Δώδεκα Ἀποστόλους. Ἀναγραστικὴ ἐξάπλωσις τῆς αἱρέσεως σημειοῦται εἰς τὰ χωρία καὶ κείμενα ὀλίγον ἔξω θι τῶν Χανίων, οἱ κάτοικοι τῶν ὁποίων προέβησαν εἰς ἔντονα διαβήματα διαμαρτυρίας πρὸς τὸν Ἐπίσκοπον.

Θ. ΑΜΟΥΤΖΟΠΟΥΛΟΣ

---

**THE HERESY OF THE PENTECOSTALS AND THE ACTION
OF ITS THREE LEADERS IN THE REGION OF CHANIA
—THEY TURNED A SIMPLE HALL INTO A CHURCH—**

CHANIA, 15 [September, 1953] (By our correspondent). — The disclosed action of the leaders of the heresy of the Pentecostals, who were accused of acts of proselytism at the expense of credulous persons, is effecting a reasonable emotional stir within the community of our city. The accusation was brought by the Very Reverend Bishop of Kydonia and Apokoronou, Agathangelos, and it appears that the gray-haired bishop is in possession of devastating material evidence which will be made known in the course of the upcoming court trial.

Because of the energetic Pentecostal leaders, Panos Zachariou, Stavros Yannarakis* and Evangelos Baletakis,* the heresy, which made its appearance locally two years ago, has been able to gain a significant number of followers, about one hundred. These have rented a hall in Syndrivani Square and have turned it into a church.

This church was established following the issuance of a license by the Ministry of Education because the Pentecostal heresy has been recognized. However, the recent discovery that the number of the members of the heresy is increasing by means of proselytism implicates its leaders in the criminal law which punishes such acts severely.

The heresy leaders allege that they know the will of God through the descent of the Holy Spirit, which speaks to them in twelve languages,† as it happened on the day of Pentecost, when the Spirit descended upon the Twelve Apostles. A disturbing expansion of the heresy is noticed in the villages of Gyros* and Istos,* which lie a short distance outside Chania, the residents of which proceeded with strong measures of protest to the Bishop.

TH. AMOUTZOPOULOS

---

My initial shock faded into a chuckle when I realized that the two names following mine were not Joseph and Evangelia De Julio's, but of two Orthodox theologians outside Chania who had no association whatsoever with our work and ministry!

Newspaper still in my hands, I caught myself dwelling on vengeful thoughts. "Lord, forgive me!" I prayed, as I realized that the enemy was leading me to an ambush paved with human reasoning. Logically, I should go straight to the reporter to examine the source of his mistakes; or I should demand an explanation from the bishop; or I should see an attorney about a libel suit against the bishop.

Prayerfully pondering the bishop's blunder, I began to see that what I was up against was not merely human injustice, but

* The names have been changed
† Or tongues

the element of confusion used relentlessly by Satan to influence human reasoning when it yields to hatred and is governed by pride.

Our prayer meeting that afternoon was interrupted by Socrates Patronas, a reporter who had previously refused to write about our views. Suspecting he had a part in the bishop's scheme, we invited him to observe the rest of the service. When it ended, we entertained a barrage of questions from him with regard to what we believe and the doctrinal differences between Orthodox, Pentecostals, and Evangelicals. I also made sure he understood that we had no connections whatsoever with the two Orthodox theologians whose names appeared next to mine in *Ethnikos Kiryx*. After taking a few pictures, the reporter left.

That evening, Christos, the retired policeman who had with tears accepted Jesus into his life, informed me he had just run into Patronas, who told him that he was going to write about the Pentecostals only what the bishop wanted him to write!

I could hardly believe my eyes two days later when I picked up the *Acropolis* and saw my picture right in the center of the front-page news under bold headlines.

ΟΙ ΚΑΤΑ ΚΑΙΡΟΥΣ ΕΜΦΑΝΙΖΟΜΕΝΟΙ «ΣΩΤΗΡΕΣ ΤΟΥ ΚΟΣΜΟΥ»

# Η ΕΞΑΠΛΩΣΙΣ ΤΗΣ ΑΙΡΕΣΕΩΣ ΤΩΝ ΠΕΝΤΗΚΟΣΤΙΑΝΩΝ ΚΡΑΤΕΙ ΕΝ ΑΝΑΣΤΑΤΩΣΕΙ ΤΟΥΣ ΦΙΛΟΘΡΗΣΚΟΥΣ ΚΑΤΟΙΚΟΥΣ ΧΑΝΙΩΝ

**ΕΧΟΥΝ ΕΓΚΑΤΑΣΤΗΣΕΙ ΤΗΝ «ΕΚΚΛΗΣΙΑΝ» ΤΩΝ ΕΙΣ ΠΟΛΥΤΕΛΗ ΟΙΚΙΑΝ ΤΗΣ ΠΟΛΕΩΣ ΧΩΡΙΣ ΕΝΤΟΣ ΑΥΤΗΣ ΝΑ ΥΠΑΡΧΗ ΟΥΤΕ ΕΝΑ ΕΙΚΟΝΙΣΜΑ**

**ΑΙ ΕΚΚΛΗΣΙΑΣΤΙΚΑΙ ΑΡΧΑΙ ΕΖΗΤΗΣΑΝ ΤΗΝ ΔΙΩΞΙΝ ΤΩΝ ΗΓΕΤΩΝ ΤΗΣ ΑΙΡΕΣΕΩΣ**

'Ο ἀρχηγός τῆς αἱρέσεως τῶν Πεντηκοστιανῶν Κρήτης Π. Ζαχαρίου

— ΒΛΕΠΕ 4ην ΣΕΛΙΔΑ —

THE SEASONALLY APPEARING "SAVIORS OF THE WORLD"
**THE SPREAD OF THE HERESY OF THE PENTECOSTALS THROWS
THE DEVOUT RESIDENTS OF CHANIA INTO CONFUSION**
THEY HAVE ESTABLISHED THEIR "CHURCH" IN A LUXURIOUS
BUILDING IN THE CITY WHEREIN NOT A SINGLE ICON EXISTS
THE CHURCH AUTHORITIES HAVE REQUESTED THE OUSTING OF
THE HERESY LEADERS

CHANIA, 17 [September, 1953] (By our correspondent). — The devout and religious society of our city, as well as of all the surrounding areas, is experiencing a great degree of agitation and restlessness due to the noted activity recently of the Pentecostals.

This newly-seen heresy which, on account of its energetic local leaders and their exploitation of the naiveness of certain individuals, has unfortunately found also our area to be an unrestricted field of operation, which has allowed it to expand to dangerous proportions, reaching a total of 100 followers.

Its leaders are Panos Zachariou—formerly an Evangelical—De Julio, an American of Italian descent, his wife, Evangelos Baletakis, and Stavros Yannarakis.

These conduct their services in a very central place in the city....

During their services their leaders pretend to teach the Bible, in actuality distorting it with anti-religious interpretations. They believe, in other words, that in their services the Holy Spirit descends upon their head as it happened on the day of Pentecost to Christ's disciples who, being uneducated fishermen, spoke languages. During this. . . descent they utter incoherent words which they claim they are the revelation and wisdom of God.

Despite all this coarse teaching, there are unfortunately many, especially simple and naive women, who have filled their

The leader of the heresy of the Pentecostals of Crete, P. Zachariou

classes to the point of disturbing Agathangelos, Bishop of Kydonia and Apoko-ronou, and forcing him to request of the authorities caution and the closure of their church.

As I have been informed, in the hands of Bishop Agathangelos there is already ample material evidence that the heresy leaders are reportedly proselytizing unlawfully by giving away clothing and money.

This heresy has unfortunately spread also to the outskirts of the city, and according to similar reports the Pentecostals have already spread their heresy to several villages, especially the villages of [Gyros] and [Istos], where many women have been proselytized and have departed from the bosom of the Eastern Orthodox Church....

—SEE PAGE 4—
[S. PATRONAS]

Similar accusations and reports appeared again the next day in *Bradyni* (Evening Paper).

## Η ΑΙΡΕΣΙΣ ΤΩΝ ΠΕΝΤΗΚΟΣΤΙΑΝΩΝ ΕΙΣ ΤΑ ΧΑΝΙΑ

ΧΑΝΙΑ, 18 Σεπτεμβρίου. (Τοῦ ἀνταποκριτοῦ μας). — Πληροφεροῦμαι ἐξ ἀσφαλοῦς πηγῆς ὅτι κατόπιν τῆς ἐπικινδύνου ἐξαπλώσεως τῆς αἰρέσεως τῶν Πεντηκοστιανῶν, τόσον εἰς τὴν πόλιν, ὅσον καὶ εἰς τὰ προάστια τῶν Χανίων, ὁ θεοφιλέστατος ἐπίσκοπος Κυδωνίας καὶ Ἀποκορώνου κ. Ἀγαθάγγελος Ξηρουχάκης ἀπέστειλε πρὸς τὴν Γενικὴν Διοίκησιν Κρήτης καὶ τὰς οἰκείας εἰσαγγελικὰς ἀρχὰς ἐκτενεστάτην ἀναφοράν, ζητῶν τὴν λῆψιν οὐστηροτάτων μέτρων πρὸς περιστολὴν τοῦ κακοῦ.

Ἡ ἐμφάνισις τῶν Πεντηκοστιανῶν εἰς τὰ Χανιὰ ἐσημειώθη μετὰ τὴν ἀπελευθέρωσιν, χωρὶς αἰσθητὴν ἀπήχησιν. Τελευταίως, ὅμως, οἱ ἡγούμενοι τῆς αἱρετικῆς αὐτῆς κινήσεως, χρησιμοποιοῦντες, ὡς καταγγέλλεται, μεθόδους ἀπροκαλύπτου προσηλυτισμοῦ, κατώρθωσαν νὰ παρασύρουν πολλοὺς ἀπλοϊκοὺς — ἰδίως

γυναῖκας — μέχρι τεῦ σημείου ὥστε ὁ ἀριθμὸς τῶν παραπλανηθέντων νὰ κυμαίνεται σήμερον μεταξὺ 90 ἕως 100. Οὗτοι προσέρχονται τακτικώτατα εἰς κεντρικωτάτην αἴθουσαν, χρησιμοποιουμένην ὡς ἐκκλησίαν ὅπου οἱ «Ἀπόστολοι» τῆς νέας θρησκείας διδάσκουν τὸν λόγον τοῦ Θεοῦ κατὰ τὸ δοκοῦν, ἰσχυριζόμενοι ὅτι ἔχουν τὸ προνόμιον νὰ ἐπικοινωνοῦν ἀπ' εὐθείας μὲ τὸν Ὕψιστον, διὰ τῆς ἐπιφοιτήσεως τοῦ Ἁγίου Πνεύματος, ὁμιλοῦντος πρὸς αὐτοὺς εἰς... δώδεκα γλώσσας!

Ἀνησυχητικὴ ἐξ ἄλλου εἶναι ἡ διάδοσις τῶν αἱρετικῶν αὐτῶν δοξασιῶν καὶ εἰς τὰ πλησιόχωρα χωρία καὶ , ὅπου δύο «Ἀπόστολοι» ἀναπτύσσουν ἐξαιρετικὴν δραστηριότητα, πρὸς μεγίστην ἀγανάκτησιν τῆς πλειονότητος τῶν κατοίκων, οἱ ὁποῖοι προβαίνουν καθημερινῶς εἰς ὁμαδικὰ ἢ κατὰ μόνας διαβήματα πρὸς τὴν ἐνταῦθα Ἱερὰν Ἐπισκοπήν.

Θ. ΑΜΟΥΤΖΟΠΟΥΛΟΣ

### THE HERESY OF THE PENTECOSTALS IN CHANIA

CHANIA, 18 September (By our correspondent) — I am informed by a reliable source that, following the dangerous spread of the heresy of the Pentecostals as much in the city as in the suburbs of Chania, the Very Reverend Bishop of Kydonia and Apokoronou Agathangelos Xyrouhakis forwarded to the General Administration of Crete and to related district attorney authorities a very extensive report requesting the strictest measure be taken toward curbing this evil.

The appearance of the Pentecostals in Chania was noticed after the liberation, without any perceptible commotion. Recently, however, the leaders of this heretical movement, utilizing as reported methods of unchallenged proselytism, have managed to tempt many naive ones—especially women—to the point that the number of those led astray today ranges between 90 and 100. These convene frequently in a very central hall, using it as a church where the "Apostles" of the new religion teach the word of God at will, alleging that they have the privilege to commune directly with the Most High through the enlightenment of the Holy Spirit, which speaks to them in...twelve languages!

Disturbing also is the spreading of these heretical beliefs as well in the nearby villages of [Istos] and [Gyros], where two "Apostles" are developing extraordinary activity, effecting a great deal of indignation among the majority of the residents, who go daily collectively or individually to the local Holy Bishopric.

TH. AMOUTZOPOULOS

I almost paid no attention. I simply went about my business, setting aside the day for fasting and prayer and waiting upon the Lord for wisdom, strength, and direction.

Two things happened that day, however, that shed light on the situation. First, that morning a reporter confided in me that all reports and descriptions were sent to him by the bishop, and that he simply had to cooperate. Then Yannarakis' wife, whom I had seen but twice in four years, came running to the shop to tell me she had just seen the bishop and had grave concerns about what was going to happen to her husband, who had recently become a target of the bishop's ire.

"Oh, Mr. Zachariou—" Yannarakis' wife said, trying to catch her breath. "The bishop—he says that you have proselytized us and the village with lots of clothes from America and—and seventeen thousand dollars!"

"Seventeen—what? The bishop said that?"

"Yes, Mr. Zachariou, and—"

"He's been totally misinformed! Who gave him such ideas, do you know?"

"I don't know, Mr. Zachariou. He's come up with all kinds of weird ideas, and blames my husband for everything—and he's going to take him and you to court!"

"And where is your husband right now? What does he have to say about the bishop's claims?"

"He's in Athens, Mr. Zachariou, and he's going to be shocked when he gets back. It's all so scary!"

"In Athens? When did he leave?"

"He's been there for ten days now, and has no idea what the bishop has in mind!"

Instantly, the whole scenario became clear to me. Yannarakis' two cousins, both Orthodox priests, had unintentionally provoked the bishop through their style of preaching and teaching, which resembled that of the Evangelicals. Too liberal for the bishop, the two brothers had uncompromisingly enlightened their parishioners with the truth of the gospel, openly declaring that salvation from the death penalty of sin comes through true repentance and forgiveness, rather than through church tradition and rituals or man-made things. The pair, with whom I had been seen by the bishop, had often half-jokingly told me that the bishop would think that I had proselytized them. Two months ago they moved to Athens in self-exile to avoid the threats and ire of the bishop. By going to Athens now, Yannarakis, previously the bishop's favorite preacher and theologian, must have stirred the bishop's suspicions that he, too, was going to desert him so he could seek freedom away from Chania—another slap in the bishop's face. Somehow, the bishop had to stop him. But how?

It must have occurred to the bishop that his beloved theologian had been influenced by the heretic Panos Zachariou, as evidenced by the fact that Yannarakis, along with his follower Baletakis, had conducted Pentecostal-style services among the villagers in Gyros and Istos where, as the two theologians claimed, the "Church of Ephesus" had been rekindled and Pentecost revived. Valid or invalid, such claims had reached the bishop, but he had no reason to make trouble because his theologians operated under the umbrella of the local Orthodox churches.

But ever since the deluge of deceptive accounts by Dendrinos was unleashed upon the entire religious community of Greece, the word "Pentecost," in the eyes of uninformed and ignorant citizens, had carried a stigma—to the bishop, an anathema. This was the word broadly displayed on our church sign in Syndrivani Square, and a word now used by Orthodox theologians in nearby villages. What a timely opportunity for the bishop to persecute those under the banner of Pentecost—namely, Panos Zachariou and the De Julios—and at the same time get back at Yannarakis.

What the bishop needed now was an element that could link Zachariou and Yannarakis and at the same time implicate the American couple: proselytism. Proselytism with American dollars. A handy concept, and potent enough to cause turbulence in the legal system. Who could deny that poor, naive people could be lured against their will to become "followers" of a heresy when coaxed with clothing and big money? Yes, American dollars. Why, everybody knows that Panos Zachariou has connections with Americans....

The timing was perfect for the bishop. Aware that the De Julios had been in Greece for one year and needed to have their visa renewed, he pressured the authorities in Chania to deny them an extension on grounds of proselytism. Fortunately, the De Julios were able to get an extension through the American Embassy and the Office of Foreign Affairs in Athens, but that did not prevent the bishop from taking further action.

VISIBLE in the distance, the round gray tower of the bishopric loomed uninvitingly as I headed for my afternoon appointment with the bishop the following Monday.

As I went up the steps to the tower entrance, I felt alone. Who was I to meet with the authorities? I was only an ordinary citizen—one despised by many.

I rang the bell. I remembered the bishops of the provinces of Rethymnon and Irakleion who had been supportive a few years back when I requested permission to distribute tracts in their area. Was God's intent to perform a miracle again this time?

As I rang the bell a second time, I sensed boldness in my spirit—it was the power of Pentecost. It was what Jesus had promised to His disciples when He told them to wait in Jerusalem for the Holy Spirit. It was not tongues He had promised, it was power—the power that comes from the Holy Spirit that indwells this human temple.

An attendant opened the door and led me to the bishop, who was seated behind his desk.

"Good afternoon, Reverend," I said.

"Come," the bishop said coldly as he got up. He went into another office, and I followed him. He walked behind another desk, stood by a chair, and turned toward me, his eyes averted. "If, Mr. Zachariou, you start your stories and accounts, I will not hear you. But if you have come repentant and willing to enter into the arms of the Orthodox Church, then I will offer you a strong handshake."

His words reminded me of Xanthoudakis, who had been a chanter in an Orthodox church for thirty years before joining the Evangelicals and who had now become the bishop's informant.

"I came to inform you that I have no connections whatso-ever with Yannarakis and Baletakis—"

"I am not hearing you! I am not hearing you!" the bishop shouted.

"But Reverend—how can I come into the bosom of the Orthodox Church if you do not allow me to share my pain so you might comfort me and admonish me? Remember before the war? Instead of asking me why I had chosen to go with the Evangelicals, you threw me in jail!"

My logical attempt to get him to hear me intrigued him. Staring at me, he waited.

"Tell me, Reverend, is it true or not that you told Mrs. Yannarakis that I received seventeen thousand dollars, which I shared with the villagers of Gyros?"

My words were like the seconds counted after pulling the pin of a hand grenade.

"I'm not telling you—I don't know—I will not respond!" the bishop roared, motioning with his hands for me to leave.

"Very well, Reverend," I said, with my voice raised so he could not but hear me. "I will find out. The truth will speak!" I said, and headed for the door.

That afternoon I went to see the district attorney.

"I am an ordinary man, and the burden of a problem this size is too heavy to bear, sir," I said to the district attorney after briefing him on my encounter with the bishop.

"Sue him for libel," he said curtly.

"The bishop?" I exlaimed. "We wish to cooperate with those in authority rather than create enmity."

"Well then, why don't you go after those whose name is behind whatever was publicized. Then the bishop's turn will come."

The secretary general happened by, and the district attor-ney invited him in. After I repeated the story of my encounter with the bishop, the secretary general said, "What would you like us to do about it?"

"First, we would like for those in authority like you, gentle-men, to know that our mission is to point men and women to God. In so doing, we never tell anyone to leave the Orthodox

Church, for it is not religion that brings us to God, but the Spirit of God. And second, should we be brought to trial, we would beg of those in authority, whose sole purpose is to bring justice according to law, to examine every fact in full detail before reaching a verdict; else we are liable to be judged unfairly."

As I stood up to leave, I told the two officials that I would be praying for them.

The secretary general followed me out in the hall. "Be praying for me," he whispered. "I am suffering from headaches. Pray for my healing."

Oh, what marvelous evidence of our Christian testimony in the city of Chania! Oh, that God would continue to use us to touch those in leadership like this man, was my prayer.

Soon the truth began to surface. Upon returning from Athens, Yannarakis made a public declaration.

### HE IS NOT "PENTECOSTAL"
[Acropolis, 22 September, 1953]

Mr. Director,

In No. 8102 of your distinguished paper I am referred to as one of the leaders of the so-called church (?) of the Pentecostals. I request that you would do me a favor by announcing, to the effect of lifting the above accusations, that I have not had, nor am I having, any relations with this heretic gathering, whose beliefs I do condemn and have always condemned, living as a genuine child of the Orthodox Church of Christ, attending the church in our village frequently, and even chanting and partaking of the Mysteries with all my family, a thing which is known to all.

With honor and gratitude
S. YANNARAKIS

ΕΠΙΣΤΟΛΑΙ ΠΡΟΣ ΤΗΝ «ΑΚΡΟΠΟΛΙΝ»

### ΔΕΝ ΕΙΝΕ «ΠΕΝΤΗΚΟΣΤΙΑΝΟΣ»

Κύριε Διευθυντά,

Εἰς τὸ ὑπ' ἀριθ. 8102 φύλλον τῆς ὑμετέρας ἐγκρίτου ἐφημερίδος φέρομαι ὡς εἰς τῶν ἀρχηγῶν τῆς ἐν Χανίοις λεγομένης ἐκκλησίας(;) τῶν Πεντηκοστιανῶν. Παρακαλῶ ἐάν ἔχητε τὴν καλωσύνην δημοσιεύσατε, πρὸς ἀναίρεσιν τῶν ἀνωτέρω κατηγοριῶν, ὅτι οὐδεμίαν σχέσιν εἶχα ἤ ἔχω μὲ τὴν αἱρετικὴν ταύτην παρασυναγωγήν, τῆς ὁποίας τὰς δοξασίας καταδικάζω καὶ ἀείποτε κατεδίκαζον, ζῶν ὡς τέκνον γνήσιον τῆς Ὀρθοδόξου τοῦ Χριστοῦ Ἐκκλησίας, ἐκκλησιαζόμενος τακτικῶς ἐν τῇ Ἐκκλησία τοῦ χωρίου μου, ψάλλων μάλιστα καὶ μετέχων τῶν Μυστηρίων μετὰ πάσης τῆς οἰκογενείας μου, ὡς τοῦτο εἶνε τοῖς πᾶσι γνωστόν.

Μετὰ τιμῆς καὶ εὐχαριστιῶν
Σ. ΓΙΑΝΝΑΚΗΣ

Although it was not Yannarakis' intent, his public declaration greatly restored our credibility in the public eye, and also gave us leverage. Editors who until recently had refused to offer us even a corner of space in their papers now feared that perhaps we might file a libel suit against the bishop that would implicate them, so they were extremely cooperative in allowing us to publish our views. When I submitted a letter to the editor of *Acropolis*, correspondent Patronas, alluding to the lies he had written about us, said, "Well, Mr. Zachariou, you see, we didn't do you a whole lot of disservice. After all, we advertised you!" As if we needed to increase our sales and net higher business profits! I looked at the man with pity, thinking that if sin could make the best of Christians look filthy in God's eyes, how much more so a godless and hopeless sinner!

My letter was published in its entirety, as I submitted it to the editor:

## ΟΙ ΠΕΝΤΗΚΟΣΤΙΑΝΟΙ ΧΑΝΙΩΝ

### ΜΙΑ ΕΠΙΣΤΟΛΗ ΤΟΥ κ. Π. ΖΑΧΑΡΙΟΥ

Κύριε Διευθυντά,

Κατόπιν τοῦ δημοσιεύματος τῆς 18ης τρέχοντος, εἰς ὃ φέρομαι ἀρχηγὸς τῶν Πεντηκοστιανῶν ,δηλὰ ὅτι ἀρχηγὸς εἶνε ὁ Ἰησοῦς Χριστὸς καὶ οὐδεμίαν συνεργασίαν ἔχω μετὰ τῶν κ.κ. Γιαν<sup></sup> ἀκη καὶ Βαλ<sup></sup> ἀκη διότι ἡ διαφορά τῶν θρησκευτικῶν ἀπόψεών μας εἶνε, ὅση τοῦ Ὀρθοδόξου ἀπὸ τὸν Διαμαρτυρόμενον.

Ἀποροῦ δὲ, πῶς, ἐνῶ Ἔξωσα γραπτῶς καὶ σαφῆ ἀπαντήσῖν ἐξ τὸ ἐρωτηματολόγιόν εἰς τὸν ἀνταποκριτήν σας, ὅστις μᾶλλον ἐπήνεσε καὶ ἑδράδευσε τὰς ἀπόψεις μου, ἐν τούτοις, τὸ σχόλιόν του ἦτο διάφορον.

Περὶ τῆς συμπεριφορᾶς αὐτῆς οὐδὲν ζητοῦμεν, διότι γνωρίζομεν ὅτι θὰ εἴμεθα οἱ ἐμπαίζόμενοι, οἱ μισούμενοι καὶ οἱ διωκόμενοι ὑπὸ πάντων, διότι ἀγαπήσαμεν Ἐκεῖνον, ὅστις μᾶς ἠγάπησε μέχρι Σταυροῦ. Ἀνάλογα δὲ μὲ τὴν μεταχείρισίν τοῦ ὑποκείμεθα, ζυγίζομεν καὶ τὴν δόξαν τοῦ Πνεύματος τοῦ Ἁγίου, τὴν σκιάζουσαν ἡμᾶς.

Σᾶς βεβαιῶ, ὅτι χαίρομεν διὰ τοὺς διωγμοὺς αὐτοὺς καὶ οὐδὲν μῖσος εἰς οὐδένα ἔχομεν εἰς τὰς καρδίας μας, προσευχόμεθα ὑπὲρ αὐτῶν.

Ἰδιαιτέρως χαίρομεν διὰ τὴν δήλωσιν τοῦ κ Γιανν<sup></sup> ἀκη εἰς τὸ φύλλον τῆς 22ας, ὅτι εἶνε ὀρθοδόξου δόγματος, καὶ ἐπικρίνει μάλιστα ὡς αἱρετίζοντας ἡμᾶς, ἀλλὰ δι' ἡμᾶς, λέγω, μέγα τρόπαιον καὶ σπου-

δαιοτάτη μαρτυρία, κατ' ἐναντίον ἐκείνων, ποὺ ζητοῦν νὰ παρασήσουν ὡς ξένην προπαγάνδαν καινούργιας θρησκείας, ἐνῶ πρόκειται περὶ τῆς, πείρας, τῆς Πεντηκοστῆς, ἥτις δὲν ἔπαυσε νὰ ὑπάρχη ἀνεπίσημα ἀπὸ τῶν αἰώνων ἐκείνων, καὶ ποὺ ἐσχάτως ἤρχισε νὰ ἐκδηλοῦται τὸ γεγραμμένον ἐπισημότερα μὲ δογματικὴν ἐμφάνισιν.

Εἶνε αὐτὰ ποὺ παραλαμβάνει ὁ Ἀπόστολος Πέτρας ὑπὸ τὸν προψήτην Ἰωὴλ β΄ καὶ τὸ ἀναφέρει εἰς πραξ β΄ 39: Θέλετε λάβει τὴν δωρεὰν τοῦ Ἁγίου Πνεύματος, διότι πρὸς ἐσᾶς εἶνε ἡ ἐπαγγελία καὶ πρὸς τὰ τέκνα σας καὶ πρὸς πάντας τοὺς εἰς μακρὰν, ὅσους ἂν προσκαλέσῃ Κύριος.

Πρόκειται περὶ ξενιμιστῆς πείρας ἀπὸ τὴν σωτηρίαν, διὰ τὸν σκοπὸν νὰ διασώση τὴς σωτηρίαν μας, διότι μεγάλη πίεσις θὰ ἐξασκηθῆ ἐπὶ τῆς χριστιανικῆς πίστεως, ἀπὸ τὸν "Ἀντίχριστον—καὶ ἡ ἐκδήλωσις αὐτὴ φανεροῦται διὰ τῶν γλωσσῶν.

Διότι λέγει ὁ Λόγος (Α΄ Κορινθ. ιδ΄ 2):
'Ὁ λαλῶν γλώσσαν ἀγνώριστον δὲν λαλεῖ πρὸς ἀνθρώπους, ἀλλὰ πρὸς τὸν Θεὸν διότι οὐδεὶς ἀκούει αὐτόν, ἀλλὰ μὲ τὸ πνεῦμα αὐτοῦ λαλεῖ μυστήρια.

λος κοινωνὸν τῆς ἐν Χανίοις Εὐαγ. Ἐκκλησίας δίδων ὁ Θεὸς τὴν ἴσην δωρεὰν πρὸς πάντας τοὺς αὐπιστοῦντας κατὰ τὸ γεγραμμένον, ἃς προσέξουν οἱ διώκται ἡμῶν καὶ οἱ κακολογοῦντες τὴν ἀλήθειαν, μήποτε εὑρεθοῦν θεομάχοι. Διότι ἐὰν μὲν εἶνε Ἐργον ἀνθρώπου, θέλει ματαιωθῆ. Πᾶσα θλασφημία κατὰ τοῦ Πατρὸς καὶ Υἱοῦ θέλει συγχωρεθῆ, ἀλλὰ ἡ κατὰ τοῦ Πνεύματος θὲν θέλει θι...

Δὲν ἀλλάξαμεν ἀρχηγὸν (τὸν Ἰησοῦν μας), ἀλλὰ ἀλλάξαμεν ὅπλον καὶ ὑπηρεσίαν καὶ μετετέθημεν ἀπὸ τὸ Πεζικὸν εἰς τὴν Ἀεροπορίαν, μὲ τὸ τρομερὸν ὅπλον καὶ τὸν στρατιωτικὸν θάνατον τοῦ Ἰησοῦ σώζει ἀμέσως, ὡς τὸν λησστὴν τοῦ Γολγοθᾶ, πάντα τὸν εὐπιστοῦντα, δι' αὐτὸ ἔχομεν ὄχι ἁπλῶς ἀριθμὸ ἀφελῶν καὶ εὐπίστων, ἀλλὰ ὄντας μετανοημένων πιστῶν τοῦ Εὐαγγελίου.

Εὐχαριστῶ διὰ τὴν φιλοξενίαν
Π. ΖΑΧΑΡΙΟΥ

### THE PENTECOSTALS OF CHANIA
### A LETTER BY MR. PANOS ZACHARIOU
(Acropolis, 25 September, 1953)

Mr. Director,

In regard to the publication of the 18th of this month, in which I am referred to as the leader of the Pentecostals, I declare that the leader is Jesus Christ, and I am not in collaboration with Mr. Yannarakis or Mr. Baletakis, since our dogmatic differences are as those between an Orthodox and a Protestant.

But I wonder why, after we gave written and succinct responses to your correspondent, and who also commended us for our views, his comments were different.

We are not going to press the issue about his kind of behavior, for we know we will be ridiculed, hated, and persecuted by all, because we have come to love Him who loved us till the Cross....

We assure you that we rejoice in these persecutions and have hatred toward none, rather we are praying for them.

We are particularly glad about Mr. Yannarakis' declaration in the issue of the 22nd, in which he states that he is an Orthodox believer and criticizes our being heretical....

The experience of Pentecost is what the Apostle Peter is talking about in Acts 2:39, where he refers to prophet Joel Ch. 2....

It is about an experience distinct from and for the preservation of salvation...and whose expression is manifested through tongues (1 Cor. 14:2): "He who speaks in an unknown tongue speaks not to men, but to God, for no one understands him, but in the spirit he speaks mysteries." If, therefore, the Holy Spirit falls upon Orthodox people such as Yannarakis and Baletakis, as it happened to me, formerly an Evangelical, let our persecutors and the slanderers of the truth beware lest they be found enemies of God....

We did not change our leader (our Jesus), rather we changed weapon and service, as we were transferred from the Infantry to the Air Force, having the formidable weapon of the atomic bomb of Pentecost.

We consider proselytizing an abomination, which is an illicit act according to law. To us it is abhorrent, because we hold the Gospel of Christ, persuading through the Word that Jesus' death on the Cross saves instantly him who believes, as it saved the malefactor on Golgotha. For this reason we have, not just naive and gullible persons, but rather persons who are truly repentant and faithful to the Gospel.

Thank you for the courtesy,

P. ZACHARIOU

TOWARD the latter part of September 1953, I went to Athens to participate at the Unification of the Pentecostal Churches of Greece Conference. The conference was a most refreshing spiritual bath for me.

After the conference, Diktos and I visited some churches in northern Greece where, according to Diktos, a couple of surprises awaited me. One surprise turned out to be the work among Orthodox parishioners in Thessaloniki by an Orthodox preacher, Gregorios Zacharopoulos, who ministered through the gifts of the Spirit. Part of Zacharopoulos' ministry also was the translation of Protestant tracts. Officially appointed by government and church officials to authorize the dissemination of such tracts and literature, this man of God furnished me with thousands of tracts and pieces of literature bearing the approval by the Orthodox Church.

A similar surprise was the work among Orthodox parishioners in Thessaloniki by a God-fearing woman, Nitsa Bousaki. I was blessed to see that the believers in this group worshiped God in a truly Pentecostal way. How I wished the same blessings for the city of Chania!

WHILE I was in Athens, the De Julios sent me a telegram to tell me that government officials in Chania were asking them to leave immediately. I ran to the Office of Foreign Affairs, where officials telephoned Chania in my presence to assure me that the officials in Chania had been given explicit orders not to override their approval. Despite all assurances, however, I feared that someone would take advantage of my absence and oust the De Julios, so I sailed back to Chania.

Alas, I arrived too late. The De Julios, God's gift to the work in Chania, had been forced by the police to leave without delay and in a most humiliating manner. In vain did my son Demetrios (Jimmy) try to track them down in Athens. They were gone.

My heart was breaking as I ascended the steps to the place where only hours earlier my beloved fellow-workers had been. On the floor lay Evangelia's white accordion, a silent reminder that the De Julios had been snatched away.

Streams of tears began to flow from my soul. I fell on my knees. "God, Your will be done! Your will be done! But now the church is like orphan nestlings, left deserted. I beg You to strengthen me so I can feed them, for I feel so alone!"

"Your battle, brother, now begins," wrote my beloved De Julios to me as they departed from Greece.

# 17

# In Paul's Steps

THE JANUARY SKIES WERE dark and dreary, and the streets leading to Syndrivani Square were crowded with people. It was Theophaneia (Epiphany), a day when all the city's religious leaders, clad in their sacerdotal splendor, were led in pompous procession by the Very Reverend Bishop Agathangelos.

The slow-paced procession reached Syndrivani Square. I looked through my window and saw an impressive retinue of emblem bearers and icon bearers, priests, deacons and chanters, all following their venerable leader.

Just then the bishop stopped. At once the procession, too, stopped. The bishop lifted his gray head, graced with a splendid crown, and looked straight up at our church. Pounding his staff twice on a cobblestone in the square, he summoned the chief of police standing nearby, and began to speak. What was he saying?

Immediately the Spirit of God fell heavily upon me, and I went down on my knees. God impressed upon me that the words I was uttering through the release of God's Spirit were a rebuke to the powers of darkness and an intercessory prayer for the souls of the spiritually blind. Tears streaming down my face, I pleaded with God that in His mercy He would open the eyes of those who would now persecute the cause of our faith in total ignorance.

TWO weeks later our church sign was vandalized. Although the newspapers characterized the incident as "sacrilege," we were met with refusal by every technician we approached about making us a new sign. It was no surprise to me when Christos informed me that when the bishop stood in the middle of Syndrivani Square on Theophaneia and summoned the chief of police, he said to the chief, "How long are you going to leave that sign over there?"

During a religious procession in January of 1954, the bishop complained to the chief of police about our church sign. Two weeks later the sign was vandalized.

A larger, more attractive sign was eventually put up which displayed an additional feature, a cross. It was a deceptive sign, according to critics, because we did not believe in the Cross, but used it to proselytize the naive and innocent. The sign was enough to arouse once again the anger of the short-tempered Bishop Agathangelos during the Easter procession. Stranded in the middle of Syndrivani Square for about ten minutes, the procession waited for a flouncing bishop to decide whether to proceed as planned or use an alternate route.

ON FEBRUARY 22, 1954, I stood before the judges on grounds of proselytism. Along with me stood two codefendants: the Orthodox theologians Stavros Yannarakis and Evangelos

Baletakis, with neither of whom I had any ecclesiastical relations. Our prosecutor was the bishopric of Chania. Because no witnesses showed up, the trial was postponed. (The day before the trial, the bishop had ordered Papagiorgis to notify all witnesses not to show up in court, due to unsubstantiated evidence.) The bishopric was fined 5,000 drachmas; but even so, the court chose not to declare me innocent by default.

A week later I was subpoenaed for a May 14 trial. At first I took it to be the date of the postponed trial, but upon examining the subpoena more closely, I realized it was for a different trial. Two days later I was also notified that the postponed trial was rescheduled for May 28. In other words, I was summoned to appear in court for two different trials in the same month, both for the same reason—proselytism.

MAY 14. Standing before three judges, I was facing charges of proselytizing by giving clothing and money to people. The prosecution (the bishopric of Chania) produced four witnesses: a relative of Evangelia De Julio, Sahinian the Armenian, Papagiorgis, and Papantonis. Because it became obvious to the court from the very beginning that the witnesses were unable to substantiate any claims, it decided instead to establish an understanding of what elements within the doctrine of the Pentecostals might be punishable by law.

Addressing Papantonis, Judge Galanos asked, "Is it possible for one to speak in tongues beyond the Apostolic times?"

"Yes, your honor, it is possible as long as one exercises faith in the written Word," the priest readily replied, to my utter surprise—though I understood that his statement was made in the interest of the codefenfants' reputation and their spiritual claims. I could hear some of the believers behind me whispering praises.

"Well, then, we can also say that the defendant received by faith, which is in accordance with the law."

Papantonis turned my way and said, "This impostor? He's able to pretend anything. One time he's Orthodox, then evangelist, and other times a Jehovah Witness, because in my parish there was a man whom he told not to pick up arms."

"Why, Mr. Zachariou, did you leave the Evangelical church?" said Rekkas, the presiding judge.

"I left, your honor, for reasons clearly doctrinal. I love my Evangelical brethren and I have a good relationship with them, but they simply do not espouse identical views with the Pentecostals in the area of the gifts of the Spirit, particularly tongues, saying that the gifts were operative in the Apostolic days only. There is no other doctrinal difference between us."

The judge nodded and seemed to want me to go on, so I summarily presented my testimony from the time I accepted God into my life in 1938 until my experience with the gift of tongues in 1948—within me raising praises to God all the while for the opportunity to share my testimony in court!

"Well, you've got something, you believe something. Is it necessary for you to keep telling others?" said the judge.

"But that's exactly what the Christian faith is all about, your honor," I said excitedly. "It is the law of God and the commandment of Christ."

"When again did you speak in tongues after 1948?" inquired the third judge.

"Nearly each time I pray."

I could hear people whispering, "Each time? Oh!"

At that point the judges exchanged a word with each other, and I could tell they were seeking ways to tie my oral testimony to the legal definition of proselytism, which deals with exploiting a person's ignorance and naiveté by entering his conscience, as in the case of speaking in mysterious tongues and thereby imbuing the hearer's mind with fear and awe, which could be construed as spiritual coercion.

"It may be, your honor, that this court is under the impression that we utilize tongues as a means of attracting converts. On the contrary, tongues are used not during the preaching of the Word, but during prayer among the body of believers. The Apostle Paul in 1 Corinthians 14:23 stresses order among the Christian believers by saying that if everyone in church speaks in tongues at the same time, an unbeliever would think they are all mad. Therefore, if we were to speak in tongues to impress others, they would flee from us thinking we were crazy."

The judge nodded.

"—And I couldn't agree any more with the Reverend, your honor, as when he pointed out that it is possible for one to receive the Holy Spirit if he exercises faith in the Word," I said.

I could hear believers praising God in the background.

One of the judges held out a New Testament. "There's a message written on the cover of this New Testament which is propaganda. It reads, 'Whoever benefits from this must pass it on to someone else.' Is this a practice you follow?"

"We have distributed these New Testaments by the thousands. Aren't we all supposed to do so?"

There was dead silence. Judge Rekkas was nodding his head.

The rest of the witnesses were asked to testify, but all they could say was that they had heard this or they had seen that—all hearsay and lies. When Papagiorgis spoke, all he had to say was that one day he saw a woman coming out of our church after the service holding a bag in her hands!

That afternoon the court read the verdict: "Not guilty."

The church praised God and rejoiced!

THE day before the May 28 trial was my Gethsemane. I found myself in extreme agony—it was even hard to pray. My fears and doubts were getting in my way. I kept thinking that at the trial I would stand alone.

Trying to be optimistic, I thought, Justice will prevail. Haven't they already found me innocent? Why not again tomorrow? All the accusations are lies and nonsense, and the judges know it.

As I lay in bed that night, I sensed God's Spirit tugging me out of bed for prayer. He wanted to detach me from dependence on human justice, and in His mercy enable me to deal with my confusion and fears by allowing me to understand His perspective. Obediently, I got up and knelt to pray a prayer of surrender.

Instantly, I knew what the verdict was going to be the next day; but I felt no fear now. The burden of my resistance had fallen off my shoulders, and God had given me strength. "Let

Your will be done, Father, not mine," I prayed. "Don't let me be content serving You only outside of prison, for it is also the prisoners without hope who need to hear Your words of comfort. But I am afraid. I feel alone. Help me to see You standing by my side tomorrow. It's going to be very dark, so stand by me!"

Still on my knees, I tore up all the notes about what I was going to say in court and instead sang my plea to my heavenly Father, using the words we often sang at our group meetings:

*Oh, my Lord God, my Savior*
*In this world only You and Your face*
*I always desire to behold*

*Oh, my Lord, when I walk this road with You*
*Don't let me go far from your side*
*For I will wander*

Chorus
*Don't let me wander far from Your side*
*Don't let me go away*
*For I am afraid in the dark*

*Oh, My Lord, if You will*
*That I should suffer for You*
*Help me in my pain always to praise You!*

MAY 28. The same court and the same accusers, but this time more witnesses and more priests. The prosecution had nineteen witnesses—four priests and fifteen laymen. The two co-defendants, Yannarakis and Baletakis, were but an extension of that list.

Presiding Judge Tsilingeridis took an aggressive approach from the very beginning of the proceedings. As the witnesses came forward, he would ask them questions, then direct their responses so as to limit them to a simple yes or no.

Two witnesses testified that they had come to our services and that at the end of a service Panos Zachariou gave them one coat each. One after another, the false witnesses stepped forward hesitantly and timidly, burdened with guilt, but relieved in the end because the judges did most of the speaking for them, so they did not have to repeat the bogus allegations and lies recorded in their depositions. None dared to look straight at me, for they could not tolerate the convicting power of the One standing by my side.

Tsilingeridis referred to a letter I had written Yannarakis in 1951, which the priests had used in their deposition to show that I had tried to proselytize him.

"What did he write you in the letter he sent you?" the presiding judge asked.

"He wrote me that icons are pieces of wood," Yannarakis said.

I couldn't believe my ears! I jumped to my feet to tell the judges that I could have a carbon copy of my letter brought to them within an hour to show that Yannarakis' allegations were not true, but I wasn't given a chance to speak.

Ironically, at that moment defense attorney Fronimos, who was sitting next to me, leaned over and said, "If they convict you today, it's because of what this man has just said," pointing to Yannarakis, who overheard him. Upon explaining to the attorney about my carbon copy of the letter, he stood up to speak. The presiding judge told him to stop. When the attorney made a second attempt, the judges reprimanded him. At that point I told Fronimos to forget about the carbon copy since the court was obviously determined to incriminate me.

Yannarakis, his head hanging low, looked sad. (As he explained to me a few months later, he had promised the priests to say those words in court only if they promised in turn to make no allusions to tongues in court. But when I asked him why he had so capriciously accused me of writing him that the icons were pieces of wood—I had a copy of the letter, I told him, and no such thing was mentioned in it—he replied, "I said that on purpose—because I knew you would agree and because the Church Pilot says it." I was flabbergasted by his reasoning!)

In his testimony, Papantonis contended that one witness had been persuaded through a letter from his Pentecostal uncle in California not to waste his life locked up in a monastery.

The priest then turned around and asked the witness to verify what he had just told the court. Grylos, the witness, apparently fed up with all the false accusations and rigmarole going on in court, suddenly got up, jabbed his finger at Papantonis, and yelled, "You came to my house, didn't you? And you said to me, 'Come on, let's get this Mason all wrapped up!' Well? What do you want now? Here—take the man and crucify him!"

The whole court burst out laughing, except Sgrekas, one of the three judges.

It was now the turn of the defense witnesses, the so-called naive ones, to step forward and testify.

One witness, Tsamantakis, told the court that he used to be a Communist, but as he watched my life since the days of the black market in the war, he became interested in attending our services and found that I lived what I preached.

Astropalitis, a new brother—a neoproselyte, according to court—testified that prior to joining our church he used to break dishes on his wife's head, and that no one had influenced him because he came on his own and decided it was good for all his family as well.

Resentful of being called naive, Joseph the mailman boldly stood before the judges and told them that his daughter had been healed and that he is fully aware of what he's doing when he attends our services.

Another brother, Basilaras, faced the judges and said that the first time he came to our church he was drunk, and that he used to be drunk more often than not. But after coming to our church, he stopped getting drunk because God turned his life around, and his whole family could attest to that.

Some women spoke, too, but mainly men, which showed the court that the "proselytes" were not "mainly naive women," but men with families and responsibilities, who were representative of the average citizen.

But the truth fell on deaf ears. When all the witnesses had spoken, Judge Sgrekas referred to the passage in the Gospel of John about the Greeks who came to see Jesus (12:20-28), emphasizing verse 3: "The hour has come for the Son of Man to be glorified." Then, for nearly an hour, starting with Socrates, the judge acclaimed and euphemized the Greek spirit of the Byzantine times and of the Greek Revolution of 1821 that ended the 400-year Turkish occupation of Greece, pointing out that if it had not been for the Greek clergy that preserved the Greek spirit, today we would all be talking to each other in Turkish.

"Behold," he said, "now come to us from foreign lands those whom the Greek spirit has enlightened, supposedly to give to us their lights, but whether they are called Evangelicals or Pentecostals, all of them are psychological scums and Satans, who infest the land for the sake of shameful material gain."

The trial went on for eight long hours, at which point the court reached a verdict: The two codefendants were acquitted. Panos Zachariou was pronounced guilty!

The police came and placed chains around my wrists, like a criminal, and took me away through the crowds waiting outside to see me. It was the church! Raising my chains high, I greeted my tearful brethren. "Hallelujah! May God keep you strong when it's your turn!" I said.

"Thank you! Thank you!" they resounded, just like in our meetings, when their sweet voices lifted words of praise unto the Lord!

As if Satan wanted to deal a final blow, before being taken to the detention area, I was served yet another subpoena. From depositions by the prosecutors, I discovered that this time the bishop was using Odysseas, a wife beater who had boldly told me that he was the devil himself, who coveted the bishop's favor for his precarious job assignment at the sanatorium.

A prayer of gratitude and praise welled up in my spirit as I marveled that the Lord had equipped me with the strength and endurance I needed to go through such battles. We often fail to recognize the degree of worth He places upon us, I thought to myself. There was a time when I believed I was worth nothing—zero—and saw no use in staying alive. Later I found it hard to imagine that I was worth so much that Christ would even offer Himself to save my soul from dying. Now I see myself as a zero of immeasurable worth, because I follow behind Number One whose name is Wonderful, Counselor, The Mighty God, The Everlasting Father, The Prince of Peace

(Isaiah 9:6). I was humbled that God had taken me one small step closer to the drama of Gethsemane.

My sentence was announced publicly the next day:

SENTENCED FOR PROSELYTIZING

The three-member Magistrate's Court of Chania sentenced our fellow citizen Panos Terp. Zachariou yesterday to 4 months in prison, a monetary penalty of 2,000 metallic drachmas, and 6 months police parole because while as pastor of the heresy of the Pentecostals he was actively engaged in the proselytization of Orthodox Christians to this heresy.

[Paratiritis of Chania - 29 May, 1954]

ΚΑΤΑΔΙΚΗ ΕΠΙ ΠΡΟΣΗΛΥΤΙΣΜΟ

Τὸ 3μελὲς Πλημμελειοδικεῖ ον Χανίων κατὰ τὴν χθεσιγὴν του δικάσιμον κατεδίκασε τὸν συμπολίτην μας Πᾶνον. Τερπ. Ζαχαρίου εἰς φυλάκισιν 4 μηνῶν, χρηματικὴν ποινὴν 2.000 μεταλλικῶν δραχμῶν καὶ 6 μηνῶν ἀστυνομικὴν ἐπι τήρησιν, διότι ὡς προέκυψεν ὡς ποιμὴν τῆς αἱρέσεως τῶν Πεντηκοστιανῶν ἐνήργει προ σηλυτισμόν τῶν ὀρθοδόξων χριστιανῶν εἰς τὴν αἵρεσιν ταύτην.

"HELLO, everyone!" I said to the prisoners, as we met out in the open the first morning. "See? They brought me here to tell you that heaven's porter is a murderer," I said. The half-dozen prisoners nearby laughed, but two young men standing farther away asked me to repeat myself.

"I assure you that the doorman of paradise is a murderer. That's the malefactor who repented on his cross!"

I noticed a glow in the eyes of Philip, one of the two young men. Only twenty-one, he was in for life for murdering his father-in-law.

As the curious prisoners gathered to hear words of comfort and hope, the guards told us to stay away from each other.

Philip did not want me to stop talking to him at night. His bed and mine were joined at one end, so I would reach for his head and rub it with my hands and tell him that God loved him to death. "Be glad, my son," I kept telling him, "because you are no longer a prisoner!"

Stelios, another prisoner, had been in for six years and had a couple more years to go. He kept following me, watching me, listening to me singing, and saying nothing. One day he found me sitting on my bed eating grapes. He leaned against the wall, folded his arms and said, "You never look depressed, so it's because you're either genuine or you're a great actor."

Other prisoners would walk by me out in the yard and say, "God's grace can cover me, too, right?" Or, "Are you sure God can forgive me?"

"Yes!" I would reply.

At the end of the second week of my imprisonment, I was isolated from the rest of the prisoners so I would not be able to talk to them anymore. As I was being whisked away, I saw Philip standing next to Stelios. The youngster raised the Bible I had given him and held it open to show me he had already underlined many verses.

To my surprise, I was released the day after my isolation. My mission of sowing the seed of the Word in prison had been accomplished. What I had left with my friends there, especially Philip, was the meaning of grace. God's grace. It is a word every prisoner understands, because it is what each of them constantly dreams about and hopes for.

I WAS deeply moved by the love shown by brethren throughout Greece and in America who contributed toward my temporary release from prison. It was not the imaginary thousands of dollars I was accused in court of giving away, but the love of God in the hearts of poor laborers and breadwinners that bought out my release. And this is how the body of Christ—the Church—operates. Those in need exercise faith, not by going around advertising their needs and begging for help, but by presenting their earnest petitions before God, who through His Spirit guides people's hearts to respond. That's when the Spirit of God moves among the saints, making needs known through discernment and prompting them to pray for one another—not randomly, but by targeting needs effectively and according to God's will.

After my release, I was fed like Elijah. I asked my wife, who had just informed me that there was no food in the house, to prepare the table for the evening meal, for we were all going to sit down as a family and give God thanks, anyway. Chrysa had no sooner finished setting the table when someone knocked on our door—it was a delivery boy, bringing us a huge bag full of groceries and an envelope with money in it!

The next day I went back to my shop for the first time in two weeks. Thaleia's sister was there, waiting.

"This is for you," she said, handing me an envelope. "It's just a small loan."

"A loan?" I said. "And who told you I needed a loan?"

"God did," she said with a smile, while I thanked Him for His provision.

God knew my daily needs. Through them He blessed me by teaching me diligence in prayer and dependence upon Him.

ON AUGUST 26, my case was appealed. But the court, not persuaded that the testimony of the witnesses was not a cover-up aimed at protecting their leader, burdened me with additional punitive charges. At the end of the trial, public defendant Fronimos, exasperated by the injustice of our courts, recommended that I appeal my case to the Supreme Court (Areios Pagos) in Athens, and offered to make the arrangements for me immediately.

Meanwhile, I examined the court records of my appeal and found that Yannarakis and Baletakis had been acquitted because of their ". . . foolishness, not having the senses developed enough to discern their punishable acts." How incredible, I thought to myself. The court attributed their innocence to their stupidity and acquitted them, yet ascribed my guilt to the smartness with which I duped them!

Furthermore, according to court records the two theologians ". . . invited Orthodox believers, isolated them, and told them that the Holy Spirit, which enlightened them by descending upon their head as in the days of the disciples of Christ during Pentecost, gave them the power and the right to forgive their sins through the sacrament of confession, at which point they would utter incomprehensible sounds which they claimed to be foreign tongues. . . ." (Court of Appeals, 26 August, 1954.)

What a classic example of the type of questionable encounters that stigmatize the genuine experience of Pentecost, I thought to myself. Now I understand better why Yannarakis had begged the priests not to talk about tongues in court—he would have been too vulnerable. As for my "crime" of proselytizing the two theologians and through them proselytizing the villagers, the very reference to the "sacrament of confession" alone should have sufficed to nullify my indictment, since the sacrament and proselytism are mutually exclusive. But pressure from the bishop had squeezed justice out of our courts.

THE court records were the handwriting on the wall. I was not surprised when I received a call from the police on October 21, 1954, to show up immediately with the church license in my hands. When I did, the chief of police read me a directive from the Department of Education and Religions:

Through the Command of the Police of Chania:

The license of Panos Zachariou to pastor the Pentecostals in Chania is hereby revoked.
   Be it known to you that Ordinance No. 16776/ 27.2.52 granting you the license to pastor the Pentecostals who gather in Chania is revoked. . . and you are henceforth enjoined from pastoring these even at any other place inasmuch as your personal file is filled with court actions against you for a series of violations of the law. Individuals burdened with unlawful acts, even as you, cannot be used in leading nor can be commissioned to the guidance and right direction of Christian groups.

In vain did I try to persuade the chief that the directive was aimed only at my pastoral responsibilities, not the closure of the church itself. The chief even went a step further: he demanded that the church sign be taken down before midnight that very day.

At a meeting that night, the church board agreed that the matter should be taken to the Supreme Court and voted for a petition to have the church license reissued under the name of another member. Meanwhile, my letter of protest appeared in the newspaper the next day.

And so we returned to our "catacomb" days. Ironically, most of our meetings were held a very short distance from the police station.

# THE PENTECOSTALS
## [Paratiritis of Chania]

Concerning the decision by the Department [of Education and Religions] whereby my license to pastor the Pentecostal Church in Chania was revoked because my personal file is filled with court actions against me, I do admit that it is true [that my parsonal file is filled with court actions against me]; besides, there are many other things which I did in my sinful past that did not come under the scrutiny of human justice.

[God] forbid that I should boast in nothing but my wretched past, for I did find mercy and I was forgiven by our Lord Jesus Christ, who granted all things to me, because He found my repentance to be genuine and true and I received perfect propitiation through His eternal and Holy blood.

Concurring with Paul, in this world I will be slandered, persecuted, cursed and treated like the scum and all filth of the world as until this day (1 Corinthians 4:13), but according to God, a new creature in Christ Jesus—behold the old things are past, all things are new.

After all, this is also my desire and my zeal, to see many of my old friends and fellow citizens enter through my ministry into the joy of salvation as new creatures.

But I do have a reasonable question to ask: I wonder, is it constitutional and just to shut down a house of worship simply because the Pastor was to blame? Or has there ever been a case where some Orthodox church was shut down because a priest was arrested for breaking the law?

Chania, October 22, 1954
PANOS ZACHARIOU

## ΟΙ ΠΕΝΤΗΚΟΣΤΙΑΝΟΙ

«'Επί τῆς ὑπουργικῆς ἀπο φάσεως δι' ἧς μοί ἀπηγορεύθη ἡ ποίμανσις τῆς ἐν Χανίοις 'Εκκλησίας τῆς Πεντηκοστῆς μὲ αἰτιολογίαν ὅτι ἔχω φάκελλον γέμοντα δικαστικῶν ἀποφάσεων, βεβαιῶ τοῦ το ὡς ἀληθές, ἄλλωστε καὶ πόσα ἄλλα ποὺ δὲν ὑπέπεσαν εἰς τὴν ἀντίληψιν τῆς ἀνθρωπίνης δικαιοσύνης εἶχα εἰς τὸ ἁμαρτωλόν μου παρέλθόν ;

Μὴ γένοιτο νὰ καυχηθῶ εἰς ἄλλο τι, παρὰ διὰ τὸ ἐλεεινόν μου παρελθόν, ἀλλὰ ἐλεήθην, καὶ συνεχωρήθην παρὰ τοῦ Κυρίου ἡμῶν 'Ιησοῦ Χριστοῦ, ὅστις μοί ἐχάρισεν τὰ πάντα, διότι μέ εὖρεν ἕν μετανοία ἀληθινὴν καὶ εἰλικρινῆ καὶ ἐγὼ εὖρων εἰς Αὐτὸν τὸ αἰώνιον Ἅγιον αἷμα Του ἐξιλεωθείς τελείως.

Διὰ τὸν κόσμον θὰ εἶμαι ὡς λέγει ὁ Παῦλος (Λοιδορού μενοι, διωκόμενοι, βλασφημούμενοι καὶ ὡς περικαθάρ ματα, σκύβαλον πάντων ἕως τῆς σήμερον Α Κορινθ. δ. 13) ἀλλὰ διὰ τὸν Θεὸν, Νέον κτῖ σμα ἐν Χριστῷ 'Ιησοῦ, τὰ παλαιὰ ἰδοὺ παρῆλθαν, τὰ πάντα ἔγιναν νέα.

Αὐτὴ ἄλλωστε εἶναι καὶ ἡ ἐπιθυμία μου, καὶ ὁ ζῆλος μου νὰ ἴδω διὰ τῆς διακονί ας μου τοὺς σαλαιοὺς φίλους καὶ συμπολίτας μου μέσα στὴν χαρὰν τῆς σωτηρίας ὡς νέα κτίσματα.

Ἔχω ὅμως μίαν εὔλογον ἀπορίαν. Εἶναι ἄραγε Συνταγματικὸν καὶ δίκαιον νὰ κλείσουν τὸν εὔκτήριον οἶκον ἐπειδὴ ἔπταισεν ὁ Ποιμήν ; Ἡ μήπως ἠκούσθη ποτὲ νὰ κλείση κάποια 'Ορθόδοξος 'Εκκλησία, ἐπειδὴ συνελήφθη ἕνας 'Ιερεύς παρανομῶν ;
Χανιά 22. 10. 1954
ΠΑΝΟΣ ΖΑΧΑΡΙΟΥ»

IN Athens I met Attorney Nikolaos Korfiatis, a man of great intelligence and full of energy. Korfiatis was held in high esteem by the courts for his expertise, talents, and published works. A devout Orthodox Christian, Attorney Korfiatis had a passion for justice.

Korfiatis and I first met with officials at the Department of Education and Religions, where he pointed out that there was no legal precedent for the closure of a religious meeting place on account of the acts of its leader. We were told immediately that the local authorities in Chania had erred in their interpretation of the directive, which did not pertain to the closure of our meeting place.

As the case was brought to the Supreme Court, I felt I was carrying a huge burden all alone. I sensed but token support from other ministries, perhaps due to the prevailing fear that an epidemic of similar persecutions throughout Greece was imminent. Some ministers, in fact, subscribed to the idea that my trials had already given rise to an outbreak of persecutions in many parts of Greece. A voice inside me kept saying, "It is for this I have called you."

At a November 13, 1954 Supreme Court session, Korfiatis challenged the justices, saying that proselytism was an anachronism and that it had been left on the legal backburner for lack of clear definition. That same day the Supreme Court dropped the charges of the August 16 decision of the appellate court in Chania for additional punitive charges.

Korfiatis next suggested that we take legal action for perjury against the prosecution witnesses in Chania, by way of restraining the prosecution's offensive disposition. I accepted the attorney's advice, thinking that the truth which linked perjury to bribery should surface, after which I could choose to drop the charges.

HIGH above the hustle and bustle of city life, the Parthenon on the Acropolis rose majestically over our heads in golden silence, as Attorney Korfiatis and I walked and talked about the absurdity of the law of proselytism and the lack of religious freedom in Greece.

"I can't believe it!" Korfiatis said. "Invading one's conscience—I just can't believe it!"

"Can you imagine, Mr. Korfiatis?" I said. "God Himself, one might say, could not penetrate the conscience of the Pharisees; yet I, with my fifth-grade education, was able to!"

Still absorbed in his thoughts, the attorney looked at me absent-mindedly and nodded. "Invading one's conscience!" he said again.

"Let it not surprise you, Mr. Korfiatis. Let it not surprise you if I dare say that the law is right about the invasion of one's conscience, for that is what proselytizing does."

Surprise rose in the attorney's face. "I don't read you, Panos," he said. "Can you explain?"

My eyes tracing the steps leading to the top of Mars Hill, I envisioned the Apostle Paul speaking to the Athenians about "The Unknown God." Turning to Attorney Korfiatis, I said, "Hebrews 4:12 says that the Word of God is sharper than any two-edged sword, piercing through until it divides the soul and the spirit, the joints and the marrows, and discerning the thoughts and the intents of the heart."

"Hmm," the attorney said, his keen mind quickly processing the meaning of the verse. "You are saying that it is God, not man, who invades the mind, correct?"

"Exactly! Only God through His Holy Spirit can 'proselytize' or convert. Man cannot."

The attorney smiled, relieved by the explanation. "That's a very intriguing thought," he said. "Very intriguing, indeed."

AS a parolee, my time in Athens was up. Soon I would be facing the same judges in Chania during yet another trial for that same unfounded reason—invading people's consciences.

丁丁丁丁

# 18

# Shining in the Dark

ODYSSEAS REPEATEDLY BEAT his little wife, Roula, in an attempt to persuade his three brothers-in-law to settle a perpetual dowry disagreement he had with them. The more they resisted him, the more he abused their sister. Afraid and frustrated, the three young men avoided facing their burly and cunning brother-in-law for fear he might do their sister even greater harm; but neither were they interested in giving a dowry to the man who had married their sister without the family's consent.

One day I went to visit the three brothers and their mother, Sofia. It so happened that Papagiorgis, who had some business connection with their father, was there also.

From that day on, things changed. Odysseas, who had been assigned to a managerial position at the sanatorium with the approval of the bishop, had a new excuse for victimizing Roula: she and their children had been proselytized, and so had Sofia. They all had better quit going to the Pentecostal church, he warned, or he would beat up Roula and his kids.

The gullible trio swallowed Odysseas' new excuse and started blaming me for their family feuds and their sister's misery. Papagiorgis, blindly subservient to his superior and sorely hateful of me, could now manipulate Odysseas and the three brothers and turn them against the proselytizer.

Until recently, I had had every reason to believe I had befriended Odysseas. Prior to the closure of our church, he had joined his wife and children at our services a few times, perhaps by way of showing me his appreciation for my counseling his wife against divorcing him. He had commended me for my faith. He had even invited me to his house for dinner. Now he was telling me that he was the devil himself.

Aroused by Papagiorgis, the brothers set aside their hatred toward Odysseas and made a compact with him to have me put behind bars for my attempts to proselytize them at their home and for proselytizing their mother and their sister. Crafty Odysseas had no problem persuading the naive brothers to sue me, assuring them he would support them in court as a witness.

As the day of the trial approached, the two godly women— mother and daughter—came to my shop teary-eyed to tell me that the least they could do was to pray for me and stand in court as my defense witnesses.

IT was Monday, January 24, 1955. The courtroom was packed, and the trial moved swiftly. After his introductory remarks, the presiding judge asked me to speak for myself—a clever method the judges used to try to get me to hang myself by my own words; for me, though, a grand opportunity to reiterate the message of Christ for the benefit of those who had ears to hear.

First, I gave a brief description of our doctrinal views, then explained that salvation from the death penalty of sin is available to every person by God's grace solely through our Lord Jesus Christ. As for me, I told the court, my hunger for spiritual truth and nourishment never seemed to be totally satisfied as long as there was more to be received, such as the gifts of the Spirit according to 1 Corinthians chapters 12 through 14. I said that many of our highly esteemed religious leaders, having no knowledge or interest in such things, wonder why we dare testify that these spiritual gifts can be received today, when faith is actively applied.

I also protested my relentless persecution by the bishopric of Chania under the pretext of proselytism through the distribution of clothing, gifts, and money, reminding the court that after an entire year of strife and endless court trials, my accusers had not been able to come up with one single piece of material evidence against me. Finally, I asked that the court consider my release as well as the protection due me under the law, because these successive lawsuits were degrading and had brought about my economic demise.

Everything seemed to be going well, until Roula was asked to testify.

"Have you received the Holy Spirit?" a judge asked.

Roula was having difficulty responding readily, thinking that the truth might be held against me.

There was silence.

"Yes—" I whispered to her from behind.

The judges became alerted.

Roula nodded. "Yes," she said.

That very instant was the turning point. The judges decided that Roula was a victim of my delusions and that I was guilty of proselytizing her.

The court summarily pronounced me guilty and sentenced me to 20 months in prison, a fine of 2,000 metallic drachmas, and one year of police parole.

As I was being escorted away by the police, I paused a moment to take a look at my good wife, who was surrounded by believers and friends. I smiled at her and lifted my chains heavenward to remind her that God was watching all this from above.

"Twenty months!" she said softly, her tearful eyes filled with pain.

That same day I petitioned for an appeal.

JANUARY 25. Last night I slept in the detention area, where the Lord gave me strength through a dream to bear the cross of my imprisonment. In my dream I saw a huge black cross, surrounded by sweet-smelling roses and other colorful flowers. I know in my heart that God would not allow the rulers of this world to keep me locked up one moment beyond His appointed time, because I am here to accomplish His purpose among the prisoners, despite the director's loud warning this morning that I had better not start teaching my theories to them again.

Today I found myself back where I was ten months ago. The first person I met was my cellmate Lakoudis, an old acquaintance, now in for embezzling public funds. Venakis, imprisoned for similar reasons, introduced himself to me as a spiritualist. He told me he was right next to the police chief last year when the bishop looked up at our church sign and said to him, "How long are you going to leave that sign over there?" I smiled and told Venakis I was impressed that he quoted the bishop correctly.

In the afternoon I stepped into the yard, where I met some friends from last year, including a discouraged Philip, the youngest of the prisoners. I also met Vasilakis, a young man who introduced himself as a born-again Jew. He was in for a suspended sentence from when he was in the army.

JANUARY 27. This morning I learned that the spiritualist had entertained some of the prisoners in his cell last night, including Philip. I am more aware now of how the Lord is planning to use me here, so I am fasting and praying. Fault-finding Lakoudis, with whom I am sharing a cell, follows me everywhere and watches everything I do. Last night he criticized me for placing my Bible on a chessboard.

JANUARY 28. I woke up this morning and headed for the toilet with songs of praise in my heart and voice. At once Lakoudis seized the opportunity to criticize me.

"It's a shame you are singing praises in this—filthy place, you—," said Lakoudis, cussing. "It shows disrespect."

"If we clean this toilet and turn it into an attractive reception room, will it continue to be a filthy place?" I said.

"No," Lakoudis said.

"So, then, this toilet in itself is not a filthy place, but it is man who causes it to be filthy or clean. Agreed?"

"Yes," he said.

"Well, then, hear now what the problem is. The toilet carries the excess of our filth, because the source of its filth is our bellies. Therefore it is illogical to say that we cannot sing and praise God in a filthy place, for in that case we should completely abolish every expression of worship and adoration, as long as we ourselves are the source of filth."

"Nonsense!" Lakoudis said.

"As for filth, look in there," I said kindly, pointing to the Bible, "and see if you can find in it the foul words that came out of your mouth just moments ago."

Tonight Lakoudis challenged me by bringing Venakis and five other prisoners to our cell to show me what the acclaimed spiritualist could do. I received them cordially into my cell and suggested that if we were going to watch "spiritual" acts, we should first have a spiritual prayer together, and raised my eyes ready to pray.

"No!" protested Venakis, as he turned around to leave.

I laughed, within me raising praises to God for His power that filled the cell. "You're welcome to visit, friends. You don't have to leave," I said.

Turning around, Venakis said, "It has been revealed to me that you are going to lose your appeal next month and that you'll end up exiled on an island," he said.

JANUARY 29. As I lay down at around 9:30 last night, Lakoudis asked me to go see Philip, who had been hypnotized by Venakis. I told him I was not interested. Lakoudis left, and the Spirit of God impressed me to pray for Philip.

Good news reached me this morning, when church brethren came to tell me that the church license was reissued by the Ministry of Education and Religions and that we were now free to hold services as before. The license, as requested by the church council on the petition I submitted in Athens through Attorney Kiorfiatis, was issued under the name of Nikolaos Manousakas, a faithful church member. Praise God! What will our opponents have to say now that the church sign will go up again? What other means will they use to stop us from worshiping God and from standing as a lighthouse in the sea of a lost and sinful world? How ironical, though, that according to man's justice it is all right to shut down a harmless place of worship while leaving wide open the doors of adultery and fornication, the clubs of debauchery and corruption, and all the centers of lewd acts and shameful entertainment! One day people will see that our lighthouse is of God.

238    *The Proselytizer*

"PENTECOST"
CHURCH BROTHERHOOD

By decision number 122278 of the Department of Education and Religions, the ban on church services at the Church of Pentecost in Chania was lifted, and church services will be conducted regularly and in accordance with the law as before, declaring the Gospel of our Lord and Savior Jesus Christ each Sunday forenoon and afternoon, Tuesday Children's Church, Wednesday Bible study.

Admittance is free to all.

(The Church Board)
[Ethnikos Kiryx, 6 Feb. 1954]

RECOGNITION OF AN
ORGANIZATION

By its decision number 13919/1953, the Court of Justice in Athens has recognized the established organization "PENTECOST Christian Brotherhood" whose seat is in Athens and whose purpose is, on the one hand, the communication of the principles of the Holy Gospel unto all conscience of the people as the only basis of salvation, of progress and civilization, and on the other hand, the moral help toward its members and toward anyone suffering.

In Athens, 10 February 1954
The Plenipotentiary Attorney

DION. N. MOURELATOS
[Paratiritis of Chania, 17 Feb. 1954]

ΕΚΚΛΗΣΙΑΣΤΙΚΗ
ΑΔΕΛΦΟΤΗΣ Η "ΠΕΝΤΗΚΟΣΤΗ,,

Διὰ τῆς ὑπ' ἀριθμὸν 122278 π. ἔ. ἀποφάσεως τοῦ ὑπουργείου Παιδείας καὶ Θρησκευμάτων ἦρθη ἡ ἀπαγόρευσις τῆς λειτουργίας τῆς ἐν Χανίοις Ἐκκλησίας τῆς Πεντηκοστῆς, θὰ λειτουργῇ δὲ αὕτη κανονικῶς καὶ νομίμως ὡς πρότερον, κηρύττουσα τὸ Εὐαγγέλιον τοῦ Κυρίου καὶ Σωτῆρος ἡμῶν Ἰησοῦ Χριστοῦ ἑκάστην Κυριακὴν πρὸ καὶ μετὰ με σημβρίαν. Τρίτη, Κυριακὴν Σχολεῖον διὰ τὰ παιδιά. Τετάρτη με λέτην τῶν Ἁγίων Γραφῶν.
Οἱ βουλόμενοι δύνανται νὰ προσέρχονται Ἐλευθέρως.

(Ἡ Ἐκκλησιαστικὴ Ἐπιτροπὴ)

ΑΝΑΓΝΩΡΙΣΙΣ ΣΩΜΑΤΕΙΟΥ

Τὸ Δικαστήριον τῶν ἐν Ἀθήναις Πρωτοδικῶν διὰ τῆς ὑπ' ἀριθ. 13919) 1953 ἀποφάσεώς του ἀνεγνώρισε τὸ ἱδρυθὲν Σωματεῖον Χριστιανικὴ Ἀδελφότης Η ΠΕΝΤΗΚΟΣΤΗ μὲ ἕδρα τὰς Ἀθήνας καὶ σκοπὸν ἀφ' ἑνὸς μὲν τὴν μετάδοσιν τῶν ἀρχῶν τοῦ ἱεροῦ Εὐαγγελίου εἰς πᾶσαν συνείδησιν τῶν ἀνθρώπων, ὡς μόνος Βάσεις τῆς σωτηρίας, τῆς προόδου καὶ τοῦ πολιτισμοῦ, ἀφ' ἑτέρου δὲ τὴν ἠθικὴν βοήθειαν πρὸς τὰ μέλη του καὶ πρὸς πάντα πάσχοντα.

Ἀθήναι 10 Φεβρουαρίου 1954
Ὁ Πληρεξούσιος Δικηγόρς

ΔΙΟΝ. Ν. ΜΟΥΡΕΛΑΤΟΣ

FEBRUARY 1. Today I met a monk who has been charged with the murder of another monk and is in for life. I told him that all our crimes are forgiven if we repent and accept God's forgiveness by faith. Though the idea of grace and forgiveness seems strange to him, he is receptive and likes to hear more.

Unfortunately, I can talk to him now only while walking past him out in the yard, because the prison director has been alerted that I continue to teach my "theories" to the prisoners in my cell.

FEBRUARY 2. There are many unpleasant and unethical things happening in this prison that I do not even wish to think of. It is an ugly place, a place filled with sin, not to mention the prevailing unsanitary conditions—the foul smell, the mice, the cockroaches, the bed bugs. As for the food, I am more fortunate than others, because my loved ones, especially my good mother-in-law, lovingly take the four-kilometer walk to the prison and back each day to bring me a warm meal. (Philip tells me his best meals in prison always coincide with my days of fasting!)

But at the same time, this prison is a spiritual gold mine. There are precious souls here, whose destinies are suspended between heaven and hell. I know of no other people out in free society who are as receptive to words of hope as the majority of these prisoners. This seems to be particularly true of the convicts serving a life term—they never cease to think of freedom. They seem to have an inner hope that they will not die in prison, that something will happen some day and they'll be free. That's not because of some false hope they choose to feed on so they can cope with hopelessness, but because there's still breath in them. Some of them are even worried about their destiny in the beyond. They are so overcome by the guilt of their crime that I would dare say they are afraid of going to hell. What makes this obvious to me is that they are better prepared to identify with the concepts of forgiveness, life, freedom, hope, comfort, and peace, all within the context of love. They are the ones who listen with greater interest to Christ's message of repentance, forgiveness, and eternal life—the only sign of comfort and hope in this place for the living dead.

Tsikoudas, a new prisoner, introduced himself to me today as a shepherd from central Greece, and told me that he liked what he had heard me say in court during my trial. He told me that he used to paint icons, which he gave to churches and friends, but when he saw how people worshiped the paints and colors and wooden frames he had assembled, he got upset and went home and chopped up all his icons with an ax and threw them in the fire. "It's plain idolatry," he said. "This nation of ours is in a state of idolatry." I listened to the man and nodded, but was cautious not to encourage this type of discussion. He is in prison for a crime that resulted from hatred and revenge, so my words to him are limited to repentance and forgiveness by faith in the work of Christ, who alone is able to deliver us from the wages of sin and give us eternal life.

FEBRUARY 4. Vasilakis and I were approached in my cell today by two other prisoners. One is in for killing two bank employees, the other for killing a police sergeant.

"Why did God let me commit a double crime—me, who couldn't even say a cuss word before?" complained the first prisoner.

"Through this, God is showing you your spiritual weakness," I said. "You considered yourself morally strong and invincible, and while you are now a convict and bound for hell, God has already made arrangements for your forgiveness through the sacrifice of Christ. There was a criminal crucified right next to Christ, yet he repented and Christ forgave him instantly."

"Oh, yes," said Vasilakis excitedly. "A big criminal, yet God forgave him because he really repented!"

"Suppose, now," I said, "our judges told you today that if you truly repent of the crimes that brought you here, you are free to go. You wouldn't wait for them to come and drag you out of here, would you?"

"I'd run out!" the other prisoner said with a chuckle.

"Well," I went on, "it's even better with God. As you know, it's easy to feel sorry for something wrong you did because of the consequences of getting caught. Repenting is different. Deep inside, you hate your sin. God loves you enough to help you repent, if you ask Him. He not only forgives you, He lifts your guilt. God's forgiveness is your freedom from the prison of hell. And when you leave this earthly body, forgiveness is your ticket to eternity with Him. Imagine! That's how much God loves you."

The two men listened with great interest. A glimmer of hope lit their faces.

"I like hearing such good words, regardless who says them," said the first convict while the other one nodded.

Oh, that our rulers and religious leaders might hear and see that we share with eternal souls words of comfort and of eternal life. We do not preach religion, for religion does not save, only God. People burdened with the guilt of their abominable crimes need to hear about the saving knowledge of Christ. If we were free to reach souls with the simple message of Christ out in the open, there would be fewer crimes in our cities and villages, and our judges would have more time to deal with other problems with more fairness and justice. Instead, they call us "psychological scums and Satans who infest the land for the sake of shameful material gain." What is the material gain to be had by talking to a hopeless convict about God's forgiveness and love? But the day will come when those opposed to us will say, "Truly, it was God's children we judged."

FEBRUARY 11. A liturgy was conducted in prison this morning by Mihalas, a visiting archimandrite, assisted by Papantonis, my relentless persecutor since 1939. The preacher spoke about faith and salvation by God's grace. I was very pleased by the message itself, but common folk like these prisoners do not comprehend such truths when they are filled with archaisms and delivered in eloquent language.

After the liturgy I greeted Papantonis, then introduced myself to the preacher.

"Oh, yes!" said the archimandrite, upon hearing my name.

"I am one imprisoned for the sake of the gospel; according to some, a delusional heretic," I said.

"Yes, yes," said Papantonis.

"In my estimate, not being Orthodox means being delusional," said the archimandrite. "Martin Luther was right to leave the pope's church; but if he had steered his eyes a bit more to the right, he would have entered the arms of Orthodoxy, the church that remains unchanged since the apostolic times."

"What Luther ascertained was that the Catholic Church and the Orthodox Church were in many respects identical, so he steered away from both," I replied.

"The Protestants have deviated from the true doctrine, and they err."

"Isn't it a fact that Orthodox theologians and writers today borrow Protestant literature?"

"We take only the best parts of their works, but that does not mean we believe that they possess the truth."

"He doesn't even baptize his children—" Papantonis suddenly said. "And you dare call yourself a Christian!"

My eyes examining the faces of the dozen prisoners listening with their ears perked up, I said, "If you read your Bible more carefully, you'll see that it does not say 'He who is baptized and saved' but 'He who is saved and baptized' (Mark 16:16). You must first be saved, then you should be baptized."

Papantonis stared at me, speechless.

"One of Luther's biggest fallacies," Mihalas went on—much to Papantonis' relief—"was his misinterpretation with regard to Holy Communion. He viewed the bread and the wine as being symbolic of Christ's flesh and blood, not His actual flesh and blood. Jesus said, 'This is my body,' meaning that without transubstantiation during Holy Communion, there is no salvation possible."

"Remember?" I said, "Jesus said, 'This is my body' while holding the bread in His hand, Himself sitting among the disciples in His visible person. So the bread stands for His body representatively."

"Then why did He say, 'This is my body,' if it was not?"

"Didn't Jesus also say in John 6:54-55, 'He who eats my flesh and drinks my blood has life eternal,' and 'My flesh is true food, and my blood is true drink'? Did He mean that literally?"

"Well, of course not," the archimandrite said, hesitantly.

"Then why did He say that, if He did not mean it that way?"

"Because—that's why He broke the bread—"

"Exactly. So the bread is symbolic of His flesh, the wine symbolic of His blood."

The prison director walked in at that moment and reprimanded me for disrupting the liturgy. Though the preacher kindly explained that the liturgy was over and that we were simply having a discussion, the director ordered the warden to lock me up in my cell the rest of the day. As I was being whisked away, I heard Vasilakis shout, "Why aren't New Testaments allowed in this place, despite my repeated requests?"

"You've been proselytized by Zachariou, too?" Papantonis said with glee, anxious to accuse me of proselytizing even in prison.

The warden gave me a chance to pause and look back a moment.

"I was Protestant before I met this man of God," I heard Vasilakis say loudly. "In fact—"

"Well," cut in Papantonis, "we can verify the truth of that."

"—In fact, I am a Christian Jew."

"I see you are from that cursed race," said Papantonis.

"I am proud to be a Jew. Proud to be from the tribe of Judah from which our Savior came," said Vasilakis, appalled by the priest's hollow heart.

Vasilakis told me later that, after being interrogated by the police on his first day here, he could not remember being asked about his religious affiliation, and suspected that his police file showed that he was Orthodox—a routine clerical practice of police personnel filling out forms on any Greek subject. He made sure on his second day, he said, that the police had crossed out "Orthodox" and entered "Protestant" instead, even though at the time he didn't think the correction was of any significance. Immediately I raised my eyes and thanked God, then explained to Vasilakis that that "insignificant" correction was made by God's providence. "Without that correction," I said, "not only would I be losing my upcoming trial at the appellate court, but soon I would be facing Papantonis and the archimandrite during yet another trial for proselytizing you in prison. Despite your personal protests in court as my defense witness, I wouldn't have a leg to stand on." Vasilakis marveled, and praised God with me.

FEBRUARY 13. My soul cries out to God, as waves of homesickness sweep through me and leave me with a longing to be free and see the faces of my children and all my loved ones. I long to be with my dear brethren, to sing songs of praise with them, to have fellowship with them, and to seek God's face together. But my heart also aches for the prisoners who come to my cell one after another to hear words of hope. How I need God's wisdom! And I need His protection even in prison from Metaxa's inhumane law of proselytism 1363/38, Satan's muzzle on the mouths of God's servants who desire to reach souls throughout this land but are faced with injustice.

FEBRUARY 15. I was touched and uplifted in my spirit today when brethren from the Evangelical church visited me to tell me that a church in Sweden has expressed an interest in publicizing my ordeals and persecutions; and that a group of Presbyterian churches in America has petitioned to the Greek government to be lenient to those imprisoned on grounds of proselytism and to release them. I also learned that churches throughout Greece are given to fasting and prayer on my behalf. What a blessing to know that Christians at home and abroad, even those who do not know me, are praying on my behalf! Paul knew the value of corporate and intercessory prayer (Romans 15:30, 2 Thessalonians 3:1, 1 Timothy 2:1). What a source of sustenance and strength during my imprisonment!

FEBRUARY 18. Today I met another monk, who came to my cell and told me about his ascetic life in Agion Oros (Holy Mountain) in Northern Greece—a simplistic life of abstinence from meats and certain other foods. When I asked him about the way a man can be saved from the penalty of sin, he spoke humbly of good works and said that in order to be a good Christian, a person must love his neighbor as himself.

"In other words," I said, "one should not hate his enemies nor speak evil of them."

"That's right," said the monk.

"So, then, you must now be condemned to hell, because a moment ago you spoke blasphemous words against those who convicted you."

"Yes, yes," he said sadly, his head hanging low. "But in time I will forgive and forget."

"Suppose tonight you were to leave this life and enter eternity. Would your soul be lost?"

"Unfortunately—"

"But without protection against our enemy's wiles, we are all hopelessly condemned and lost!"

"I—suppose so," the monk said, his eyes examining mine quizzically.

I shared with the monk my experience of trying to do good works in the past, but never feeling that I could measure up to the standards of a good Orthodox Christian, and how I had thought that spiritual perfection could be attained only by monks and priests. One day I realized that my salvation from the curse of sin is God's free gift through faith, faith being a part of the gift, so that I could not brag about earning God's salvation through my own faith or through my good works (Ephesians 2:8-9). Now I am free from the condemnation of sin (Romans 8:1) and a partaker of God's promise of eternal life (Romans 6:22).

The monk looked thunderstruck. "Do you know any good prayers?" he asked.

"Well, of course," I said, and prayed a sinner's prayer asking Jesus to forgive the monk of all his sins and to save his soul, which the monk humbly repeated after me.

The monk asked if I would write down that prayer for him, because he wanted to memorize it, as he had all other prayers.

"You do not have to memorize any prayers, though it's not a bad idea," I said. "When you pray, pray as if you were talking with a very close friend you love and respect. Just tell God how much you love Him, express to Him your gratitude for knowing Him as your Father, ask Him to forgive your sins, and simply voice your needs to Him. Jesus taught us to pray that way in Matthew 6:9-13 and John chapter 17."

Today I am thanking God for my imprisonment. It has afforded me grand opportunities to plant the seed of the Word by ministering to some of the most desperate people on earth. I am convinced beyond doubt that I am here by divine appointment.

Tonight my cell is filled with God's presence. Lakoudis walked in just before curfew, paused curiously and looked at me, then asked me to forgive him for insulting me in front of the others earlier in the day.

FEBRUARY 21. It's Monday morning. My fellow prisoners know of my upcoming trial at the appellate court this Wednesday and are already saying that they will miss me, as if they are sure I'm not going to return. Last night I invited several of them to meet in young Philip's cell, where I shared an interesting story. The nine prisoners who showed up listened attentively as I told the story of a mother who did hard labor in a field just outside the prison where her son was held. Upon his release from prison, the son realized that his mother had paid the ransom for his redemption by pulling thorny weeds and thistles and removing rocks, as evidenced by her bloodstained hands and bruised and aching body. That's what Jesus did for us, I said. He uprooted and removed our sins, and with bloodstained hands and a bruised and broken body bought our freedom from the prison of sin. No one reacted to the allegory, or to the chorus of praise I sang at the end.

Everyone remained still. The curfew bell was due any moment. To prevent drawing sarcastic remarks from anyone, I thought of leaving, but the Spirit of God prompted me to stay. A couple of prisoners were wiping away tears. "If any of you sense a tug in your heart to repent of your sins and receive God's free gift of salvation today, this is a grand opportunity," I said. "Would you let me know by raising your hand, so I can pray with you?"

"We've been so moved tonight," said Lakoudis, probably with a degree of honesty, which sounded better than his sudden spurts of abusive language and shocking stories.

"This kind of talk suits me right," said Philip. "We all need to hear such wonderful words. I don't know about you, but I know I need to repent!" Then, looking at me, Philip said, "Mr. Zachariou—"

"Yes, Philip?"

"We all know you are a godly man and—and you don't belong here."

There was dead silence.

I smiled at Philip and pointed heavenward.

The curfew bell rang three minutes later than usual.

FEBRUARY 22. Today is the anniversary of the onslaught of Satan's bombardment of our church through the court system, aided by the artillery of the news media. His first attack through the bishopric of Chania on February 22, 1954, was aborted due to lack of evidence, and the trial was rescheduled for May 28 of the same year. A second attack on May 14 left the toothless lion roaring as the courts pronounced me not guilty. Ironically, at the rescheduled trial on May 28, the courts pronounced me guilty of virtually the same thing I had been found innocent of only fourteen days earlier. And upon appealing my case, I was charged with an additional sentence, which was repealed by a Supreme Court decision in Athens.

Today is my fourth day of fasting and prayer in preparation for tomorrow's trial. I have been praying specifically that Judge Sgrekas and Judge Tsilingeridis, who are extremely prejudiced against us, will not be behind the bench tomorrow.

I learned today that Attorney Korfiatis has been sent by the churches in Athens to defend my case tomorrow morning. I am moved by the brethren's generous gesture. This would not have been necessary if our local courts had not succumbed to pressures created by ignorance, prejudice, and pride; and though I find some comfort in the attorney's presence, it will not make any difference if it is God's will that I remain in prison another eighteen months. In any case, I feel that my mission in prison has been accomplished, and I take this development as God's sign that I may now return to the flock God has entrusted into my care. Besides, tomorrow's outcome may be God's way of eventually eradicating this uncivilized law of proselytism 1363/ 38,* which only promotes the exploitation of our justice system to satisfy those who would have no other way of channel-

---

* The law against "proselytism" was enacted in 1939, just as Panos Zachariou became a Christian and launched out his ministry. This law is still on the lawbooks of Greece, a land of today's free world and the birthplace of the ideas of freedom and democracy.

ing their jealousy and pride against us. May God use tomorrow's outcome to uproot this heinous law from our lawbooks and to open the doors for ministers of God's Word to reach perishing souls in our city and throughout our needy nation. And may our opponents begin to see us not as a threat to their parishes and churches, nor as religious fanatics rebelling against customs and tradition, nor as profiteers motivated by the pursuit of power and material gain, nor as delegates under the banner of some foreign heresy, but as co-workers in God's vineyard who are eager to obey Christ's command to spread the light of the gospel to lost souls who deserve a chance to choose to come out of their prison of darkness.

# 19

# The Verdict

IT WAS THE MORNING OF FEBRUARY 23, 1955. The heavy metal door slammed, breaking the chilly morning silence as the warden called the names of eight prisoners, above the cold sound of clinking chains.

"Your right hand—your other hand," the warden ordered. Their wrists in chains, the seven prisoners watched silently as the warden moved toward me. I stretched out my right hand, eyes raised high, and said, "Lord, I thank You for this humiliation!"

The warden hesitated. "You're a godly man," he said. "I am not putting chains on you."

"Thank you," I said.

As I entered the courtroom, I saw my dear wife and a good number of the church brethren. I raised my hands, palms pressed together, to remind them to be in prayer.

The presiding judge walked into the courtroom and took the bench. It was Judge Moustakas. I kept praying. Two other judges followed—neither Sgrekas nor Tsilingeridis. Attorney Korfiatis wasn't in sight yet. There were more than six trials scheduled for the day, and I wasn't sure if my defense witnesses were going to wait for my turn.

Judge Moustakas announced that the order of the trials had been switched. At that point Attorney Korfiatis walked in, with an assistant attorney. "Great are Your miracles, Father!" I prayed in my heart, for had the order not been changed, my trial would have been the last one.

Korfiatis, his quick-moving hands and big eyes bespeaking alertness, opened his satchel and bags, plus two more bags my son Jimmy brought in for him, then spread his lawbooks and papers on the table as if he were about to conduct some book exhibit.

"Panos Zachariou!" called Judge Moustakas.

I got up, walked to the familiar dock, and sat down. I counted the times I had sat there as a defendant for Christ's sake since 1939—eleven!

Pastor Panos in conversation with some of his chief persecutors and accusers outside the courthouse in Chania after a trial in 1954

The first of the three brothers was called to the witness stand.

"Witness, did Panos Zachariou give you any money or clothing in order to proselytize you?"

"No, your honor, but—"

I was surprised to hear him say "no," because in his deposition two months earlier he had accused me of trying to proselytize him with clothing. Were the judges aware of this?

"But what?" the judge insisted.

"He proselytized my mother and turned our home into a volcano."

It became obvious from the next couple of questions that turmoil and strife had already existed in the witness's home for years.

The second brother was called to testify, then the third. One of them said that I had used motion pictures to do propaganda, alluding to a motion picture of the crucifixion of Christ I had shown publicly a number of times. All three brothers seemed to have thought things over, because they were more truthful this time and consequently said nothing incriminating.

Odysseas, too, limited his responses to a few words, perhaps because he was afraid that the truth about his treatment of Roula would surface.

The prosecution produced no other witnesses, and the judges started calling the defense witnesses. The first one was my good neighbor, Andreas Papadakis.

"He's my neighbor, your honor," he said. "When he first moved next door to me I was a bit defensive, because he had been introduced to me as a bugaboo of some sort. That's why I always kept an eye on him. I am Orthodox, and the priest of our parish advised me to beware of him, and said if I ever saw him do anything weird, to catch him. So I went to his meetings a couple of times to check him out; but soon I changed my mind about him, because nothing I had been told against him was true."

"Witness?" Korfiatis called. "Did the defendant know that you were watching him?"

"Does it behoove the thief to inform the shepherd that he's going to steal his sheep?" Papadakis replied.

"Do you know that he is poor and has many children and can barely get by?" Korfiatis asked.

"Extremely poor, sir. Is it possible for a poor man to hide his poverty?"

"What did you hear others say about him?"

"They told me that he claims that at their meetings the Holy Spirit descends upon their heads and they speak in other tongues, and so he thinks he's someone important. But what I observed was that he explains the Bible."

"What kinds of explanations do you do, defendant?" inquired the presiding judge. "What are these tongues? Do you understand what you are saying?"

"Your honor," I said, "I wish you could follow the Scriptures as I am speaking to you, and you would see that we are not unlawful. Tongues have to do with the individual's edification. In 1 Corinthians 12 and 14 the Apostle Paul talks about the spiritual gift of tongues, which is used in worship as the Spirit gives utterance—"

"Come on, now, Zachariou. Drop that nonsense," another judge said suddenly.

Judge Moustakas first called Roula to the witness stand, then her mother. Both of them testified that they attended our church of their own volition and that their households had been aware of that from the very beginning.

Seeing that there was no material evidence against me, Moustakas turned to me and asked if I baptized my children.

"No, your honor, I—"

But before I had a chance to finish speaking, he started crossing himself, saying, "Oh, my God! Remember me when you enter into your—so what kind of Christian are you?"

The judge's reaction triggered a fit of laughter among some in the courtroom. I felt a catch in my throat, and prayed for the right words.

"Your honor—you see, I will—my children will be baptized when they are of age. That's what the Bible teaches," I went on, my tongue suddenly coming unglued. "Water baptism follows the confession of faith. The Bible teaches us not to be baptized first and then believe, but that we should be baptized after we have believed. Shouldn't we follow the teachings of the Bible?"

There was absolute silence. No one stirred. Judge Moustakas kept nodding and staring at me for a long moment, as if he understood what he had heard.

"Do you take communion? Do you fast?" he asked.

"Certainly. We take communion every month. And we do fast—"

"When they fast, they eat nothing!" said the assistant attorney.

"They eat nothing?" echoed judge Moustakas in amazement. "Then do you confess and forgive sins?" he said in a more serious tone.

"This is the heart of the issue, your honor," I said, "for we do not introduce ourselves as pardoners of men's sins nor do we receive confessors for the forgiveness of their sins. It is Jesus Christ alone we introduce as the pardoner of men's sins, for the Bible says in 1 Timothy 2:5 that there is only one mediator between God and man—Jesus. That is a basic difference between us and the Orthodox Church. Nor can we buy people's consciences with gifts and money, as we have been accused of doing. Christ Himself never tried to attract people through material means. He fed them and healed them, yet he was grieved by their attitude because, as He told them, they followed Him not because they saw His miracles and believed in Him, but because He fed them. People cannot be persuaded to believe in God and receive salvation through material means. But your honor, all this agitation on the part of our persecutors is not due to what we do or do not believe, but the fact that we are so visible in a central part of our city. If their main interest was the welfare of people's souls, they would even let us cooperate with them."

"Enough," said Moustakas. "Sit down."

The three judges whispered among themselves, then the presiding judge turned to me. "There's something here in your files—smuggling."

"Smuggling? There must be some mistake."

"Let me read it to you," the judge said. "Back in 1936 and 1937—"

"Oh, yes, your honor," I exclaimed. "That tells you of only one such incident. How about the ones you do not know? That was when I lived in sin. Now I am a new creation in Christ Jesus. The old Zachariou is gone. By the grace of God, I have repented of all my sins and no longer walk in sin."

The judges sat in stony silence. Korfiatis stood up. Fixing his eyes silently on the three justices for a long moment, he waited. Was he going to address the court once more?

"All right," finally said Judge Moustakas. "You can go now."

Two policemen came and took me out of the courtroom. Two trials later I was called back in.

Presiding Judge Moustakas stood up to say that he thought that in essence I was guilty, though not through evidence produced by the prosecution, and recommended that I be pronounced guilty.

The assistant attorney got up and protested the presiding judge's recommendation, contending that the judge was endorsing my guilt on a blank piece of paper. Moustakas retorted by telling the attorney to get to the point, because it was rather he who spoke from a blank piece of paper.

Attorney Korfiatis then stood up. With refined speech and firm voice, he first reminded the court that on May 28 and August 26, 1954, as well as on January 24, 1955, the defendant was pronounced guilty despite the lack of material evidence. He then commended the November 13, 1954, Supreme Court decision that dropped the additional punitive charges against the defendant and immediately tied the cases to the status of the law of proselytism 1363/38 for clarification. Questioning the nature of the law of proselytism, the attorney stressed the fact that no legislative act had enabled the lawmakers to determine how to interpret this law, and reminded the court that it had cost the State Council many a meeting trying to decide how to deal with it. In 1951 the State Council, still not sure what to do with this law, decided to set it aside, giving the legislative world some respite from its nightmarish burden. However, yet today, the courts continue to utilize this archaic law.

The courtroom had turned into a university lecture hall. Korfiatis' eloquent style captured the interest of judges and attorneys alike. He carried on, now quoting from this or that publication, now referring to this or that code of law, and reading definitions and descriptions from the numerous works spread before him. After referring to the findings of my previous trials, especially this appellate court's most daring decision of August 26, 1954, for additional punitive charges, then finally recapitulating today's proceedings, he brought the ax of justice down upon the risky decisions of this court. As a coup de grace, he picked up his copy of the May 14, 1954 court decision, and as he waved it back and forth, reiterated the decision of this very court, which on that day found the defendant not guilty!

Oh, how I wish for my accusers to have been here today, I thought to myself. But none dared come, since legal action against them for perjury is pending—Lygerakis, S. Valadakis, Priest Apostolos Mylonakis, Basileios Doumeliotakis, Priest Georgios Bourlakis (Papagiorgis), Priest Antonios Strongylakis (Papantonis), Emmanuel Katsifarakis, Markos Mygiakis, and Mihael Sahinian—all residents of Chania.

After a short recess, the judges reconvened and Judge Moustakas called me. I stood up and walked to the dock. "No, not there," he said. "Over here, close to us."

I stood before the judges.

"Look here, Zachariou," said Judge Floros, who was also in my previous appellate court trial. "Why don't you just look after your little shop and drop all this stuff?"

"Listen to me," said the presiding judge again. "Make sure they do not bring you in here again."

At that point the assistant attorney leaned over and whispered in my ear, "Tell the judge, 'Your honor, I won't do it again.'"

I looked at the man sideways, saying nothing. I noticed that Attorney Korfiatis was talking to the judges, and I thought of the prisoners I had left behind only a short distance from the courtroom. Yes, they are telling me not to do it again, I thought to myself. But they do not realize that even prison has not stopped me from doing the very thing they are accusing me of! Oh, Lord, "Not to do it again!" What did I do? What is my crime? I wish these people could see the harm they are doing to weary souls.

Looking at the presiding judge, I said, "Your honor, you are under the impression that my speaking to others about God creates trouble. Is the sharing of the Word of God with others a crime? We are not in violation of the law."

"And do you have a license?"

"Why, yes!" I exclaimed joyfully. "From the Ministry of Education and Religions! The public has been informed through the newspapers—"

Judge Moustakas' face froze. Good Lord! I thought to myself. Can it be that all this time these judges had no idea that our church license was reissued over a month ago? Is this why they think that we are in violation of the law? I wonder, on the other hand, if this judge, having just been warned by the attorney about this court's risky decisions—which, if pushed, will reach the Supreme Court in Athens—will now conveniently camouflage his fears by using this timely bit of "surprising" news about our church license as his excuse for reversing his capricious decision?

The judge sat straight up in his chair. "How can it be? There must be a mistake—this license has not been mentioned at all!"

Within a few moments the court announced that I was released!

As I was being ushered out of the courtroom, I went straight to my good and deserving wife and kissed her first. Her eyes were filled with tears of joy such as I had not seen for a long time. The police gave me a few moments to greet my dear brethren and loved ones.

"Come by my shop," I said to the four young policemen ushering me out of the courtroom. "I'll treat you all to coffee!" I noticed then a teary-eyed police sergeant standing by and smiling at me.

"Yeah, so you can start talking to us?" one said jokingly, as the rest of them laughed.

Emotions ran high among my friends in prison when they realized that I was no longer going to be with them. Philip was in tears. He promised me he would stay strong, and I promised I would pray for him and that I would return to visit him. Vasilakis tearfully said he was going to be left alone now, but that he and I would have a praise session together after his release. As I hugged Venakis, who came to congratulate me, I reminded him that the spirit that had told him I was going to lose my court trial had deceived him. He said he did not remember ever saying such a thing to me. Lakoudis told me I was going to be missed and that a man like me deserved to be free. I greeted the monks, the shepherd, and the other two dozen souls the Lord had enabled me to touch, and told them once more that God is real, and His love for them is unconditional and far beyond man's ability to measure it.

"Zachariou!" someone shouted through the small opening in the heavy metal door at the end of the ward. "Get your things and out you go!"

I picked up my things and walked to the exit. Looking back one last time, I saw the faces of my friends as they waved good-bye. "Lord, I thank You for giving me the strength to accomplish the mission for which You sent me here. Please protect from the enemy the souls You touched through me."

The heavy door opened. "Don't forget the New Testaments!" Vasilakis shouted as I stepped outside.

"Oh, I am free! I am free!" my lips whispered, as my soul shouted within me. A short distance from the prison was a one-horse carriage with my teenage son Jimmy waiting in it.

When we arrived home, my mother-in-law greeted me at the door with a kiss. There were people waiting inside. I told my mother-in-law to prepare for a feast. She hesitated a moment, then nodded and smiled. "As soon as Chrysa gets back, we'll do some shopping," she said.

Chrysa returned with an envelope in her hands. She had gone to borrow some money for groceries, but first had stopped by the church to see if there was any mail. I opened the envelope. It contained a gift from the Greek church in Campbell, Ohio—thirty dollars! "Oh, God, You will for ever provide for Your faithful children!" I said, as together we praised God for His love and mercy.

THAT same night, family and guests rejoiced around our dinner table. With us were Attorney Korfiatis and his wife, Helen. Mrs. Korfiatis was particularly thrilled by the good news of my release.

As we talked joyfully around the dinner table, the thought occurred to me that, just as Attorney Korfiatis had interceded on my behalf for the release from prison of my earthly body, so does Jesus intercede on our behalf for the release from the bondage of sin of our spirits. As I shared this analogy, the attorney showed great interest, and asked me to explain further. Using Scripture verses, I talked about the redeeming work of Jesus Christ, who offered Himself as a ransom to redeem us from our sins. All along, the attorney asked questions and further clarification. Seeing her husband's interest, Mrs. Korfiatis became concerned and said to him that they could not change religion. Smiling, her husband assured her that his interest had nothing to do with changing religion, but rather with enlightenment and the discovery of something he was missing.

Later Mrs. Korfiatis expressed her concern once more. "You see, I agree with what you are saying but—but just the thought of changing from Orthodox to another religion makes me feel dizzy."

"I assure you, Mrs. Korfiatis," I said, "that there is no need to think that you have to change religion. We never recommend this type of thing."

"You mean that I can believe these things and still remain in my church?" she said.

"Of course," Mr. Korfiatis said, happy to reassure his dear wife.

"Well, then—agreed, agreed," she said excitedly.

"What's more, Mrs. Korfiatis," I added, "it is also possible for a person to claim he is Evangelical or Pentecostal and still not be a Christian, if he has not accepted the free gift of salvation through Christ. A Christian is not one who goes to a particular church or who does good works. A Christian is one who has received Christ in his life whether he is Orthodox, or Protestant, or Catholic. A particular church or religion does not make one a Christian, only the acceptance of Christ as one's Savior. There was a time when I had similar questions," I continued, "and I had to have the answers. What I discovered was that the answers were already in the Bible. So, whatever you do not comprehend now, leave for later. Just keep meditating on the Word and ask the Father to give you insight."

"And how do I ask?" inquired the eminent counsel, whose great mind examined every detail from all angles.

"Through prayer. Simple prayer. Pray by the authority of the name of Jesus. Just like sending registered mail."

"I understand, I understand," said the attorney.

As I lay gratefully in my bed late that night, I felt God's presence permeating my being. I was grateful that He had answered my prayer to speak to this great man and his good wife about my Savior, the Savior of the world. I was grateful also to be with my loved ones again. And I was grateful to be free!

WALKING to Agora in downtown Chania to do some shopping the next day, I witnessed a most unforgettable and touching sight, as people stepped out of their shops and stores, one after another, to shake my hand. Rich and poor alike—bankers, grocers, fishermen, bakers, policemen, street cleaners, taxi drivers, restaurant employees, shoemakers, teachers, street vendors, kiosk owners, money exchangers, even a priest!—they all came to congratulate me and tell me that they were glad for me and my family, that justice had finally prevailed, or that they were ashamed of the unwarranted actions of our opponents. My soul rejoiced, for it was a testimony of how the average citizen viewed our ministry in our community. I thought to myself, Many people respect us for what we stand for and believe, for our character and life match what we preach, and our love for souls is genuine. It is not the people who persecute us, but those few who stir the people against us.*

I was in the center of Agora when Mr. Drakos, a retired customs controller who for years had shunned me because of my faith, walked up to me, grabbed my right hand with his two hands, and shook it for a long time. Those watching were amused because he kept opening his mouth but could not talk. "Yes, my friend, say it now. What is it?" I said, wondering for a moment if his aim was to make a public spectacle of me. Giving me a hearty smile, Mr. Drakos finally said in a clear and loud voice, "You have overcome the world!"

"Hallelujah!" I exclaimed, pointing heavenward. "It is He who has!"

---

* Among those who stepped out of the business places to congratulate Panos that day was a photographer near Agora who invited him into his studio for a free photograph (as shown on the cover).

A few days later I visited my friends in prison. It was like a family reunion. One of the monks told me that he and Vasilakis spent time meditating together, and that now one big goal he had in life was to lead someone to Christ. I looked into a sincere face, its dark eyes alight with concern. That was a supreme goal in this life, I told him, and being Orthodox, he had every opportunity to do so because no one could accuse him of proselytizing.

IN MAY of 1955, after again visiting my friends in prison, I went to the courthouse and withdrew the charges against the nine false witnesses in the trials of May 28 and August 26, 1954. I wanted my opponents to know, not by way of elevating myself above them, but for Christ's sake and for our testimony as Christians, that I had hatred toward none, for the Bible teaches that we should love and pray for those who hate us and persecute us. I wanted them to know also that, even though they had allowed themselves to become the enemy's agents—as I attempted to explain to most of them over the ensuing two weeks—I never considered them my enemies. Odysseas and the three brothers were speechless when I offered them a warm handshake and suggested that we put our differences behind us. Never again did Odysseas or the three brothers demand that Roula and her children or Sofia stop coming to our church.

Of the dozen I visited, only Papantonis refused to hear me. He was quick to say, however, that if I ever needed public assistance in terms of verification of our poverty status, he would prefer having his "two hands cut off first."

FOLLOWING another visit to the prison, during which I was able to bring a supply of New Testaments, I met a judge and two attorneys engaged in conversation outside the courtroom.

"Say, Zachariou, why don't you teach us a tongue or two," joked Vlazakis, one of the attorneys.

"Is it possible to get some people to speak in tongues, so they can stop talking nonsense?" teased Judge Kremmydas, implying that in his daily encounters in court he had to deal with people's nonsense.

"That's right, sir, it is possible," I said, doubting that the judge was capable of comprehending the spiritual import of my response.

"Do you think Christ is coming?" said the other attorney. "You've waited for him since 1914."

"Unfortunately, you are confusing us with the Jehovah's Witnesses," I explained. "We know He is coming soon, but no one knows exactly when. The signs do indicate that the time is at hand."

"What signs?" asked Vlazakis.

"The wars, the earthquakes—right?" said the judge.

"Exactly," I said. "And especially the restoration of the nation of Israel."

"What do you mean by 'restoration'?" asked the judge.

"The fulfillment of prophecy regarding the re-establishment of Israel in our times," I said. "It was prophesied in the Old Testament that before the coming of the Lord, Israel will become a nation again. I saw this event happening before my very eyes in the port of Souda back in 1948, when hundreds of Jews aboard the ship Patma were headed for Palestine, their homeland. In fact, that was one event that fired up my faith one hundred per cent back then, and made me want to delve deeper and deeper into the truths of the Bible."

"Isn't one hundred converts enough, though?" quipped the other attorney. "What's your goal now, two hundred converts? Five hundred? A thousand?"

"The whole city!" I replied with a cordial smile.

"I kind of believe you!"

"Let me tell you, friend, our Great Master, who holds this whole universe in His hand, has no need of this preacher, his talents, or his services. But I, as His servant, am in need of serving Him. It's not numbers that please God. For instance, a missionary may not reach even one native with the message of Christ for many years. On the other hand, one of our churches in Sweden has over six thousand members, but—"

"Six thousand!" said the attorney in amazement.

"That's right—but God looks at the heart of His dedicated servant. He takes note of His servant's faith and faithfulness. Faithfulness in serving Him, faithfulness in desiring to serve Him. Total faithfulness. The faithful minister who speaks to thousands of persons on a Sunday morning does not please God any more than the faithful missionary who has spent years seeking to reach the soul of one person. To be sure, I would like to see the whole city of Chania and our whole nation reached with the message of Christ; but numbers and outcomes are God's department. My goal is to be faithful in God's service while trying to reach as many hearts for Christ as any opportunity according to His purpose may dictate."

Judge Yannopoulos happened by and joined our conversation as I was saying that I had "proselytized" a Communist.

"Why didn't you tell us about it in court?" said Judge Yannopoulos earnestly. "We would have acquitted you!"

"Suppose, your honor, you check the court records of my May 28, 1954 trial and find out that a former Communist himself was one of our defense witnesses?"

"Incredible!" said the judge. "That's incredible!"

The three men signaled to each other that it was time to go. Judge Yannopoulos kept shaking his head as he turned around and walked away with them. I thought to myself, These are men who hold the power of the law in their hand. These are also the men who decide how the law should be applied— often according to expediency or personal taste.

I MADE it a point one day to visit Judge Sgrekas in his own home, so I could talk to him in private to be sure that at least one of our judges was well informed about our position as servants of the gospel. It was "a very daring and risky thing to do," the justice told me, but he said he was willing to hear me.

Away from the pressures of his office and in the privacy of his home, Judge Sgrekas appeared relaxed and treated me courteously. I gathered from his sparing remarks that he preferred to remain noncommittal and did not wish to be asked questions.

"We hold in very high esteem and dear to our heart our matchless Greek heritage—" I said to the man who had boldly stated in public one day that he who is not Orthodox is not

Greek, "—our history, our ideals of democracy, our culture, our influence on civilization and human thought, our language and its role in the spread of Christianity, and our unique image and identity among the nations of the world. We hold especially dear the gospel of Jesus Christ. We believe it in its entirety, and in its power to transform lives. We believe our government is ordained by God. We are law-abiding citizens who respect and obey our government leaders. We respect our religious leaders, and believe they are in an extremely important position in that they have the grandest of opportunities to reach people with the Christian gospel. We believe we are in the last days before Christ's return, and that the harvest of eternal souls in our nation is great and the laborers are few. For this reason, our aim is to do our part in God's work by sharing the gospel message with our fellow citizens. To that end, we reach people with the love and truth of Christ, for His message is timeless and universal—not only for the Greeks, but for all people, all races, all languages, all nations, each and every human being.

"Our aim is not to supplant religion nor to condemn any religious practices. We do not infiltrate people's minds through proselytism; we are not a cult or a sect interested in inducing people and making them our followers. We are not agents of any foreign or domestic influence or force, nor do we serve or promote the personal or gainful interests of any individual, group, or organization.

"There are many people living in our city today who have expressed their gratitude and appreciation for our ministry, yet have not come to our church even once. We force no one, exploit no one, elude no one, deceive no one. For, as with the first Christians, the motive of our faith is rooted in the unadulterated message of Jesus Christ; and our foremost desire is to serve the living God in the name of Him whom He sent to the cross to redeem humanity from sin and to offer every person His free gift of eternal life.

"As for me, I was convicted for proselytizing others by offering them money, gifts, and clothing. I should first be found guilty of proselytizing my own family, for I provide food, clothing, and shelter for them, and they all attend our church. But I assure you, sir, that never once did I force my family to accept and follow my beliefs and convictions through intimidation, force, or the exploitation of their ignorance or lack of spiritual insight.

"Nor did I ever take advantage of anyone's psychological need or weakness in order to impose my predilections regarding my faith—though there was ample opportunity for that. People have thanked me for ministering to them or to their loved ones, for praying for their sick, or for showing genuine love and concern. Yet I never used the opportunity to appeal to their conscience or good will by asking them to come to our church. Many transients did come to our church for help, and we prayed for them and ministered to them even while we knew they would not come to see us again.

"I love people. Their souls are eternal. They are created in God's image. That is why every soul is priceless in God's eyes. Therefore I am determined, sir, regardless of the cost, to use the days God gives me in this precious life as faithfully in His service as I possibly can by reaching people with His message. For I am persuaded that in this life there is no mission or honor greater than to reach another human being, in obedience to God's command, with the love and message of Jesus Christ, our Savior."

# 20

# Breath of Praise

A S THE GUNS OF OPPOSITION AND INJUSTICE suddenly fell silent, our church entered a period of renewal and growth. The body of believers grew in spiritual blessings and maturity, and new souls were added to the flock.

Teamwork. Panos Zachariou and his six sons working together in the mid-1950s on the publication of the *Manna* magazine.

But the enemy did not cease to be at work. Seeing that his attacks through the courts against our faith had ended in defeat, he made various direct attempts on my life. While I was preaching one Sunday morning, a woman rushed upstairs screaming and shouting incomprehensible sounds. Perceiving this to be the work of the enemy, I kept preaching. As she entered the sanctuary, still ranting and howling, she fixed a stare at me as her fingers fumbled for an object concealed in a red towel. A young sailor sitting near the entrance jumped to his feet and apprehended her, but as he tried to escort her outside, she somehow managed to escape from his hold and push him down the stairs. She then threw a hatchet at the sailor, the hatchet barely missing the sailor's head and cutting a deep groove into our front entrance.

As my son Jimmy and I were leaving the church building two weeks after that incident, we greeted a man who was sitting in front of the small cafe right across the cobblestone alley from our church entrance. Agathangelos, notorious for his war exploits, family feuds, and vendettas, responded with a nod. Moments later, Jimmy and I were turning the corner at the end of the block when we heard footsteps behind us. We looked back and saw Agathangelos some thirty yards away. Farther along, as Jimmy and I were engaged in the discussion of a passage of Scripture, we looked over our shoulders again. Agathangelos, grim-faced, was gaining on us, and Jimmy warned me that the man was carrying a weapon under his belt.

I stopped a moment to face Jimmy—as I habitually did during discussions in order to emphasize a point. Agathangelos, now only about twenty yards from us, froze in his steps. As we resumed walking, we looked back to see whether Agathangelos was still following us, only to witness a most peculiar thing: not only was he not following us, he was running like mad in the opposite direction as if pursuers were at his heels. Jimmy and I reckoned this to be God's intervention.

The next day Agathangelos came to church to find me. "Please, Mr. Zachariou," he said to me on his knees, "do not let those giants hurt me—"

"What giants?" I said, as I helped Agathangelos to his feet.

"Those two big giants that came to join you when you stopped, remember?"

"Oh, those giants!" I said, as I marveled at God's angelic protection.

"Yes, Mr. Zachariou, they suddenly turned around and—and ran after me. It wasn't my idea, you know—"

Agathangelos confessed that Papagiorgis had instructed him to harm me. But as I explained to Agathangelos, God had sent his giant angels to protect us; and that they would not hurt him as long as he asked God to forgive him. And so it turned out that, through God's intervention, the man who hours earlier had sought to harm me—ironically, again with a hatchet—was now letting me lead him in a prayer for the forgiveness of his sins.

DURING the summer of 1956, the enemy devised a new way of attacking me directly. Seeing that his relentless attacks against me had been to no avail, he fashioned a "thorn in the flesh" with which to afflict me.

While working at the soap factory one day, I slipped and scraped my right leg along the shin. I thought nothing of the incident, especially because the redness of the skinned area subsided and the healing process seemed normal. A few weeks went by, and Chrysa began to notice persistent bloodstains on my pajamas. Examining my leg more closely, we noticed a bit of bleeding coming from a mole on the side of my leg which had also been scraped when I fell. Chrysa cleansed the area with alcohol, applied antiseptic, and used gauze. The discomfort I felt was not significant enough to stop me from going on with my busy schedule as usual.

Early in September, at the request of some brethren from northern Greece, I went to Thessaloniki to participate in plans for a new church. By now the mole on my leg was inflamed, causing me to limp. The brethren prayed for my healing and also urged me to see a doctor. It would cost 500 drachmas ($17) to treat the infected sore, a doctor told me, but since I did not have the money, he would accept verification of the number of my dependents so I could qualify for government aid. Chrysa wrote back to tell me that the person who issues verifications in our parish was he who would have his "two hands cut off" before helping us.

On the way back to Crete, I stopped in Athens to see a surgeon, a close friend interested in the things of God. Immediately, the doctor performed surgery and removed the mole, free of charge. It was a malignant melanoma, the doctor informed me, and if left untreated, my leg might have to be amputated.

Going for electrotherapy in Chania, I asked the Lord to strengthen my faith, for I knew in my heart that the situation had already progressed beyond human intervention. Aware of Job's encounter with Satan, I knew that the Lord was in control of my situation also, and He would not allow the enemy to touch my soul. Churches throughout Greece joined our church in prayer. "Lord, let Your will be done," I prayed. "Give me Your healing touch, or use this 'thorn in the flesh' to bless Your name."

By November, going up a small step to reach the pulpit was a painful effort. While preaching I sat on a high stool, and as I spoke my breath would sometimes catch from the pain suddenly shooting up through my spine. "Hall—elujah!" I would shout in the middle of my sentence, in preference to "Ouch!"; and some of the brethren would echo my praise. Unable to move, I spent my days and nights in the church building.

By December, the most comfortable position for me was squatting with my back against the wall, as brethren would gather around me and pray.

God used my condition to strengthen the church by drawing lukewarm Christians into the fold as they prayerfully begged God for my healing. God blessed us also by bringing our way ministers from various parts of Greece to strengthen and encourage us.

FRIDAY, February 15, 1957. Generous and loving brethren arranged for Chrysa and me to go to Athens so I could receive better care. The church in Chania sent us away in a taxi, as we all lifted a favorite chorus as our final prayer:

> ...Oh, my Lord, if You will
> That I should suffer for You
> Help me in my pain
> Always to praise You!

FEBRUARY 16. Chrysa and I are staying at Hotel Olympus. As soon as we arrived today, we were visited by Pastor

Konstantinides, Pastor Karakostanoglou, Dr. Gerasimos Metaxatos and his wife Mary (Orphan), the pastor of the Aiolou church Dr. Louis Fengos, and other ministers, believers, relatives and friends. My hotel room is packed with love and prayer. Chrysa is overwhelmed by the love and support of each person who comes in and out of our room. Impressed by the rush of visitors, the head of the hotel asked if I am running for some office. What a massive expression of love from the hearts of God's children!

FEBRUARY 17. My body is in pain. Fengos and Metaxatos, both medical doctors, informed me this afternoon that only a miracle of God could save my life, because the cancer is spreading upwards. They urged me to consider going to the cancer ward of Laikon Hospital. After fifty years of good health and strength, I am suddenly told I may depart from this life. Without confirmation from the Lord Himself, I wonder if I should even think of dying. It sounds so absurd. It seems too soon. But what if the Lord has decided to take me? I am thinking of my six sons—the youngest is not yet eleven. And my good wife— they all need me. And the church. Would the Lord have me now leave them all behind? Lord, is my reasoning correct? You have blessed my life abundantly with the lives and ministry You gave me. If it is Your will that I be restored like Job, do smite this affliction from my body now. For in my spirit I am ready to meet You, but for the sake of my loved ones—Lord, keep me strong. Help my heart not to be shattered.

Lord, prevent me from being like Asa, who sought not You when his feet were exceedingly diseased, but the physicians (2 Chronicles 16:12). You know, Lord, that I chose to be in a hotel, not in a hospital, because of Asa's example; but tonight I must decide whether to remain here or be taken to the hospital tomorrow. I am also thinking of my loving brethren, who are making tremendous sacrifices on my behalf. Remaining in this hotel places an extra burden on their generosity. Lord, give me wisdom. Reveal to me Your will so I will not pray amiss.

FEBRUARY 18. This morning I shared my heart with the brethren. "It's not the doctors I am avoiding," I said to them.

"Two of my brethren here are doctors. Luke was a physician. God uses doctors to accomplish His purposes. I just need to exercise the faith God has given me to seek His divine healing first."

"You have sought the Lord, brother Panos. You have not ignored God's healing power," said my beloved brother Konstantinides, giving me courage and leading me to reconsider the heart of the issue: though Asa's heart was perfect with the Lord all his days (1 Kings 15:14), in the throes of his crisis he not only failed to seek God, but he probably sought ungodly "physicians."

At noon, as the brethren knelt to pray, a nurse came to give me a painkiller. While she was giving me the shot, I could read brother Konstantinides' lips: "Poor Panos!" Oh, how hurt my beloved brother was on my behalf, this staunch believer of the gospel whose faith I so admire.

"Praise!" my soul shouted as the nurse turned me over and flashes of pain rushed through my body. Still on their knees, the brethren looked up. "Halle—lujah!" I cried out aloud.

FEBRUARY 19. Yesterday brother Louis made arrangements for me to be brought here to Laikon Hospital. The pain this morning is intense, the pain killers more frequent. I am lying in bed on one side and do not wish to be moved. I have resigned myself to God's will. I feel peace. I still believe in God's touch. I still can't believe I may be dying.

My condition is worsening by the moment. Without the pain killers, the pain is incredibly intense. This afternoon the nurses came to change me and found me drenched in a cold sweat.

God is using my crisis to help me ponder that He may have chosen not to heal my body. Only two days ago it seemed that it was much too soon to be leaving this life. However, my condition makes the last two days seem like weeks, the past two months like years.

FEBRUARY 20. God gives me peace when I think of meeting Him soon. To meet God! I am overwhelmed at the prospect.

All the searching, the prayers, the preaching, the service since Christ came into my life—all in preparation for meeting the Almighty God now! People keep coming in. They smile, they pray, they cry. A group of brethren gathered on the left side of my bed to pray as two doctors and a nurse reverently stood on my right. I looked at warm faith on one side, cold science on the other. But alas, even faith now looks lukewarm, for I noticed the expressions on my brethren's faces, who would first direct their eyes toward me as they prayed, then let their sad faces hang low. Perhaps faith and science should lie down by my side and look up toward heaven. Things do look different from here.

My mother keeps looking at me so lovingly through her tears. It's been years now since she accepted Christ. And so did my father and my sister and my brother and their families and mine and, oh, so many others! It all started twenty years ago, when she prayed for me and handed me the "forbidden book" which she had intended to place on my casket. How marvelous are Your counsels, O God! I try to encourage her with smiles.

It's so difficult to talk now. I am out of breath. I feel weak. People come in. I smile and point toward heaven.

My faithful and loving companion looks into my eyes. We exchange a slow smile, saying nothing. She knows with absolute certainty that I understand her.

Lord, keep my loved ones in Your care. Bless my good wife. Bless all my children.

The Aiolou choir has come to sing and uplift my faith. What a moving expression of love!

It's hard to write. I am weak. The pain is excruciating whenever I move. I've asked Chrysa to make two signs and hang one on each side of my bed—the left side for the unsaved, and the right side for the saved. With my eyes, I can direct my visitors' eyes to either sign. I want the signs to read:

REPENT, THE LORD IS COMING!
and
I WILL BE WAITING FOR YOU IN HEAVEN!

During his last four days, my husband was unable to speak. The cancer had worked its way into his lungs, and he had to be on a life-support system. Each time visitors walked into the room he would welcome them with a faint smile, raise his eyebrows, move his eyes to direct their attention to the signs by his bed, then slowly raise his forefinger to point to the Bible by his side.

It seems like yesterday that the three nurses walked into the room to change his clothes and switch oxygen tanks on that cold morning of March 1, 1957. My husband's mother and I had sat by his side all night, so the doctors suggested that she and I go outside for some fresh air. As we were closing the door behind us, we heard a very loud voice: "Hallel. . . !" Instantly, we knew it was the word that linked my good husband's last breath on this earth with life everlasting.

He had expressed a desire to be taken to brother Konstantinides' church before his burial. It meant so much to him to know that his lifeless body would rest for a while at the altar where nineteen years earlier he had first learned to forgive and ask God for forgiveness.

It has been over forty years now since my husband prayed for our six children and for all our loved ones for the last time. Our Father has honored those prayers. He has abundantly blessed our children, grandchildren, and great-grandchildren. Many people have come to know Christ as a result of his ministry, and many more through our children's and grandchildren's ministries. God has blessed his seed, as He has blessed the seed of the Word he so faithfully planted wherever he went, until the very end.

—Chrysa Zachariou

Chrysa Zachariou, wife of Pastor Panos Zachariou,
reading the Bible in 1997 at age 87

# Aftermath

JOHN paced back and forth on the raised platform in the middle of Syndrivani Square, flexing his muscles and preparing for his next superhuman feat. Hundreds of onlookers, startled by seeing him break a stack of bricks with a single butt of his head, anxiously waited to see what incredible thing he would do next. Was this big American really going to bend that solid metal rod around his neck?

John stood still. Heaving his huge torso in rhythmic breaths, he filled his lungs with the fresh ocean breeze. "I have stayed away from drugs!" John shouted in English, as I in like manner repeated his words in Greek. "I have abstained from drugs and let God's Spirit fill my life!

The Power Ministries team from the United States had arrived in Syndrivani Square under police protection after I secured the approval of the mayor of Chania. Following the team's performance, I spoke to the crowds. As I spoke, my mind went back to 1954, when Bishop Agathangelos Xyrouhakis stopped his venerable procession in Syndrivani Square, instructed the chief of police to see that our church sign be taken down, and then began to persecute my father in the courts. Now, 28 years later, on this beautiful spring afternoon in 1982, I found myself standing where the bishop had stood and declaring the life-changing power of the Spirit of God.

PRIOR to inviting Power Ministries to Greece, I had extended an invitation to the Celebrant Singers. When the group arrived in the city of Chania in 1981, Yannis Georgakakis, the son of Nick the watchmaker, secured for us a permit for the use of the auditorium of Chrysostomou Educational Society of Chania. Because we were not allowed to preach there, the Celebrant Singers ministered in song and through personal testimonies, and I conducted a question-and-answer session with the audience. People that night responded to the message of Christ. Following the service, some individuals who remembered my father came to tell me that my father was a holy man of God. One man asked me to forgive him, because he had stood in court as a false witness against my father.

As for the use of the facility, I remember my father saying to me as we would walk past Chrysostomou auditorium together, "Oh, that we could some day use this auditorium to minister the Word!"

THE next day the Celebrant Singers' bus headed for Kastelli, a town at the west end of Crete, where the group ministered in Kastelli's Spiritual Center of Bishop Irinaios, a center near the bishopric in Western Crete. The occasion allowed me a ten-minute window of opportunity to share the message of Christ through questions and answers. Following the service, our group enjoyed food and fellowship with Bishop Irinaios at his own quarters.

I remember the words my father wrote in his prison cell: "One day people will see that our work is of God!" How prophetic those words were. For on each such occasion—and there have been many—I feel that I stand where my father would have stood, speak the words he would have spoken, and accomplish the work he would have desired to accomplish in Greece for his love of God.

My father labored hard tilling the rocky soil of Crete and preparing it for the planting of spiritual seeds. Today the ground in Greece is more fertile than ever, and the harvest bountiful.

May God raise many faithful laborers to carry on His work in the country of Greece.

—D. Jimmy Zachariou

Demetrios Jimmy Zachariou is the second oldest of Panos T. Zachariou's six sons and has ministered in Greece as a missionary of the Assemblies of God for over 30 years.

# Epilogue

BECAUSE of the work of Pastor Panos and other men of faith like him, freedom of religion in Greece today has found unprecedented expression. Open-air youth rallies and outdoor church gatherings and activities are not uncommon, and may be conducted under police surveillance or protection. Foreign non-Orthodox clerics have entered the country and pursued their mission without notable restrictions. Greek Orthodox priests and religious leaders, particularly in urban areas, are more accepting of the presence of non-Orthodox Christian groups or individuals, and view their work and mission as a positive sign rather than a challenge or a threat. However, the law against "proselytism" is still on the lawbooks. Court cases in Greece still occur even today, so though the law is not consistently enforced, it continues to threaten religious freedom.

Today the church in the city of Chania, along with seven other Pentecostal churches in various parts of the island, is but a token of one man's pioneering work in Crete. The seeds of his faithful ministry keep yielding fruit in Greece and in other parts of the world through the lives and ministries of his sons and his grandchildren, and through the lives and offspring of those he touched.

The six Zachariou boys in a 1984 photo, from left to right:
Terpandros (Ted), Demetrios (Jimmy), Thedosios (Teos),
Timotheos (Tim), Philemon (Phil), and Panos

Panos T. Zachariou is survived by his wife, Chrysa, 89, who
has been blessed with fifteen grandchildren and eight great-
grandchildren. His six sons have raised families in different parts
of the world. In 1991 the oldest son, Terpandros, a radio specialist, went to be with the Lord. Jimmy (Demetrios), a missionary to Greece for over 30 years, shares his father's vision by
reaching Greeks throughout the world. Theodosios, a businessman, has been involved in church work. Timotheos is a
musician and a music teacher and has often used his talent in
church services. Philemon, an educator and a school adminis-
trator, has taught Bible classes and New Testament Greek and
has spent many years in church service. Panos, the youngest
son, is a singing evangelist and a Christian songwriter.

Presently, among Panos T. Zachariou's grandchildren, there
is one pastor, one youth minister, one Bible college graduate,
two Bible college students, and one involved in various church
ministries.

# Order Form

**Postal orders:**
Phil Zachariou, P.O. Box 278583, Sacramento, CA 95827-8583

**Please send ___ copies of *The Prosyletizer* to:**

Name:_____

Address:_____

City:_____ State:_____

Zip:_____

Telephone: (____) _____


**Book Price:** $16.95 in U.S. dollars
(Includes shipping and handling)

Special discounts for churches and for orders of 5 books or more.